THE REGION'S PLAGUES

THE REGION'S PLAGUES

THE SO CALLED "MIDDLE EAST"

NEDAL ABU-ALKHAIR

NEDAL

Dedicated to my daughters
Wedad & Jasmin

Contents

Acknowledgements

My sincere thanks are to those who found time to encourage and support me during the journey of writing this book.

This book would not have been possible without the moral support of my family and friends, in particular, my brother Dr. Khalid Abu-Alkhair who stood by my side all along, morally and practically. I also would like to thank my friend Reda Djamaa for believing in me and lending me a hand when a hand was needed.

My gratitude also goes Russell Philips at "Author Help", for reading the draft and making helpful comments, as well as assisting with all other technicalities to enable this book to be published.

Introduction

"By the time of the arrival of Islam in the early seventeenth century CE, what we now call the Middle East was divided between the Persian and Byzantine empires. But with the spread of this new religion from Arabia, a powerful empire emerged, and with it a flourishing civilization and glorious golden age.

"Given how far back it stretches in time, the history of the region — and even of Iraq itself — is too big a canvas for me to paint. Instead, what I hope to do in this book is take on the nonetheless ambitious task of sharing with you a remarkable story; one of an age in which great geniuses pushed the frontiers of knowledge to such an extent that their work shaped civilisations to this day."

— *Jim Al-Khalili*

A myth-shattering view of the Islamic world's myriad scientific innovations and the role they played in sparking the European Renaissance.

Many of the innovations that we assume of as hallmarks of Western science had their roots in the Arab world of the Middle Ages, a period when much of Western Christendom lay in intellectual seclusion. Jim al-Khalili, a prominent British-Iraqi physicist, resurrects this lost chapter of history, and given current East-West tensions, his book—The House of Wisdom— could not be timelier. With transporting detail, al-Khalili places readers in the hothouses of the Arabic Enlightenment, illustrates how they led to Europe's cultural awakening and presents the question: Why did the Islamic world enter its own dark age after such a dazzling flowering?

I admire al-Khalili's intellect and his great abilities of writing and narrating, and that is why I have singled out his remarks to kick off starting this book.

Despite the many historical injustices that have occurred to the region and its people over the past two centuries, even though this book is not a historical narrative, I will discuss historical developments throughout the book. I will not coddle the Arabs and non- Arab inhabitants and claim they are poor, unintelligent people or victims of the West or otherwise. That would not be an honest statement. I wish to point out that the "Middle East" Arab s and non-Arabs and their descendants, in the world's history, were educators and scholars who taught the world many subjects. In fact, although the Arabs never realised their renaissance, their achievements in navigation and medicine brought the world out of the dark ages.

In recent decades, the situation and the state of affairs in the region have become not only sad but heart-breaking. I come from this part of the world which is labelled the "Middle East". I am declining to call it such, due to the fact that this terminology I consider as inaccurate and biased, and serves no purpose but the purpose of its inventors, the twentieth-century imperialist powers and their associates.

Recent history of the region can't be in any sense described as anything but pathetic. The reality of the situation facing between 411 to 435 million inhabitants living in the region is growing worse by the day, without a light at the end of the tunnel. Different ills and plagues are unbeaten and taking a stronghold of the societies and their fabrics, dividing people into groups and tribes to wipe out each other and corrupting the atmosphere of tranquillity and harmony. Other ills are crushing the virtues of the people, killing the spirit of cooperation and good faith among communities. Plagues that have for so many years been encouraged and cultivated by people who are presumed to perform morally and ethically for the sake of the common man, and the interest of the societies, the so-called rulers of the region. Wars, proxy wars, domestic wars and terrorism have exploded in recent years resulting in indescribable suffering, humiliations and degradation of people who had once produced a great civilisation full of knowledge, understanding and innovations.

Unfortunately, the nations of the region are led and encouraged in various ways and forms to believe that their ills and problems are someone else's fault. Someone, an "alien" is constantly there to conspire against them and to destroy them, to kill them, to reduce them into beggers etc. Every plague-infested in the region is someone else's fault. The West blames the region's dictators and what they call extremism for the problems confronting the region. So, East blames West, and West blames East, and the blame game runs on. Yet, I believe that both parties are losing the bigger picture and more important is the fact that the common man of the region's street is the end sufferer. I do not believe in the game of blame. I believe that there are substantial issues and complicated problems in the region which require addressing, by the indigenous people, in reasonable, constructive and non-prejudicial means, to try to resolve these plagues as a matter of necessity.

I wrote this book as I believe that governments are just a product of the societies they represent. Therefore, addressing political problems are also linked to addressing social problems. They are nevertheless, both sides of the same coin. Having a dictator at the helm of government produces another dictator in the workplace, in school, in the university, in the family, and so on. Violence produces more violence, hate produces more hate. But morality, understanding, intelligent argument, and transparent conversations produce a durable peace and peaceful coexistence.

In this book, I might contribute and shed lights on some problems challenging the people of the region, but my primary purpose is to encourage the masses of the region to consider, contemplate, contribute and above all act responsibly for the benefit of each individual and for the benefit of the societies they represent, for their offspring and their unborn children.

My other objective in writing this book is to try to contribute, in a frank and straightforward manner, on some important issues — I call them "plagues" — confronting the region. Some of them are rarely debated among the societies concerned and some of these plagues are regarded as taboo. I wrote this book as the themes illustrated are subjects close to my heart and, I believe, close to the heart and conscience of so many millions of people in the region.

I am not concerned about Western governments and their perception of the region or their interests. In mentioning the West, in this book, I target the US and the UK and some of their allies, of which Israel is one. My concern, in seeking to convey my message in writing to a wider audience, is to inspire some sort of authentic and meaningful exchange of points of view and conversations among the region's media, intellectuals and non-governmental organisations, to try to save the region from further sufferings and humiliations.

For so many long and agonising years, and despite its enormous natural and human resources, the region and its people are drifting ever further towards poverty, economic stagnation, political chaos, extensive unemployment and complete discord. Looking at the region as an insider and from afar, and contemplating its future, I can hardly see or predict a positive outlook. The region's states are plagued with regimes determined to serve their own interests and the interests of the US, UK and their associates, regimes which are inherently corrupt, ruthless and distant from the masses. Economic mismanagement is widespread and plagued with corruption and nepotism. An original and meaningful education system based on thinking outside the box can hardly be found in any political entity of the region. Long-term political strategies are nowhere to be found or even exist and are at best described as reactive. Inhumane, ill-treatment and brutality by the police and security services towards the people, who expect to be protected, are sometimes incomprehensible. Wars, civil wars, conflicts and violence are becoming the norm. Above all, the scariest issue is the airy silence pervading the streets of the region, as if this vast region is becoming a land without people.

Foreign powers have played a significant part in defining and dividing the modern "Middle East", from the Sykes-Picot agreement of 1916 between Britain and France which was described by Lawrence as "Each part making the terms considered only what it could take, or rather what would be most difficult for her neighbours to take or refuse her, and the document is not the constitution for a new Asia, but a confession, almost an advertisement of the greed of the conquerors. No single clause of it will stand the test of three years' practice, and it will only be happier than the German treaty in that it will not be revised — it will be forgotten." It was not (1). And thereafter, to the Cairo Conference of 1921 chaired by Winston Churchill as colonial secretary at the time, to the battlegrounds between the Soviet Union and the United States which took place in the region during the Cold War, and to the perpetual interferences by various foreign powers, directly or in secrecy, in the affairs of the region to advance the well-being and welfare of their own people regardless of the indigenous people of the region and their aspirations. The US, the UK and their other Western friends tailored their policies towards the region to their broader interests and desires, specifically their commercial interests, irrespective of moralities, human rights or democracy which they have a full mouth to propagate. As usual, meaningless slogans and empty rhetoric.

In the belief that history is an essential subject, because we cannot fully understand the present situation of a region without considering its history fully or partially, the following is relevant to the present situation confronting the so labelled "Middle East".

So many authors and so-called "experts" of the region attribute the on-going violence and miseries on the nature of views the Islamic societies hold and to the Arab culture specifically, in which I differ and condemn. The factors that are responsible for the current sorry affairs of the region and the intolerance that is prevailing are just a few of the results of the arbitrary boundaries that created the modern states of Syria, Iraq, Lebanon, Jordan and Palestine/Israel. These Sykes-Picot boundaries were drawn by the British and French to break up the Arab parts of the Ottoman Empire for imperial convenience. The British wanted Iraq for its oil, Palestine in order to implement the Balfour Declaration that promised a homeland for the Jews, and Trans-Jordan, to compensate the Hashemite Prince Abdullah Ibn Hussein for losing Hijaz to the Saudis — and to show their recognition to the Hashemite clan for leading the so-called Arab Revolt against the Ottoman Empire.

Implementing the Sykes-Picot agreement as modified by the Balfour Declaration created weak states lacking the political and social cohesion that only an autonomous process of state-making could create. The legitimacy of these states' borders has been constantly challenged since their inception, particularly during the heyday of Arab nationalism under the leadership of President Nasser of Egypt in the 1950s and '60s, when various abortive plans for the unification of Egypt, Syria and Iraq were attempted. (2)

However, from the 1970s through the 1990s the challenge subsided. Nasser's defeat at the hands of Israel in 1967 took much of the wind out of Pan-Arabism's sails. This coincided with the coming to power of strong men in the two most important states of the Fertile Crescent — Hafez al-Assad in Syria and Saddam Hussein in Iraq. Their heavy-handed rule not only crushed regime opponents; the states over which they presided began to exude a sense of permanence that had eluded them until the 1970s. The situation changed utterly in 2003 with the American invasion of Iraq and the subsequent decimation of the country's military and civilian state apparatus. This resulted from a deliberate policy of de-Baathification, and led to Iraq's descent into chaos. (3)

The upheavals of 2011, collectively known as the "Arab Spring", let loose forces that made a bad situation even worse. Libya, Yemen and above all, Syria, began to totter on the verge of collapse as their strong men either fell or were seriously challenged. Iraq's situation was compounded by the Maliki government's short-sighted and overtly sectarian policies, which alienated Sunni Arabs, as well as Kurds, almost to a point of no return. The Iraqi state, like its Syrian counterpart, began to unravel as well. (4)

What this shows is that it was not the rise of extremism or radicalism that created anarchy and state failure in the Middle East. It was set forth that failure and the anarchy surrounding it provided the opportunity for such groups to flourish. Therefore, jihadism and extremism are not the independent variables that many imagine them to be, but merely the products of anarchy and chaos that typically accompany state failure. It also demonstrates that artificially-created states are more vulnerable to state failure than those, such as Turkey and Iran, which are products of a largely autonomous historical process of state formation and consolidation. (5)

And while speaking about history, I would like to invite the reader's attention to two important facts in relation to the Islamic political lexicon. 1. During the Islamic civilisation/empire and under different dynasties, there never was a capital city as we know in modern times. In Arabic capital means (Aleasima), and this term they employed to describe the boundary between the Islamic Empire and the Byzantine Empire. They used to have centres or important cities, such as Baghdad under the Abbasids or Istanbul under the Ottomans. 2. The term boundary is also an alien term to Muslim political culture. A boundary in Arabic means (Hudud) which literally means limits, which in Islamic culture relates to some kind of punishment under Islamic law. Nowadays boundaries around the region, and in the minds of so many millions of inhabitants, make no sense to them. A merchant who used to trade freely between all Muslim territories, he/she is now called a smuggler if they do not possess what is called a passport and a visa.

I do not believe that the US and its allies want to see any kind of political democracy in this region. For a simple reason, it won't consolidate with their long-term interests, for example:

In Tunisia and Egypt, the popular uprisings of 2011 have won an impressive victory, but the Carnegie Endowment reported, while names have changed, the regimes remain: "A change in ruling elites and system of governance is still a distant goal." The report discusses internal barriers to democracy but ignores the external ones, which as always are significant. (6)

The United States and its Western allies are sure to do whatever they can do to prevent authentic democracy in the Arab world. To understand why it, is only necessary to look at the studies of Arab opinion conducted by US polling agencies. Though barely reported, they certainly are known to planners. They reveal that the overwhelming majority of Arabs regard the United States and Israel as the major threats they face: the United States is so regarded by 90 per cent of Egyptians and by over 75 per cent of the inhabitants of the region generally. By contrast, 10 per cent of Arabs regard Iran as a threat. Opposition to US policy is so strong that a majority believes security would improve if Iran had nuclear weapons — in Egypt, 80 per cent. Other figures are similar. If public opinion were to influence policy, the United States not only would not control the region but would be expelled from it, along with its allies, undermining fundamental principles of global dominance. (7)

From the perspective of US foreign policy, democracy was acceptable as long as the results worked in favour of securing American strategic interests in the region. If the elections did not, then democracy was a problem.

From a different perspective, the events of 1921 (a reference to the Cairo conference) had a mixed effect on the "Middle East" region. Partition of the Fertile Crescent, an idea initially subscribed to by the European powers in 1915, was taken for granted at Cairo. In addition to creating artificial entities, arbitrary and therefore illogical boundaries, and narrow national loyalties, partition also provided a basic obstacle for the late struggle on behalf of the idea of Arab unity. (8) The disunity and other massive problems facing the region's inhabitants are grave and are the creation of these entities that were created and appointed (mainly by Britain and France) to rule the region. So far, the region's so-called "governments" have immensely, throughout the past decades to present, succeeded in three main areas 1. In oppressing the region's population. 2. In stealing the wealth of a nation. 3. In serving their masters based in the West.

In Jeremy Bowen's book The Arab Uprising he writes: Jihadist suspects were captured and even abducted under a programme that was given the euphemistic name of 'extraordinary rendition' and were sent to Arab countries where there were none of the tiresome legal constraints that made life difficult in Western democracies. A former CIA agent called Robert Baer said, 'If you want a serious interrogation, you send a prisoner to Jordan. If you want them to be tortured, you send them to Syria. If you want someone to disappear – never to see them again – you send them to Egypt. (9)

What I can understand from this statement is a simple conclusion. The region as a whole is becoming the wild jungle of the world. You want someone to go insane, send him to Jordan. You want someone to be physically and mentally scarred forever, send him to Syria. You want someone to completely vanish from the face of the earth, send him to Egypt. Hence, the region has been turned into an innovation centre for torturing human souls, an excellent international laboratory for inhuman, ugly, and degrading treatment of human beings, and a spacious graveyard for the unwanted human species.

I am asking every moral, responsible and caring person of the region this question, what do you want for yourself, for your sons, daughters and grandchildren? Are we turned into machines just to kill, torture and suffocate our own fathers and mothers, our brothers and sisters and our children? Are we becoming so immune to the horrors and atrocities committed in my name and yours? Are we so okay with corruption and dishonesty perpetrated mainly by the so-called governments of the region and its cronies? Are we becoming just content to breathe some air, even if it's polluted, and have a crust of bread before going to bed? Are we pleased to become so unresponsive to the many plights taking firm hold of the region and its progress? These questions and many more need to be answered, not only by me as an individual, not only by you as an individual, but by all as a society, as a region and as a whole.

But I also must salute the people of the region who say and still say the truth, many of whom are imprisoned and tortured by the ugly security services in their respective countries and some of whom have died or been assassinated at the hands of their mad governments such as the recent assassination of the prominent Saudi journalist Jamal Khashoggi, and with regret, there are too many other Jamal's who were killed for daring to be an honest voice in a region where few moral and honest voices are being heard. Here, I salute everyone and exclude not one of them be they Sunni or Shia, Arab, Barber or Kurd, Muslim, Jew or Christian, light skin or dark skin, I salute them all.

It seems to me that the discovery of the black gold in the region is more of a curse than a blessing, not only to Baghdad but to the region as a whole. The nowadays sad story of Baghdad and its sorrows and miseries are not confined to it, no it is not. The region of the so-called "Middle East" consists of twenty two political entities, these entities in different degrees suffer from endemic poverty, rife corruption, widespread killings and torture, extensive lack of justice, rulers with an extreme lack of morals, to the lack of reasonable knowledge and innovations, and above all lack of basic human rights and dignity.

This book cannot and should not be considered as a social science book, or for that matter, a historical narrative. It is a book written to try to open the closed eyes of so many people around the world about the realities of today's region and give a glimpse to the masses of the region on the way forward if they decide to do so.

I have also written this book as I personally feel hurt and saddened seeing the way and the direction this region is heading into. A thousand years ago, the great cities of Baghdad, Damascus and Cairo took turns to race ahead of the Western world. Islam and innovation were twins. The various Arab caliphates were dynamic superpowers — beacons of learning, tolerance and trade. Yet today the Arabs and non-Arabs of the region are in a wretched state. Even as Asia, Latin America and Africa advance, the so-called "Middle East" is held back by despotism and convulsed by wars, refugees, poverty, corruption, etc. Some hopes soared some years ago — 2010-11 when a wave of unrest across the region led to the overthrow of four dictators—in Tunisia, Egypt, Libya and Yemen — and to a clamour for change elsewhere, notably in Syria. But the Arab Spring's fruit has rotted into renewed autocracy and war. Both breed misery and fanaticism that today threatens the region and might threaten the stability of the world too, if this the current situation may deteriorate further.

It is just a modest attempt on my part to try and convey my message which comprises painful and sad realities — realities which we all must come face to face with and confront, and not hide our heads under the sand. But I believe that trying to point out the truth, no matter how painful the truth might be, is far more constructive than keeping silent. Some people might find my writing aggressive and on occasion, if we are to read and understand thoroughly the Muslim civilisation, we will discover that the beauty of it was built on by many ethnicities and different religions. You find Arabs, Kurds, Turks, Armenians, Persians, and even a few Europeans. You find Muslims, Christians and Jews, all of whom were united and working together for the sake of reason, knowledge and advancement of humankind. They were all working hand in hand tirelessly to translate, learn, analyse, and add discoveries, and what united them all were their excellent attitudes, understanding, tolerance, and morality.

Baghdad once was the centre of it all; was the crown jewel of the Muslim empire. Baghdad now is the centre of all subjugations, terror, killings, tortures which makes any decent writer full of anger and despair, which is maybe true in this case, but a person with a bleeding heart, surely can be excused for being angry and to a certain degree may be aggressive.

Despite my strong reservations about the internet and how it has corrupted so many young people's minds all over the globe, it helped me a great deal in finding useful information and data without which my book would be harder to complete. But as my father once said to me "anything in this life — literary — can be used or abused." I think he was right.

As a Palestinian who was born under the label refugee, saw and experienced first-hand the true picture and facts of being labelled a refugee and what they entail, being used and abused by the hand of your own people who share the same history, religion, language, culture etc., is hard to comprehend. As a person who travelled far and wide, seeking education or shelter, and saw and experienced different countries, languages and cultures, it is quite daunting for me to believe or comprehend the injustices happening around us. Yet, I consider myself to be one of the lucky few. After almost 40 years of my life, I finally can freely travel, freely express my thoughts and beliefs, have safety protection from a state, have health care, and be treated without prejudice, etc. in which the Western people, for example, take for granted. Therefore, I thank very much the country that awarded me its citizenship. And I have no thanks whatsoever to the region's governments I was born in, to their ugly regimes and to their lack of morality and lack of compassion towards their larger family. Millions of other Palestinians, inside Gaza and the West Bank and in neighbouring lands, are trapped and incarcerated in refugee camps since 1948 and 1967, in sub-human conditions in some of the refugee camps, with no legal protection, proper education, health care or job prospects and forced to live on top of each other like animals. And with great sadness and regret, the picture is not getting any better. Now, the Syrians, Yemenis, Iraqis, Sudanese, Somalis etc. unfortunately are experiencing — more or less — the same dreadful fate as the Palestinians.

But I must stress my sincere thanks and gratitude to Algeria and Qatar for their impeccable support and compassion towards the Palestinian cause and its people. They both have proven, to the dislike of the traitors, that they are countries and people with a great sense of pride, morality and solidarity. And in mentioning the Palestinian cause, I also must stress my sincere gratitude to some Western non-governmental organisations which are still persistent, and despite all the odds, support the Palestinian people and their legitimate political and human rights.

Despite the incredible advancements of science and technology achieved so far, almost in any field of knowledge you can think of, and despite the massive accumulation of wealth and resources — albeit in the hands of the few, we still have not advanced in being human beings, human beings with morality and touch. More and more poverty, inequality, hunger, wars, war crimes, and unimaginable and unnecessary deaths and destruction of innocent human lives are accruing almost every single day around the globe, some of which are even pictured on the internet, "live-streamed" and regrettably seen by my daughters aged just 14 and 16, and I am sure seen by many other millions of children too, such as the barbaric massacre that happened in two mosques in Christchurch, New Zealand on the 15th March 2019.

I am convinced that what is happening in the world today, with special emphasis on the "Middle East region" in terms of total instabilities and wars are just one product of the collapse of the USSR, as the balance of power in the world has shifted mainly to the hand of the US and the crazy politics adopted by George Bush II, his neoconservative administration and their cronies from 2002 onwards. Since then, the region is in turmoil non-stop and deteriorating rapidly.

Throughout this book, the term "intellectuals" will be mentioned, but what I mean is only the intellectuals who are honest, honourable, free-thinkers and speak their own minds, and not the so-called intellectuals who are technocrats and policy-oriented, whom I personally call states or established institutions appeasers.

Frequently the term "Middle East" will be used, but when used by me, I will add the inverted commas, when quoting others; I leave it as it is originally written.

References for Introduction

1. Walter Reid, Empire of Sand, How Britain Made the Middle East, Brilinn Limited, 2011, P. 91.
2. Mohammed Ayoob, What is Wrong with Arab World, Middle-East Policy Council, https://www.mepc.org/commentary/what-wrong-arab-world
3. Ibid
4. Ibid
5. Ibid
6. Noam Chomsky, Who Rules the World? Hamish Hamilton, UK 2016, P.46.
7. Ibid
8. Aaron S. Klieman, Foundations of British Policy in the Arab World: The Cairo Conference of 1921, The Johns Hopkins Press, Baltimore and London, 1970.
9. Bowen Jeremy, The People Want The Fall Of The Regime, The Arab Uprising, Simon & Schuster UK Ltd, 2012, P. 14

Chapter 1: Plague One: Corrupt Terminology

"...But the human tongue is a beast that few can master. It strains constantly to break out of its cage, and if it is not tamed, it will run wild and cause you grief."

— Unknown

"All I need is a sheet of paper and something to write with, and then I can turn the world upside down."

— Friedrich Nietzsche

As a person who was born and grew up in the "Middle East", I have always taken the term with me everywhere I travelled. I stuck it in my brain and my bloodstream as a term taken for granted. My father used it, my elder brothers and sister, my community as a whole and the media in a bigger sense all used it and keep using it until this moment in time. Therefore, I took the term for granted without proper and serious thought.

So what has changed? Some years ago, I went for a job interview. The job I applied for had nothing to do with politics and was not related to the field of intellectualism. At the end of the interview, the English lady who interviewed me asked me, "Mr Abu-Alkhair, if I may ask. Where do you originally come from?" As I encountered this question (in Western Europe) so many times before, and my usual answer was I come from Palestine, yet many people did not grasp where this Palestine is, as many confuse it with Israel. So, at that moment, my brain told me to say I come from the "Middle East" instead of saying from Palestine, out of respect to her intellect. For seconds, she gazed at me, and then asked, well where is the Middle East? Her question took me by surprise. I paused for seconds and then said, well, the Middle East is the East of the West, if this makes any sense? She then with an enormous smile said, "Mr Abu-Alkhair, I assure you there is no Middle East".At this moment, I thought oh, I think she knows what she is talking about. With a big smile back to her, I said I come from Palestine, is that any better? She said that was much better and continued to say, please send my regards to Jerusalem and thanks for coming, Mr Abu-Alkhair.

Out of her office, I stood for a minute asking myself if I was a stupid idiot or is she an arrogant stupid creature who likes to show off.

I did not pause long, and I drove 80 miles back home. During the journey back home, I thought to myself that I needed to investigate the matter further to prove to myself that she is the one whose point of view was right.

Guess what guys, I was the one who is wrong, and she was the one who opened my eyes and expanded my intellect to investigate the terminology of the so-called "Middle East". Therefore, I must thank her forever that she pointed out to me something which is so important in relation to international politics and relations and to the justice which needs to be served for the people of the region as a whole.

Although I was successful in the interview and I was offered the job, unfortunately I had to decline the offer due to some health problems which crept into my body at that time. That means and unfortunately again, I was never to see this lady again whom I respect.

That takes me now to elaborate on the use of this terminology, the so-called "Middle East". I frankly cannot define this term or enlighten readers on how logically this term can be used and which countries this "Middle East" contains. But I can tell you that this term is a funny one and does not, when analysed, make any sense or stand any critical thinking.

In medieval Europe, the Romans used the term Orients that takes its roots from a Latin word "sol oriens" which means sunrise, to define the area. Then they implied the Eastern half, that is the Byzantine (395-1453), of the Roman Empire. Once again in this period, the term was also used for the east of Jerusalem, which was named as the Holy Land with its broadest sense in the context of the tradition of the Holy Bible. (1)

The area now designated as the "Middle East" was known as the Near East in medieval times. It is reputed as the cradle of civilization as it was home to some of the most ancient human developments. Such civilisations include those of Mesopotamia, ancient Egypt, Hittite, Greek, the Levant, Persia, and the Arabian Peninsula. The ancient Near East was governed by multiple empires starting with the Neo-Assyrian Empire, Achaemenid, Macedonian, Persian, Roman, and Byzantine Empires. The Islamic Caliphate began their Arab conquest of the area in the 7th century, and then the last is the Ottoman Empire.

In the middle ages, in particular, at the end of the 11th century when Europe was almost static and unchanged since ancient times, circumstances for the Europeans started to change as of the start of the sheer determination and endurance by the Crusaders, which is fully illustrated in Conor Kostick's book "The Siege of Jerusalem". The Europeans began to gain rich heritage and some sort of sophistication attributed mainly to this bloody and horrifying encounter with the Muslims in which they were completely wiped out. According to his book around 40 thousand Muslims and Jews inhabiting Jerusalem were slaughtered, sparing only the Christian inhabitants.

The term Orient was widely used in Europe to describe a vast region comprising Arabic-speaking countries and non-Arabic-speaking countries such as Iran, India and China until the 19th century. After the total fragmentation of the Ottoman Empire, race and competition between different European countries, in particular Britain, France, Germany and Russia to capture and divide the region intensified. In terms of regional geopolitics, the region was regarded as a whole by Europe and by that time, either East or Orient was used for the whole of Asia. As the Ottoman Empire was sinking, sharing the territories of the empire turned into conflict because of the different interests of the European powers.

The term "Middle East" first began to be used by the British imperial government during the 1850s, the decade that witnessed both the Crimean War, which involved all the major imperial powers of Europe and West Asia, and the assumption of rule of the Empire of India by the British government from the British East India Company. As defined at that time by the British government, India included modern India, Pakistan, Nepal, Bhutan, Bangladesh, Burma, and, at least hypothetically, Afghanistan.

Almost all political definitions relevant to the "Middle East" and the foundation of a large portion of the political boundary changes are based on the sovereignty and the beginning of the establishment of spheres of influence by the British, French, Russians and Germans in this region at the end of the 19th century and first half-century of the 20th century. In this context, a change in terminology took place in 1890 where the term Near East was used for the first time. The Near East term was rather used to describe Southeastern Europe, including the Balkan region. The region was East because of being still a part of the Ottoman Empire, whereas it was near because of being Christian European, however, it was also still the East because of remaining under the sovereignty of an Eastern state of the Ottoman Empire. (2)

In September 1902 Alfred Thayer Mahan, an American naval strategist, published an article in the British Review, a British Journal, called "The Persian Gulf and International Relations", where he used the term "Middle East" to designate the area between Arabia and India. For him, the "Middle East" was a geographical region of enormous maritime and naval significance ranging from the Bosporus to the Suez Canal and the Strait of Hormuz to Bab el-Mandeb. Mahan was called "the most important American strategist of the 19th century." His concept that countries with greater naval power have a greater worldwide impact had an enormous influence in shaping the strategic thought of navies across the world, especially in America, Britain, Germany, and eventually causing a European naval arms race in the 1890s. Yet, some historians suggest that the term "Middle East" was first used by the British India Office in the 1850s, but whatever the truth, the term "Middle East" gained momentum and started to be very widely used (until today) by and in different languages around the globe with no exception to the Arabic language, Al-sharq Al-ausat.

Two months after Mahan's article, Valentine Chirol, a reporter working for the British Time magazine published a series of articles titled "The Middle East Question" (turned into a book by him at a later stage). During his series, he expanded the definition of the "Middle East" to include "those regions of Asia, which extend to the borders of India or command the approaches to India. (The issue of the security of the Indies route also entailed control of the Persian Gulf, a bolt-hole for pirates plying the Indian Ocean. Rather than direct rule, the British navy opted for the protectorate system, initially imposing a treaty on the sheikhs of the region, which turned the Pirate coast into the Trucial coast, now the United Arab Emirates. The same approach was used in 1899 with the Shaikh of the little known town of Kuwait... and the Sultanate of Muscat [in modern Oman]). (3)" After the series ended in 1903, The Time magazine removed quotation marks from subsequent uses of the term. In his book called "The Middle Eastern Question" Chirol expanded Mahan's version of the "Middle East" to include "Persia, Iraq, the east coast of Arabia, Afghanistan and Tibet." Yes, you read correctly – Tibet! Obviously, the definition of the new geopolitical term adapted to the corresponding colonial interests that created it in the first place.

Chirol acknowledged Mahan's original use of the term Middle East, but applied it more broadly and he tied the "Middle East" to the defence of India and related it to British interests throughout southern Asia, but not yet to the Suez Canal. The view of other strategists at the time were irrelevant to the British readers, they expected their government to defend British interests between Europe and

India. How best to do that preoccupied Whitehall, Westminster, Fleet Street and the City during the early years of the twentieth century. (4) Even before the 1914-1918 war, Downing Street, the Foreign Office and the Admiralty had adopted policies that palpably altered the balance of power in the Middle East. During the war, when the British military occupied so much of Western Asia, the Middle East label would gain momentum in the newly created Middle East Department, Mahan's identification of the Middle East with the Persian Gulf and Chirol's preoccupation with India's defence expanded to encompass Iraq, Palestine, the Sinai and the Arabian peninsulas, and the Suez Canal. (5)

After WWI, Winston Churchill became the head of the newly established "Middle East Department," which redefined "The Middle East" to include the Suez Canal, Sinai, Arabian Peninsula, and the newly created states of Iraq, Palestine and Trans-Jordan. Tibet and Afghanistan were excluded from London's version of the Middle East. In the modern world, we now see Turkey changing its status from a "Middle Eastern" state to a "European" state.

The description Middle has also led to some confusion over changing definitions. Before the First World War, "Near East" was used in English to refer to the Balkans and the Ottoman Empire, while "Middle East" referred to Iran, the Caucasus, Afghanistan, Central Asia and Turkestan. In contrast, "Far East" referred to the countries of East Asia (e.g. China, Japan, Korea, etc.) (6)

With the disappearance of the Ottoman Empire in 1918, "Near East" largely fell out of common use in English, while "Middle East" came to be applied to the re-emerging countries of the Islamic world. However, the usage "Near East" was retained by a variety of academic disciplines, including archaeology and ancient history, where it describes an area identical to the term Middle East, which is not used by these disciplines. (7)

The first official use of the term "Middle East" by the United States government was in the 1957 Eisenhower Doctrine, which pertained to the Suez Crisis. Secretary of State John Foster Dulles defined the Middle East as "the area lying between and including Libya to the west and Pakistan on the east, Syria and Iraq on the North and the Arabian Peninsula to the south, plus the Sudan and Ethiopia." In 1958, the State Department explained that the terms "Near East" and "Middle East" were interchangeable, and defined the region as including only Egypt, Syria, Israel, Lebanon, Jordan, Iraq, Saudi Arabia, Kuwait, Bahrain and Qatar. (8)

The Associated Press Stylebook says that Near East formerly referred to the farther west countries, while Middle East referred to the eastern ones, but that now they are synonymous. It instructs:

Use Middle East unless Near East is used by a source in a story. Mideast is also acceptable, but Middle East is preferred. (9)

If you are getting confused ('as I am), try this simple exercise: go to an image search on your internet browser and type "map of Europe", you will get hundreds of images of the same group of countries, with the same borders in different formats. This will also be the case if you wrote "United States" or "Asia" or "Africa." Now, search for a "map of the Middle East" and see how many versions of the map you will get, with totally different borders and several countries, some will include or exclude countries like Iran, Turkey and Somalia.

Yet the fact remains, writes historian Roderic H. Davison, that no one knows where the Middle East is, although many claim to know. Scholars and governments have produced reasoned definitions that are in hopeless disagreement. There is no accepted formula, and serious efforts to define the area vary by as much as three to four thousand miles east and west. There is not even an accepted core of the Middle East. Involved in the terminological chaos is of course the corollary question of how the Middle East relates to the Near East — or, indeed, whether the Near East still exists at all. (10)

The concept of a region called the "Middle East" is a relatively recent and unstable construction. Since the term was first coined at the beginning of the 20th century, it has been applied to different sets of countries and territories. To complicate matters further, territories which have at times been categorised as "Middle East" have also attracted other designations: Near East, western Asia, eastern Mediterranean, the Arab world and so on. These designations all represent different ways of conceptualising what these territories have in common and how they relate to other parts of the world.

The term was and still is clearly conceived in the framework of European/Western geopolitical and strategic considerations, delineating the region as a realm of actual or potential political, military, and economic rivalry and spheres of influence among European/Western imperial powers. Since then, this geographic designation has assumed more fluid boundaries and has come to represent different sets of interests and considerations for the outside major powers, as the following explains.

The broadest definition of the term "Middle East" came at the 2004 conference of the G8 (Group of Eight) nations, based on the definition of the USA's Bush administration. This included the entire Muslim world, because to the Bush administration Middle East = Muslim = terrorist (or oil in the case of "friendly" regimes). Often called the "Greater Middle East", this list includes the "traditional" Middle East nations in Anatolia, the Levant, the Arabian Peninsula and Mesopotamia, as well as those in Central Asia, the Caucasus and North Africa. (11)

The nations of the Greater Middle East as defined by the G8 and the USG (United States government) include the core Middle East nations of Bahrain, Cyprus, Egypt, Iran, Iraq, Israel, Jordan, Kuwait, Lebanon, Oman, Palestine, Qatar, Saudi Arabia, Syria, Turkey, UAE, Yemen; the North African nations of Algeria, Djibouti, Libya, Mauritania, Morocco, Somalia, Sudan, Sahrawi Arab Democratic Republic (SADR; Western Sahara), and Tunisia; the South Asian nations of Afghanistan, Azad Kashmir (Pakistani Kashmir), and Pakistan; the Caucasian nations of Armenia, Azerbaijan and Georgia; and the Central Asian nations of Kazakhstan, Kyrgyzstan, Tajikistan, Uzbekistan and Turkmenistan. (12)

These G8 nations, by the way, are Canada, France, Germany, Italy, Japan, Russia, the United Kingdom and the United States of America. So here we have the absurdity of an envoy from Russia, whose easternmost border comes to a mere 82 kilometres (51 miles) from the western border of the US state of Alaska, referring to events in Morocco as happening in the "Middle East". Or that of an American cultural attaché in Athens discussing the same thing, something possible since the USG (United States government) still uses the same definition. (13)

Inhabitants refer to the area included in the Greater Middle East by other names: the Maghreb, which includes the North African nations along the Mediterranean Sea (Morocco, Algeria, Tunisia, Libya), Bilad al-Sham (the Levant), and the Mashriq (eastern Syria, Iraq, Kuwait, and the nations of the Arabian Peninsula). Egypt is not included in either the Maghreb or the Mashriq, nor is Iran included in the latter. Egypt, along with the Sudan, is assigned to the Nile Valley, considered a region in and of itself. (14)

Culturally speaking, it is difficult to limit the "Middle East" to a geographic area with hard borders. Civilisations outside of what is commonly referred to as the "Middle East" made intellectual, cultural and biological imprints in today's "Middle East" that are indelible, especially in regard to the waves of migration from Central Asia. Further, North Africa has profound cultural connections through language, religious practices and philosophical discourses. There have been continuous flows of thought and ideas, whether through the spiritual content of Muslim practices, or through practices and technologies of law, medicine, education, and food production.

With many ugly and senseless conflicts and wars raging throughout the region, in Palestine, Yemen, Syria, Iraq, Libya etc., and a delicate calm in the rest of the region, the terminologies we use, including "Middle East" in covering this region of more than 435 million inhabitants is not only hindering our understanding of the geography of the region, but also in understanding its issues and difficulties, leading to misguided strategic politics and decisions.

It is also not fair or politically correct to describe the region as the Arab World, as the region's inhabitants consist of many other races other than Arabs such as Armenians, Kurds, Turks and so on, who have been living in this part of the world alongside Arabs for centuries and Arabic is not their mother tongue.

In researching for meanings, definitions and categorisations of the term or the region, there are no definitive answers to populations, countries, sects and languages that accurately agree on what constitutes the

MENA (Middle East and North Africa). There is no getting away from that ethnocentric mindset that mash up countries, ethnicities, religions, cultures and languages by referring to the region, not as the Arabic speaking world, not as the Middle East or North Africa, but as "Arabs" and the "Arab world." We wouldn't refer to Scotland, Ireland, Australia, Canada and the USA as "English" or the "English world" but most likely the English-speaking world. (15)

A lot of what has happened in the MENA is sadly a case of unintended consequences. The struggles in these regions to a great extent have shifted from a nationalist to a religious front, which has led to the interchangeable terms of "Arabs" and "Muslims". This has been a predominantly Western perception, however, and the labelling of "Arabs" as monolithic can only be described as a fearmongering term to reflect the "war on terror". (16)

Neuroscientists and linguists have demonstrated that the language we speak and the words we use shape how we think. Terminology certainly matters in geopolitics as well, conditioning how we view entire regions of the world. Crucially, our geographic vocabulary evolves to suit the times. The Cold War, for example, was often referred to as the "East-West conflict" but today nobody thinks of Russia as the representative of the "East" — when it is China that is clearly the eastern superpower. Unfortunately, when it comes to the Arab, Turkic and Persian realms, the catch-all term "Middle East" continues to hold sway among English speakers. Subsuming any of the geographic distinctions and nuance contained in the Arabic terms Maghreb, Khaleej and Mashriq, the vague "Middle East" continues to represent so much — even as it increasingly means nothing at all. Isn't it time for our vocabulary to adapt to reality? (17)

At its most obtuse, Middle East connotes everything from Morocco to Afghanistan, spanning a melange of sub-regions stretching from North Africa to Central Asia. But North African countries from Egypt westwards have little relevance to Asia, even though they are mostly Arab-populated. It makes far more sense to refer to West Asia and Southwest Asia to capture Turkey, Iran, the Gulf States and the nations lying between them. Neutral geographic labels are ultimately much more revealing than colonial artefacts. Of course we can blame colonialism and the Cold War for fragmenting what was once a far more fluid and integrated picture of relations across Asia's Silk Road. But it has been nearly three decades since the collapse of the Soviet Union, more than enough time for Arab leaders to come to terms with the new global circumstances. (18)

Some have suggested that the term "Middle East" is problematic because it is, unquestionably, a Western term reflecting a Western perspective. India's first Prime Minister, Jawaharlal Nehru, once observed that the region should really be called West Asia, and there have been occasional efforts to adopt terms like "Southwest Asia" in academic circles. Yet there are plenty of countries whose names imply a relative geography that we hardly notice — Norway (north) and Austria (east), for example. And Arabic speakers have long referred to North Africa as the Maghreb — from a word meaning west — because it is on the western side of the Arabic-speaking world. (19)

Anti-imperialist critics of the concept might also take comfort from knowing that no less an imperialist than Churchill never much liked the term he helped create. In 1950, he lamented: "I had always felt that the name 'Middle East' for Egypt, the Levant, Syria and Turkey was ill chosen. This was the Near East."

The imperialists at the time labelled the region to serve their own interests. They created artificial entities, arbitrary and therefore illogical boundaries, which the people of the region never knew or experienced, and grew the seeds of narrow national loyalists to serve them and not the masses of the region, as they are still doing now. In addition, to all the confusions they have successfully created, including their terminologies, labelling and stereotyping, there are dark yet strong and influential elements behind the scenes and the so-called intellectuals and experts who are investing heavily in creating, with good success, the notion that Muslims in general and Arabs in particular hate them, want their destruction and so on.

Genuine intellectuals are aware that, like everyone else, they have their blind spots and should be willing to remain open-minded. Therefore, together with the responsibility to awaken society, they also need to be constantly aware of their own shortcomings, which may limit their understanding and cause harm to society. I believe that intellectuals are agents of change, particularly in those parts of the world, like the so-called "Middle East" where the unjust and aberrant behaviour are the norm. Therefore, I urge honest and open-minded intellectuals around the world, and the region's intellectuals in particular to do some justice and eliminate the term "Middle East". Call it West Asia, or call it a thousand and one nights, I don't care, yet I need to see it called and labelled by the region's indigenous people and by their intellectuals and not by aliens who do not even bother to learn the Arabic language and did nothing for the region apart from exploiting it and dividing it according to their own greed and interests.

The problem of the new "Middle East", created out of the ruins of the old order, was that it was a constant reminder to

Arab nationalists of the betrayal of their aspirations. They regarded the system of mandates as merely imperialism in disguise, a fact that was borne out in their eyes by the constant military presence and the exploitation of their raw materials. Moreover, the Allies had fashioned it in their own image, creating a state system, with arbitrary frontiers and governors whom they nominated, that was based on European ideas and as such held no legitimacy in the eyes of local people, both secular and religious. This has been the cause of turmoil and instability in the region ever since, at the root of uprisings, territorial disputes, revolutions and wars. The Versailles Peace Conference should have left a better world for the subjects of the Ottoman Empire. Instead, what it ended up doing was best summed up by Field Marshall Wavell, who was the Brigadier-General of the General Staff in Palestine in 1919. "After the war to end war," he said, "they seem to have been pretty successful in Paris at making a peace to end peace." These turned out to be prophetic words indeed. (20)

References for Chapter 1: Plague One: Corrupt Terminology

1. Where is the Middle East? The Definition and Classification Problem of the Middle East as a Regional Subsystem in International Relations. YJP Turkish Journal of Politics Vol.2 Winter 2011, by Osman Nuri Ozalp

2. Ibid

3. Kassir Samir, Being an Arab, Paperback Edition published by Verso 2013, P. 70.

4. Adelson Roger, London and the Invention of the Middle East, Money Power, And War, 1902-1922, Yale University Press, 1995, P. 24-26

5. Ibid

6. Wikipedia, https://en.wikipedia.org/wiki/Middle_East

7. Ibid

8. Ibid

9. Ibid

10. Ibid

11. Roderic H. Davison, Where is the Middle East? Council on Foreign Affairs, https://www.foreignaffairs.com/articles/middle-east/1960-07-01/where-middle-east

12. Online article, Let's Eliminate the Term Middle East, by Chuck Hamilton, Saturday, January 25, 2014 https://www.chattanoogan.com/2014/1/25/268217/Le t-s-Eliminate-The-Term-Middle-East.aspx
13. Ibid
14. Ibid
15. Ibid
16. Neheda Barakat, Let's banish the term 'Arab World'. What does it mean anyway? https://www.theguardian.com/commentisfree/2018/apr/18/lets-banish-the-term-arab-world-what-does-it-mean-anyway
17. Ibid
18. Parag Khanna, The National Opinion Online, Why do we still use the term Middle East when West Asia is more relevant to Arab nations? https://www.thenational.ae/opinion/comment/why-do-we-still-use-the-term-middle-east-when-west-asia-is-more-relevant-to-arab-nations-1.822994
19. Ibid
20. Christopher Simon Sykes, The Man Who Created the Middle East, A Story of Empire, Conflict and the Sykes-Picot Agreement, William Collins 2016, P. 338-3

Chapter 2: Plague Two: The Puppets

We've seen over time that countries that have the best economic growth are those that have good governance, and good governance comes from freedom of communication. It comes from ending corruption. It comes from a populace that can go online and say, "This politician is corrupt, this administrator or this public official is corrupt."

— *Ramez Naam, American Writer*

Dictatorships have dominated global politics for hundreds of years, from the pharaohs of Egypt to the absolute monarchs of Europe. In the region labelled as the "Middle East" all types of current government systems, in my view, represent and resemble complete or partial dictatorial regimes, irrespective of the label they are given. And yet, compared to democracies, we know very little about how dictatorships work, who the key political actors are, and where decision-making powers lie. Political processes are muddy, and information is often intentionally distorted. Political survival depends not on maintaining the favour of voters, as in Western democracies, but on securing the backing of a considerably smaller coalition of supporters i.e. family members, tribes, clans, etc. The absence of a reliable third party to enforce compromises among key players means that power-sharing deals lack credibility and the threat of forced ouster is omnipresent. Uncertainty pervades authoritarian politics and their decision-making process.

Modern autocrats respond to this uncertain environment in a variety of ways. They use political parties, legislatures, elections and other institutions typically associated with democracies to lessen their risk of overthrow. Despite the facade of democracy, these institutions are key components of most autocrats' survival strategies; those that incorporate them last longer in power than those that do not. The specific ways in which autocratic institutions are used and the extent to which they can constrain leadership choices to prevent consolidation of power into the hands of a single individual, however, vary enormously from one dictatorship to the next. Better understanding the conditions that push autocracies down a path of reciprocal versus strongman rule remains a critical task, particularly given that the latter is associated with more war, economic mismanagement and resistance to a meaningful change of government system, which we see in the region's so-called sovereign countries.

We typically view dictatorships as brutally repressive, which is the case of the region's so-called modern states, regimes where power lies in the hand of a single individual. Some dictatorships fit this portrait well, such as Saudi Arabia, Egypt, Syria and so on. This is only a small problem, as the bigger problem in modern dictatorships in the region (which is not one of the same) is that they are fully supported and enhanced by the modern, civilised, and democratic governments (as they call themselves) of the West, in particular, the United States and the United Kingdom. Take, for example:

In the lead-up to the 2003 US invasion of Iraq, the Bush administration was hoping to open a second battlefront into Iraq from the north, across the Turkish-Iraqi border. The newly elected government in Turkey was subjected to considerable pressure from Washington to acquiesce to this request, including as an incentive a $32 billion dollar aid package that was desperately needed to bolster a sagging Turkish economy. While initially Ankara seemed to be receptive to the offer, Turkish public opinion was strongly opposed to any role Turkey might play in the invasion of Iraq (about 90 per cent of the Turkish public strongly opposed Turkish involvement in the invasion of Iraq). After an extensive public debate in the media and parliament, the Turkish government, bowing to overwhelming public sentiment, refused the American request. After the toppling of Saddam in March 2003, Deputy Defence Secretary Wolfowitz travelled to Turkey. In a famous interview on CNN-Turk, he publicly criticised the Turkish government for its non-cooperation in the invasion of Iraq and then he stated "[l]ets [sic] have a Turkey that steps up and says we made a mistake." Wolfowitz then added a revealing comment that he wished the Turkish military would have stepped forward and played a more prominent role in shaping Turkish foreign policy in the lead-up to the war. "I think for whatever reason they did not play the strong leadership role on that issue that we would have expected ... [A]ll I'm saying is that when you had a[n] issue of Turkey's national interest and national strategy, I think it's perfectly appropriate, especially in your system, for the military to say it was in Turkey's interest to support the United States in that effort."

These controversial comments unleashed a furious debate in Turkey. Wolfowitz's desire that the Turkish military play a more prominent role in politics was shocking in light of modern Turkish history. At the time, Turkey was just emerging from a long period of authoritarian rule dominated by the intrusive role of the armed forces that had toppled four civilian governments, most recently in 1997. One year earlier, in 2002, Turkey's freest and most inclusive election took place bringing the Justice and Development Party to power. While Wolfowitz's statement was shocking from a political development perspective, it was completely understandable from a US foreign policy point of view. As this case amply demonstrates, it is much easier for the US to deal with military regimes than with democratic parliaments who reflect the will of the people. One can project forward and imagine the complications and difficulties that might arise if Washington has to deal with democratically elected governments across the region in countries such as Saudi Arabia, Kuwait, Jordan, Qatar, Bahrain, the United Arab Emirates, and Oman instead of the pro-Western monarchies and family dictatorships that are currently in power. This example establishes a key principle that has long guided US foreign policy in the Middle East. Greater democracy does not always translate into greater support for US geostrategic interests in the region. There is often a chasm between popular indigenous nationalist sentiments on key geostrategic issues versus the foreign policy preferences of the United States. In this context, Tamara Coffman Wittes has correctly observed that the broad problem that haunts American democratisation efforts is that... "[the] general preference for democratic politics has long been tempered, in regard to the Arab world, by the knowledge that the victors of a democratic process in most Arab countries are unlikely to be the parties who share America's policy preferences in the region. In other words, as former

Secretary of State Madeline Albright once observed, 'Arab public opinion, after all, can be rather scary.'" (1)

The irony of this matter of dictatorships, who are ruling the region, is that they are created by the West. In particular by the UK and its famous Winston Churchill who in 1921 as colonial secretary, held the infamous Cairo conference (the forty thieves, as dubbed by Churchill) that consolidated the hands of the British Empire on the affairs of the region. The assembled officials at the conference had before them three immediate objectives:

First to consolidate gains and effect economies through more efficient administration at the local level in various parts of the Arab world; second to reconcile the different representatives held by the British officials and governmental agencies involved in the Middle Eastern affairs by means of a centralised control exercised effectively in London; and third by means of the above, to arrive at a comprehensive framework, incorporating previous commitments and existing realities for the future relations with the Arabs. (2)

At the same time as Amirahmadi puts it, Orientalism was promoted in Western policy circles, academia and media, exaggerating and distorting the differences between Arab peoples and cultures and those of the West. Arabs and Muslims were viewed as exotic, backward, uncivilised, and at times dangerous. For many years the thinking of Western scholars was dominated by the idea that Arabs were not ready for democracy and were indeed even incapable of living under democratic rule. The racism and stereotyping went so far as to claim that there was an "Arab mind" bent on rejectionism, fundamentalism and terrorism. Cultural demonization complemented the Western economic domination and murderous political humiliation; while

Britain was seizing control of Arab oil resources, for example, France was killing a million Algerians. Worse, Arabs and Muslims were also humiliated by their own corrupt, inept, or ignorant rulers — dictators and populists alike. These rulers, many of whom had been nurtured and supported by outside powers, made the national state their private property, extended their rule to lifelong terms, and limited elite circulation to their immediate families, allies and stooges. They created oligarchic economies, mismanaged their countries, and misappropriated the public budget and wealth. Middle Eastern rulers, aided by foreign powers, destroyed all nationalist, reformist and socialist opposition. (3)

The division of the region with sandy borders, and the appointing of the puppets who were already receiving pay cheques from the queen at the time, including al-Saud, current leader of Saudi Arabia and the Hashemite of Jordan and some others, in real terms all have same one main objective which is to stay in power by all means possible. In the modern history of the region, I do not recall any puppet has ever retired voluntarily or been voted out of office. The historical pattern is that if they are not toppled during the first few months, they are set to rule — usually for life.

The longevity of the leaders and their regimes is indeed puzzling. They hang onto power until they are dead by natural causes, but before their deaths, they make sure that they clone themselves for the next one to appear. If people revolt against them, they never surrender in peace, instead they are ready to destroy their whole country before they go, and that is if they go. There is also a huge disconnect between the leaders and the common man, therefore, these leaders face serious legitimacy issues which they tend to deal with by all kinds of brutality and intimidation in dealing with their citizens. The picture in this region is that there are governments without people and people without governments.

The biggest and most deadly plagues taking firm hold of the region and its people are the heads of state. Those who are so-called Kings, Emirs, presidents, etc. are the main and most serious plague and main obstacle that is holding back the development of the region and its people, directly or indirectly stealing its wealth and its valuable resources, and destroying the main source of pride for any nation, the human brain.

Those who are at present called the leaders of the so-called "Middle East" have a job description. This job description is written mainly by their masters in the West, and it says the following:

1. Always maintain the West's interests as the highest priority, irrespective of your people's wishes or desires.

2. The natural resources your territory has must always be maintained to serve the Western world's interests.

3. Always ensure (by all available means) that the good brains of your people are automatically transferred to our horizon.

4. Always ensure the stability and security of the Zionist state and its interests.

5. Ensure that your people are always divided and weak by fuelling the sense of tribalism and kinsmen.

6. Ensure that the corruption culture, however small, is enriched and encouraged in the mind of your subjects.

7. If your country is rich with natural resources, ensure that you give them the crumbs falling from the table and for non-rich countries, just give them the leftovers.

8. Ensure that Islam and Islamic culture are subjugated and looked down upon as a primitive, backward and irrelevant religion in the current age.

9. Ensure that you and your extended family(s) spend your holidays and money in our lovely capitals and different resorts, but above all, encourage your wife(s) and children to purchase the most expensive homes, yachts, pieces of jewellery ever brought to market.

10. Ensure that you have solid and sophisticated chambers of torture in filthy and inhuman underground rooms and basements.

11. Ensure that illicit drugs, such as Hashish, are widely available to your subjects for them to have some relief before dawn.

12. Above all ensure that the oil fields and the gold mines are in our hands, no matter what the circumstances are.

13. Full compliance and adherence with our monetary systems and its policies and procedures.

14. The above job description is not exclusive and may, at any time, change according to our needs and interests.

Aims and Objectives of the Job:

1. To enhance and protect your master's vital economic, political and diplomatic interests in the land you're appointed to rule.

2. To keep validating the purchase of weapons and ammunition from your master's factories.

3. To kill, imprison or expel your opponent (your opponent is automatically ours too) who might be a risk towards our interests and intentions towards the region.

4. To enrich the field of ignorance, confusion and hopelessness among your subjects by all means possible.

5. To develop a heavily restricted media and promote highly corrupt personnel to run it according to our ideas and opinions.

6. To establish and propagate (through different means) an atmosphere of consumerism and individualism according to our great civilisation.

7. To build a society that looks down upon its teachers and intellectuals as irrelevant, and where knowledge is discouraged.

8. To create no meaningful or effective research institutions in particular scientific institutions or think tanks.

9. To ensure that creative thinking and problem-solving are discouraged and reduced and looked upon in your schools and other learning institutions as just rhetoric.

10. By all means to enrich and encourage the sense of tribalism, kinsman, nepotism and favouritism.

11. Again these aims and objectives are not conclusive and may change or be adjusted according to the circumstances of the day.

Benefits and Reward:

1. Security and stability of your land and regime for life. No need for you to look for another job or consider another field of work.

2. Full pay and subsidies from your masters every month, or if your land is awash with oil, then you're allowed to steal as much as possibly can be tolerated to enrich yourself and your corrupt gangs.

3. Full backing of our military and security services including intelligence services to protect you in case of an emergency.

4. Complete cover up or looking the other way, if our free media reveals or criticises your doctrinaire, repressive and

ugly actions towards your subjects (we might consider them people, yet for now, they are just a sack of subjects).

5. You and your extended family(s) are welcome in our magnificent cities and beaches to have inordinate holidays free of charge, and middlemen/women can be arranged to hide any trace of our government's link. As you well know, we care about our election(s) to power.

6. Full reception with full honours as a head of a state in our lands including the lounges of the Whitehouse or the Court of the Queen.

7. Complete induction and full training for your intelligence services on the modern techniques of surveillance and how to use our equipment effectively to this noble aim of ensuring that your subjects are fully controlled.

8. Intelligence cover ups and support for your atrocities committed against your subjects, as and when required. Therefore, no fear of any court including the one in The Hague.

It is highly important and vital that for you to preserve the job forever you must ensure that, at all times, full compliance and submission to your paymaster(s) is observed. Non-compliance will trigger some mild warnings initially. Yet, further commitments to violate the contract will be met by severe and lasting punishments including, but not limited to, severe sanctions against you and your subjects and/or regime change.

To our candidates: keep in mind that your master(s) control and dominate all international institutions including, but not limited to, the impotent United Nations and its wings, as well as the International Bank, etc.

For a region I grew up in and can fairly say is the most volatile and explosive region in the entire globe, yet I always wondered how on earth are their rulers surviving and in some instances even flourishing? Are they geniuses? Despite the massive economic poorness, lack of respect to human dignity, lack of accountability, lack of the vital importance of the rule of law, lack of basic human freedoms such as the freedom of speech or assembly, lack of proper and effective civil servants, lack of basic health care in some countries of the region, lack of any leading scientific researchers in any field, and I can go on and on and on.

I think the most reasonable explanation of how they and their regimes survive are three main factors (1) their brutality and aggressiveness in which they suppress their opponents, whoever they might be. (2) They've cultivated among their ministers etc. a strong culture of corruption and favouritism to the end of protecting their chairs forever. (3) The robust protection of their paymasters in the West in supporting them directly or discretely in every way possible to ensure that the status quo is safeguarded for the paymaster's benefits and vital interests in the region according to their job description stated above.

Concerning point one, examples can come from two so-called countries i.e. Saudi Arabia and Jordan. The former is the richest (in terms of wealth) and the latter is one of the poorest in the region. Both of their regimes have survived for ages, but the big question is how have they survived to the present day?

In the case of Saudi Arabia, which is an autocratic regime, their main survival tool is their vast and unimaginable wealth (petrodollar) which they exploit to meet the end target of staying in power. They basically buy their legitimacy by bribing the different tribes and their heads scattered in the desert kingdom. So the heads of the tribes accordingly also buy their legitimacy from their tribesmen. Therefore, the cycle of corruption and bribes is endless.

The so-called Saudi Arabia monarchy has no system of accountability to the people. Meaning that they (the Al Saud family) can do virtually anything with the wealth of the land generated mainly by the vast amount of oil the land has. Yearly, millions of dollars are given to their extended family members as allowances and their numbers are estimated to be in the thousands. That is why, for example, you see young Saudi men/boys racing in their highly luxurious cars through the streets of London or Saudi women chasing the most expensive pieces of jewellery or brand clothes that ever came to the shops in any European capital.

Some people would say that not all Saudis are corrupt and content with the current situation. Yes, that is a true and fair point. So what does the Saudi government tend to do with them, if they try to oppose their rule publicly? Usually, what the agents of the government tend to do is two main things (1) calmly and politely, ask the "rebel" to change their mind and go along with the mainstream herds. (2) If this policy does not work, and the rebel insists in his opposition, then he/she will be labelled all sorts, including but not exclusively Muslim extremist (the most popular label) which equates to terrorist, Marxist which equates to Kafir (infidel), or any other label(s) which is overwhelmingly known to all us in this age.

The fate of that person will be as follows:

1. Life in prison with the accompanying lovely humiliation and torture.

2. Complete degradation of their livelihood and tarnishing of their reputation by all means possible including the use of the media.

3. And at best, a life-long exile to another country (usually to the puppet's paymaster/supervisor in the West).

In the case of Jordan, which is one of the poorest states in the region, as it has virtually no natural resources to speak of and no real economic development to sustain a nation? Now we have a dilemma of what to do with the people who might cause a risk to our autocratic regime? This small country with its monarch at the head (the Hashemite family, who claim to be the descendent of the Prophet Muhammad) has established through the years an extremely strong sense of tribalism and at the helm of their tribes are the Bedouin of Jordan's deserts. These tribes essentially control and administer the internal security agencies of the country and its wide and ruthless branches. Of course, their main task is to keep a close eye on the people in general and persons who might be considered a risk to the establishment in particular.

As the head of the country (the monarch) is subsidised by their masters in particular Britain and the US, to ensure these countries' interests are protected. The internal agents are also rewarded for a good job done. Their rewards include a permanent job for life as well as good possibilities for promotion, securing jobs and benefits for their clan/relatives as well as an audience with the ultimate court.

Their basic skills and qualifications are good measures of torture, humiliation, and destruction of body and soul to the person(s) in question.

What the ultimate power of the county (the monarch) also does is, from time to time they create some kind of reform(s) to the repressive and tyrannical atmosphere. Such as creating a parliament (a talkative one) by permitting some political parties (parties which are YES SIR) to exist. But the final aim of any reform is to release some anger towards the established order. As well as to paint a fake picture (internally & externally) that they are democratic, progressive and care for people.

The two examples illustrated above are by no means exclusive to these two countries. You can easily draw the same or similar parallel to other countries in the region. Some others are even more brutal and aggressive towards their subjects than the two counties mentioned.

But it must be said that these countries, as the creation of foreign/alien western powers, are illegitimate children of the imperialists. After the First World War (1914/19), and as a consequence, the famous Sykes-Picot agreement of 1916 was established to divide the spoils between the British and French imperial powers. And to this day, their leaders in the eyes of the region's streets have no real legitimacy or credibility and are extremely weak. As a result of their pitiful weakness and illegitimacy, they practise terrors and oppressive measures against their subjects to preserve their position. The question now is, for how long? The answer is I do not know.[1]

But on a positive note, and despite the whole destruction (more or less) of the whole region due to endless and meaningless wars from North Africa to the heart of the Arab world, the resilience and determination of the people in the streets will defeat the injustices they have for so long incurred. Yet for them to win their legitimate freedom and acquire justice they must meet certain conditions which, in my view, are essential to building a viable nation(s):

1. Elimination of the system of tribalism and favouritism as well as corruption, the issue of corruption will be tackled later in the book.

---

[1] For more readings about the point illustrated, refer to, London and the Invention of the Middle East, Money, Power, and War, 1902-1922. Roger Adelson, 1995. Or Foundations of British Policy in the Arab World: The Cairo Conference of 1921, by Aaron S. Klieman, 1970.

2. Building a family system that endorses logical conversations and enriches the notion of rational and critical thinking.

3. Family and society as a whole must acknowledge and respect differences in opinions without prejudices and ill feelings.

4. Encourage our young through family and parenting, to think out of the box.

5. The notion of pure individualism and pure consumerism, according to Western values and beliefs, must be discouraged and replaced by the sense of collective charities and collective solidarity.

6. Society, in general, must propagate and encourage as well as cultivate in the minds of the youth respect for teachers and educated people. As our teachers are very essential and one of the main constructs of any successful society or country.

Just to illustrate how vital education is to the minds of imperialism the following is said:

Education is the key to the missionaries' strategy. The best known of the schools that the Americans set up was the Syrian Protestant College in Beirut. Renamed the American University of Beirut, by 1940 it had 2,000 students on its roll, meaning the Americans had overtaken the French as the most significant providers of education in the region. It, and the American University in Cairo, which was established just after the end of the First World War, reinforced the Americans' reputation as disinterested philanthropists. Writing a few years later, a British politician reckoned that these two institutions had 'done more to promote American interests in the Middle East than all the British diplomats and armies put together'. (4)

7. I have always believed that if you want to change and create a positive impact on the situation you're in, then you must first create first a positive change(s) from within. We need to ensure that we tackle and solve our internal ills and plagues troubling our society(s) before looking any further, meaning sort out our home first before sorting out any other external issue.

8. If we want to move forward, we need to admit and acknowledge that the massive problems facing the region, at the end of the day, are our fault. We cannot afford to just keep blaming others. In my view, there is no point in pointing fingers at the centuries of foreign interference and imperialism. But yes to learning/analysing lessons from the past and move forward according to lessons learned. Therefore the blame culture must be stopped as it will essentially lead to nothing but frustration, disenchantment, and more disappointment among us all. Smir Kassir — a Palestinian/ Lebanese/French journalist, who in 2005 was assassinated by a car bomb — summarises the situation of the Arab streets feeling as follows: The Arab people are haunted by a sense of powerlessness; permanently inflamed, it is the badge of their malaise. Powerlessness to be what you think you should be. Powerlessness to act to affirm your existence, even merely theoretically, in the face of the "Other" who denies your right to exist, despises you and has once again reasserted his domination over you. Powerlessness to suppress the feeling that you are no more than a lowly pawn on the global chessboard even as the game is played in your backyard. (5)

For me, I do not think I would be able to put it as eloquently and as bluntly as he did.

In the streets of the region, many ordinary people are dissatisfied and abhor their puppets. They believe that they are oppressed and made or reduced to the level of slaves for the sake of the selfish, dishonest and corrupt regimes whose interests lay squarely in maintaining their seats of power irrespective and regardless of peoples' interests and welfare. The region's people are appalled by the heavy-handedness of the apparatus of the security forces in their lands. And they have been led to believe that if the current regime is toppled, the next one will be much worse (Sies's Egypt is an example) or at best insecurity and chaos will prevail.

These puppets with their disgraceful lifelong rule over the peoples of the region using various kinds of torture in their unrestrained security forces and subjecting the masses to daily humiliations and antagonisms in their daily lives, did not refrain at that, they have also brought to the region destruction and countless deaths through various and ugly regional wars, brought grinding poverty upon the masses, and all they have successfully managed is to corner the people and their spirits into a tiny prison cell without a window. And of course, the Western world is more than happy to support and keep these puppets nailed in their seats, not because these puppets have a lovely look, but because they have vested interests in the region's precious natural resources as well as other strategic considerations. Despite all the nonsense talk we constantly hear from Western politicians and the like, in the dishonest waves of the Western media, promoting the policies of "freedom, human rights and democracy", their real intention was, is and always will be to retain the tyrants in their position and ensure that the status quo is maintained and strengthened.

In the 1950s, an American spy (CIA officer) called Kim Roosevelt, chairing a committee tasked with defining a new American approach to the "Middle East" declared the following: 'Our principle should be encouraging the emergence of competent leaders, relatively well-disposed toward the West, through programs designed for this purpose, including where possible, a conscious, though perhaps covert, effort to cultivate and aid such potential leaders, even when they are not in power.'(6) Here we go our stooges; you are virtually nothing but a creation of your paymasters of the West. And, of course, their are so many other similar historical facts and statements to prove that you are nothing but a musical string dancing between the figures of your appointee(s).

I do not comprehend how those so-called leaders of the region, can or dare to show their faces to the public! But it seems to me that they have completely lost self-esteem, principles, pride, morality, and above all, they have lost consciousness. What a shame, but this what the common man in the streets of the region believes, in their hearts and pulses, as well as what they have to put up with, i.e. the Stooges, due to fear, oppression, vengeance or more impoverishment. Therefore, they are sadly trapped and trapped more than they've ever anticipated or thought of. They are in reality stuck between the following:

1. Vicious and ruthless 'leaders' insisting and adamant, by all means, to ensure that they stay on their seats, as they say in English by "Hook or Crook." And to put it mildly, the only description for them is that they are a punch of cankers.

2. The bombardment of too many media outlets which propagate 'above all' Western and alien propaganda and values which don't strike a chord with their religion, values and cultures.

3. What they hear and watch, day in and day out, on how their countries are progressing in terms of being civil and just, and what they're seeing and witnessing on the ground daily are far apart.

4. They are also stuck with and between the magnificent history of the Islamic empires for so many centuries with full freedom of movement, innovation, knowledge, justice and security and what they are living under at present, which consist of misery, constant destruction of their livelihoods, humiliation and lack of basic freedom and maybe, above all lack of self-existence as a human being.

The ironic part of the whole story is that, while the common man in the region blames their puppet leaders for the current awful situation in their countries, the puppets and their propagandists blame the centuries of imperialism and colonisation of the region, and then the imperialist powers blame their puppets for being dictators. Yet, there is no one willing to admit or have the moral courage to take any responsibility. So, it's a blame game that will never solve or correct any problem.

Then the big question is how to solve this problem? I might sound unfair in answering this question, taking into account how much the peoples of this region have suffered and are unfortunately still suffering, yet it's the common man who is virtually to blame. Why? The answer, in brief, is as follows:

1. Once the peoples of the region participate directly or indirectly in the daily affairs of the state, then they are (they like it not) active supporters of the ugly regimes they detest.

2. The peoples of the region believe that their 'states' represent almost always everything negative, yet, they hardly take actions to change the black realities they are living under.

3. Most significant is the fact that they long for and aspire for unity amongst the region's divided 'states', but miserably they're divided amongst themselves.

Many ordinary Arabs complain of a huge and growing disconnect between governments and people. For Egyptian Khaled Diab, the behaviour and attitudes of most Arab regimes are more akin to those of colonial rulers than a government that has genuine roots among the people. Given the history, this is not entirely surprising, he said:

Egypt, for example, apart from a few isolated episodes, wasn't an independent country ruled by native rulers for nearly two-and-a-half thousand years. It was the jewel in the crown of various empires. A lot of them were based there, but it was often a foreign elite that ruled those empires. (7)

[After independence, Arab governments] took over a lot of the instruments of state that were left behind and did not reform them, so the ruling elite became a kind of pseudo-colonial ruler. Rather than reform the system to make it reflective of the will of the people they also became distant elite. People feel just as alienated from the native government today in a lot of Arab countries as they did towards their foreign rulers previously. (8)

To summarise this chapter, if the societies of the region keep fearing their puppets (as if they were Gods) and persist in describing themselves as victims of different internal as well as external factors, then I would suggest that the status quo will endure and may endure for a long time to come.

Without a cohesion and unified front to face any enemy, which are essential elements to any significant change or victory, of the peoples in the streets of the region, I would think that there would be no real victory and the attempts, if occurred, would be considered a waste of efforts and resources, which at the end of the day, will strengthen the hands of the stooges who by their teeth and supported by the teeth of their Western friends advocate the current status quo.

Quoting George Carlin, an American stand-up comedian and social critic by saying, "governments do not want well-informed, well-educated people capable of critical thinking. This is against their interests. They want obedient workers, people who are just smart enough to run machines and do paperwork. And just dumb enough to passively accept it".

Many years after the Arab uprisings of 2010/11, most of the political entities in the region are still facing a crisis in governance, but their responses to the events have varied. Many of the regimes that did not experience uprisings insist the current regional turmoil is a consequence of these upheavals and are thus seeking a return to the stability of the pre-2011 Arab order. Countries that have undergone transitions are struggling to create more inclusive and responsive systems of government. Others are caught up in civil wars, or, as in the case of Egypt, are headed toward further repression and a new brand of authoritarianism.

The current geopolitics of the region in no doubt is characterised by failed states, political chaos, popular revolt, ignorance, and inter-state conflict, foreign rivalries and military interventions. The lands of the region are shamelessly plundered, their social systems twisted and dehumanised, their environments ruined, their cities and towns vacated by the people migrating to safer places. In such a dark scenario, a condition of despair will prevail and extremist groups and their rivals, struggling for self-preservation, will scar the region's landscape. These puppet rulers and their foreign masters must bear full responsibility and be accountable for the ugly atrocities committed. For too long they have worked, whether together or in opposition, to suppress popular demands for political reform, ruin economies, provoke regional conflict, and humiliate struggling populations. Ideologies, religions in particular, have promoted obliviousness and intolerance; they have inflicted so much suffering and hardship and therefore I can't resist calling them criminals and they must be replaced by new, honest and moral drivers for a meaningful change.

What the so-called "Arab Spring" has done is help clarify what the region's scholars have known for a long time — that the fundamental political gap in the region that shapes internal politics is not between pro-Western and anti-Western forces nor is it between Shia and Sunni or Arab and Jew, but rather it is the enormous gulf that separates long-standing authoritarian regimes from the people they rule over.

Without the formation of far-reaching and broad alliances for real change, the Arab autocrats might eventually manage to deal with internal and external pressures either by inventing a "theatre of reforms" based on cosmetic changes or by discrediting calls for political change as acts of subversion and foreign aggression against the national sovereignty. History shows that authoritarian rulers are well equipped to successfully play the game of "us against them" and in doing so to portray themselves as national heroes whose unquestioned obedience becomes a sacred duty.

I strongly believe that is exactly the dark picture dominating the region and its peoples from its north to its south, from east to west. Despite its darkness, I can't deny the fact that the people of the region, in different degrees, are a participant in the system of oppression that is prevailing in every part of the region; hence, they are to blame.

Imagining a more inventive Middle East can seem like an audacious act. In the late 1960s and early 1970s, a movement of radical Arab intellectuals began to reject the prevailing political malaise characterising the region. In 1968, one of its members, the Syrian philosopher and dissident Sadiq Jalal al-Azm, who passed away in December 2016, published "Self-Criticism After the Defeat," for which he was jailed. Although ostensibly an analysis of the humiliating Arab defeat by Israel in the Six-Day War, in fact this seminal volume was a scornful critique of Arab political culture. Al-Azm lamented that rather than accepting responsibility for the military defeat, Arab leaders instead sought to make excuses and deflect blame, thereby squandering the opportunity for cultural rejuvenation. Nearly half a century later, al-Azm reflected upon the legacy of the tumult of recent years. He argued, in an echo of his earlier critique, that the Arab uprisings have helped us to see regional realities for what they are: states that are now dominated by sectarian and ethnic identities instead of inclusive national identities, and dictatorships that have given way to civil war, state collapse and terrorism. If these uprisings have succeeded in nothing else, they have helped to illuminate the profound challenges Arab societies face in the long journey toward civility and a better future. (9)

In concluding this chapter, I need to stress the fact that these Arab regimes never represent their people. The people's aspirations and opinions are one thing and their so-called rulers are another matter altogether, certainly apart from the cronies who benefit. For example;

It is often stated that for the last thirty-three years, Egypt and Israel have had a peace treaty. This is a misleading characterisation of the 1979 Camp David Accords. It is more accurate to state that Israel has had a peace treaty—not with Egypt—but with the Sadat-Mubarak regime and with the Egyptian ruling elites that supported it. The people of Egypt were not consulted on the Camp David Accords and they have had no input on this important foreign policy decision.

The same truism applies to Israel's 1994 peace treaty with Jordan. Moshe Arens, a Likud party hard-liner and three-time Minister of Defence, addressed this topic with considerable candour and clarity at the start of the Arab Spring. "The ugly facts," he noted, "are that the two peace treaties that Israel concluded so far—the one with Egypt and the other with Jordan—were both signed with dictators: Anwar Sadat and King Hussein." He added that "the negotiations that for a while held some promise of reaching a peace agreement with Syria and with the Palestine Liberation Organization were also conducted with unsavoury dictators." With the gradual and inevitable spread of democracy throughout the region, this national security strategy is no longer tenable. Israel's long-term security in the Middle East can only be guaranteed when it makes peace with the people of the region, not with the dictators that rule over them. This can only happen if Israel is willing to give justice to Palestinians, which is a precondition for its acceptance as a legitimate state in the eyes of the people of the Arab-Islamic world. Ibrahim Kalin, an adviser to the Turkish government, captures this point quite succinctly in calling on Israel to reassess its strategic priorities. "The Netanyahu government's defiant yet eventually self-destructive approach is indicative of the eclipse of Israeli strategic thinking," he observes. "Israeli politicians fail to understand that the fundamental values of the new Middle East spearheaded by the Arab Spring are no longer occupation, dictatorship and alienation but justice, freedom and rule of law. No policy that does not take these values seriously can have legitimacy." (10)

References for Chapter 2: Plague Two: The Puppets

1. NADER HASHEMI, THE ARAB SPRING, US FOREIGN POLICY, AND THE QUESTION OF DEMOCRACY IN THE MIDDLE EAST, 15/12/2012,http://djilp.org/wp-content/uploads/2014/04/Hashemi_FinaltoPrinter.pdf

2. Aaron S. Klieman, Foundations of British Policy in the Arab World: The Cairo Conference of 1921, The Johns Hopkins Press, Baltimore and London, 1970. Preface, vii-viii

3. Hooshang Amirahmadi, Dark Geopolitics of the Middle East, how the Region's Autocrats and Foreign Intruders Created Growing disorder,https://cdn.thecairoreview.com/wp-content/uploads/2015/09/CR18-Amirahmadi.pdf

4. James Barr, Lords of the Desert, Britain's struggle with America to dominate the Middle East, Simon & Schuster UK Ltd, 2018

5. Kassir, Samir, Being Arab, London, 2006

6. Lucas and Morey, 'The Hidden "Alliance"', P. 97.

7. Brian Whitaker, What's Really Wrong with the Middle East, by Saqi, 2009, P. 83-84

8. Ibid

9. Arab Fractures, Citizens, States, and Social Contracts, PERRY CAMMACK MICHELE DUNNE AMR HAMZAWY MARC LYNCH MARWAN MUASHER YEZID SAYIGH MAHA YAHYA, https://carnegieendowment.org/files/Arab_World_Horizons_Final.pdf

10. NADER HASHEMI, THE ARAB SPRING, US FOREIGN POLICY, AND THE QUESTION OF DEMOCRACY IN THE MIDDLE EAST, 15/12/2012, http://djilp.org/wp-content/uploads/2014/04/Hashemi_FinaltoPrinter.pdf

Chapter 3: Plague Three: Corruption

Corruption has appeared in the land and the sea on account of what the hands of men have wrought that He may make them taste a part of that which they have done, so that they may return.

— *Holy Qur'an, Surat al-Rum, 30:41*

"The curse of Allah is upon the one who offers a bribe and the one who takes it."

— *Saying of Prophet Mohammed, peace upon him*

The roots of instability in the region are found in several factors: the entrenchment of governing regimes, human rights violations, government corruption, and extreme gaps between the rich and poor, rising food prices, unemployment, and (importantly) the large and growing circle of educated but unemployed and dissatisfied youth.

Political corruption is the use of powers by government officials or their network contacts for illegitimate private gain. Forms of corruption vary but include bribery, extortion, cronyism, nepotism, parochialism, patronage, influence peddling, graft, and embezzlement.

Corruption is a very costly affair, politically, economically, and socially. The plague of corruption is a very serious and destructive disease when struck upon any society. Its destructiveness is immeasurable. It consumes people's resources, wealth, and above all their spirits, but it also leads to dis-cohesion and mistrust among members of the society and the fragmentation of moral principles. I simply compare any region as the "Middle East" suffering from this plague, as a walking body but without a spirit, or as a person injected with a syringe full of morphine prescribed for slow and eventual death.

Corruption is a major obstacle to the rule of law, to the economic prosperity of any region, to good and honest governance, and also a major obstacle to social unity in which any sane regime must strive to gain support, legitimacy and defence against potential odds.

Some people of the region say that corruption happens everywhere, even at the highest levels in Western countries. It is true that corruption happens everywhere. Yet, unfortunately, that does not make corruption less bad. In particular, corruption is not as embedded in everyday life in the West as it is in the region's countries. The majority of citizens in the West have never bribed an official. The majority of people in the region's countries have. Therefore, I consider it endemic. People also say that corruption is an illness brought by the West. Yet, that does not explain why the majority of people in the region's countries participate in corruption. Thus, this seems to be rather wishful thinking.

Endemic corruption, in any society/nation, causes so many catastrophes, irrespective of the political systems, religions, race, etc. It causes major dis-functioning of coherent and viable societies, reduces economic productivity which leads to stagnant growth, increases the disillusionment and widens the gap between the people and their governments, and above all it creates a massive conscious conflict in the psyche of the individuals especially when their religion condemns and forbids corruption/bribery in the strongest terms. Of course, there are many other horrendous and lasting negative consequences relating to this plague, which can be found in other literature. But my point here in this chapter is the three following questions:

(1) Why do the peoples in this region indulge in this crime? (2) Why is it endemic and who is encouraging it? (3) And how it should be fought?

If you venture into the "Middle Eastern" streets and ask the people what are the most loathed places they have to go to attend an essential business, they would most likely say governmental departments. Why? The answer is simply and plainly a great deal of high bureaucracy and the obstacles the concerned bureaucrats will toss in your way to prevent you from completing your business, but they have one thing in mind which is to eventually break your spirit and force you to pay a bribe or to achieve some sort of favour, which is usually the end game. The corruption and favouritism in the region are not only confined to the small bureaucrats, but it's more widely spread amongst the big sharks of governments' apparatus. Even back in 1977 when shortly after David Owen took over as Britain's foreign secretary, he received a confidential letter from the British embassy in Jeddah (Saudi Arabia) clarifying the difficulties of doing business with the Saudis, and I quote:

"The exact nature of the Saudi decision-making machinery is obscure but certainly much settled by agreement between the senior princes. To secure contracts, a company must secure the support not merely of a senior prince, often through an established agent through whom very substantial commissions have to be paid, but also many ministers and officials down the line." (1)

Certainly, the example above is not, by any measure, exclusive to the regime in that land. Unfortunately for the so many millions of inhabitants of the lands of this region, this disease is wildly entrenched in every corner of governmental institutions, maybe with extremely few exceptions.

Western governments and companies connived in this, apparently without serious qualms, because they knew their export sales depended on it. It was also difficult to avoid when rivals were resorting to bribes and the use of fixers too. In the words of Sir Ian Gilmour, a former British defence secretary, "You either got the business and bribed, or you didn't bribe and didn't get the business." (2)

And what is more disastrous to the region and its people is that this disease has infected and grown as a giant in the systems of courts of police and their agents who are supposed to protect and safeguard the principles of justice and law and order. Therefore, I argue, if the apparatus of justice and its wings are corrupt and justice is for the higher bidder, then how on earth can the region and its people prosper, flourish, strengthen, and above all feel safe and secure with dignity and respect? There is no way thinkable that the people can feel safe and secure, and as a result, the evolution and progress of the region are completely hindered or even stopped.

Again it is unfortunate that the masses of this region are engaged in this evil practice, simply because they believe, or are made to believe, that they are powerless to do anything else and they have to be content with the current status quo. They simply argue that if the heads of the regimes and their strong and vast apparatus of bureaucrats are infested with corruption and greed, they ultimately indulge themselves in the practice in the hope that their lives will be a little easier and avoid problems and more hardships. Yet sadly, the bigger picture of participating in this malpractice is lost in the minds of the masses.

Corruption in this region starts from the top, and when people at the top are corrupt, they must ensure that their juniors are also corrupt, for one main reason, "their safety". And this point leads me to the second point of the argument. Who encourages corruption and dishonesty?

The following will shed light in explaining this point. The Arab Human Development Report of 2004 says about the factors in Arab countries that exacerbate the problem of corruption and makes it so widespread:

"The politico-legal structure of some states makes it difficult to differentiate between corruption in its conventional form (abuse of public office for personal gain), and an inherent failing (rigged rules) in the system itself. For example, in some states both law and custom decree that the land and its natural resources belong to the ruler, and fail to distinguish at this level between the private and public life of the ruler, while private property of the ordinary citizen becomes a grant from the ruler. In such a situation, it is difficult to talk of corruption in governance, for whatever the ruler does, he is disposing of his property.

"Some regimes set up economic institutions attached to their military or security apparatus, to finance their activities. Here again, matters become confused: it becomes difficult to draw the line between the exercise of an official function (since individual corruption may be but a reflection of the corruption of the whole situation) and what can be described as personal corruption.

"Besides, there are ways to manipulate laws that, in many Arab countries, do not allow senior officials to carry out private business while they occupy an official post. Many officials circumvent the law by allowing members of their families to set up companies and enterprises that often benefit from the official's position and relations". (3)

I certainly do not and cannot contradict or argue against the above description, as it accurately depicts the whole situation currently prevailing in the region. And that leads me to say that, those puppets who rule the region and their brutal wings of bureaucrats are the chief instigators and encouragers of the epidemic of corruption. Yet, I also must indicate that the masses of the region also bear big responsibility. It is good to say and complain that the governments and its wings are corrupt and ineffective which is true, but the essential question is how we people can change this?

I can fairly and with some certainty, say that the so-called "Arab Spring" did not emerge or erupt as mass demonstrations in the streets of some parts of the region, which unfortunately did not materialise in a massive change, for the love of the ideology of Western democracy, as the Western media wants to portray, and what this ideology entails. The "Arab Spring" predominantly was a mass demonstration of the people against corruption and its associated evils. And by associated evils, I mean the status quo in the image of the corrupt puppets and their oppressive wings of the ruling elite and bureaucrats.

Miserably, and despite the human lives lost, the tragedies and sacrifices which the people had to endure and suffer during "the Arab Spring", and to some extent, after the dust settled down and the air became clearer to see through, the situation in the region, to a great extent remains static or even worse than before, such as the present situation in Egypt.

Results from a poll conducted in 2016 by Transparency International (the survey included around 11,000 respondents from Algeria, Egypt, Jordan, Lebanon, Morocco, Palestine, Sudan, Tunisia and Yemen) suggest that 61 per cent of people in a cross-section of the Middle East and North Africa (MENA) countries saw an increase in corruption compared to the year before, while nearly a third said that they had paid a bribe in order to access basic services.

It also suggests that almost one in three respondents said they had paid a bribe when dealing with the court system in their country, while one in four had paid a bribe to the police. Furthermore, the results show that around a half or more of bribe payers to the courts and the police had to pay multiple times, indicating that this can be a frequent occurrence for some in the region when accessing law and order services. Government officials, tax officials and members of parliament were viewed as the most corrupt groups overall.

The main drivers of this endemic corruption are the puppets and their circle of power and greed. And the end game in their corrupt minds is merely political survival at all costs, rather than pursuing meaningful, viable, real jobs-creating economies, and transparent governance and economies. In this part of the world, the real commercial, financial and influential leaders are no one but the privileged elites, irrespective of their qualifications, merits or suitability, who become part and parcel of the horrid governments.

And what is really disturbing and morally corrupt, is the fact that, more or less, all the puppets of the region employ massive numbers of bureaucrats, definitely not to help their people, but only to ensure that the loyalty of the bureaucrats is maintained. Of course, each bureaucrat has a family or even an extended family to look after and sustain. Therefore, these puppets are certainly aware of the fact that these people are heavily reliant on them for the monthly crumbs or hand-outs from the state. Simple mathematics leads me to conclude the following: (only for the sake of the argument)

Total workforce of a population is 10 million people.

Employing 40 per cent (in some countries of the region) of the workforce equates to 4 million.

The 4 million people have dependents; usually on average another 4 people, which equates to 16 million people.

As a Lebanese activist noted, the "lack of meritocratic recruitment in the public administration and the prevalence of clientelist, nepotistic, and sectarian considerations often leads to the appointment of unqualified civil servants who either take part or contribute to cover corrupt practices." Clientelism across the region leads to a vicious cycle of poorly performing bureaucracies, which undermines trust in institutions, which in turn fuels further corruption. (4)

Seeing the bigger picture, the vast majority of the working population is dependent on the hand-outs (crumbs) of their puppets and its wings. Therefore, they are simplistically, just trapped behind the iron bars of their government(s), if I can call them such. Sadly and regrettably, as these people and their dependents are on extremely low monthly wages/salaries, the situation they find themselves in encourages them to resort to corruption to compensate for their low legitimate earnings. I must stress here that, by no account am I am accusing all of them of being corrupt, but sadly, the majority are.

In the Arab world, bureaucracy has traditionally inspired bitter spoofs. Tunisians remember comedian Lamine Nahdi in the role of a hapless citizen asked to provide all kinds of implausible documents, including his death certificate, as a prerequisite for government service. (5)

The problem of red tape, as experienced in many parts of the Arab world, is that it is built on the pessimistic premise that no one is to be trusted. The assumption of dishonesty reigns supreme. Each document supplied is assumed to have been forged until proven authentic. For every signed document, proof must be provided that the signature is genuine. All too often this means having a civil servant vouch for the authenticity of a signature in exchange for a fee. That surrealistic exercise can consume half a day if not more. The only redeeming quality of this time-consuming practice is that it helps keep public servants employed, or at least apparently busy. (6)

In December 2018 Egypt's Minister of Finance Mohamed Ma'it said the government cannot create new jobs but the private sector can. "The government has five million employees who cannot even find a chair to sit on," the minister said during a meeting of the parliamentary economic committee which was calling for greater investment in the country. (7)

Brian Whitaker, in his well-balanced book, "What's Really Wrong with the Middle East" writes: When the machinery of government grinds slowly and inefficiently, people look for ways to short-circuit it — and one way is with money. Realising that slowness and inefficiency can be lucrative; officials — often on low salaries — thus have every incentive to be as obstructive as possible until payment is in prospect. (8)

The author also added, the preoccupation with social status in Arab countries also infects and undermines their administrative systems. Constitutions may preach that everyone is equal before the law but the reality is different. Whether it is a matter of asking officials to do something — such as granting a permit — or seeking to avoid a penalty, status counts and is recognised by the system, allowing those with the right level of clout to pull rank. "People with a certain status in society think the rules don't apply to them, or they think that even if they do apply in theory, they can just pull a few strings and someone will sort it out." (9)

The common definition of corruption is a form of dishonesty or criminal activity undertaken by a person or organisation entrusted with a position of authority, often to acquire illicit benefits. (10) In this region, there is also another form of corruption hiding its face under the term 'Wasta' or as commonly known in the region, 'Vitamin W'. This form of corruption is also a very widespread practice in the region that bears the resemblance to pulling strings in the United States or the old boy's club in England.

In the Arabic language, Wasta means 'connection' or 'mediator'. The Wasta issue has its roots in the culture of Arab societies. Tribal leaders of old were morally obliged to help their kin and friends without a demand for this help to be reciprocated. By contrast, modern forms of intercessory Wasta are less about the performance of tribal virtues and moral obligations and more about the instrumental giving of favours in expectation of return. (11)

Organisational life in the Middle East relies heavily on personal relations, in both the private and the public sector. Employees, in their professional capacity, often cannot get their job done without the personal relationships within their own and other organisations. For this reason, having connections and the ability to function as a Wasta for one's job is a highly prized professional asset and represents valuable social capital. This is particularly the case in regard to those private corporations that inevitably have routine dealings with the state bureaucracy. For example, NGOs, industrial companies, and financial institutions such as banks and insurance companies often employ high-ranking retirees from the public sector in their administration and public relations departments to facilitate their dealings with the state bureaucracy and expedite the processing of their paperwork. Particularly in the public sector, individual employees rely on their Wasta connections to advance professionally. The career of any individual public servant is likely to include one or several Wastas. S/he may need to find a job as a day-wage or temporary employee, another to be switched to a permanent contract, another to be transferred to a different department or location within the bureaucracy, and perhaps a few others to receive promotions or allowances or to be granted early retirement. (12)

Corruption and "cosy capitalism" are emblematic features of the region's political economies. Wasta and baksheesh (bribe or tip) are integral parts of daily living in the region. Corruption and reliance on personal connections are common. They play an essential role in structuring access to opportunities in the region.

In order, for example, to obtain government documents such as identity cards, gain access to very basic social services, secure a place in a university, or secure a job. In this region, you need to rely on personal connections or have money to be able to bribe. Lack of both will certainly lead to frustration, anger and exhaustion. And that definitely leads to limited possibilities for social progression and improved well-being.

But concerning the states in terms of politics and its public resources and richness, the state of affairs is fundamentally aggravated, which evokes much public anger, disillusionment and frustration. Those in power work mostly to maintain their positions at all costs, regardless of legitimacy or adherence to the law, as well as accumulate as much wealth as they can possibly put their hands on.

For example, once a candidate is elected to parliament in the so-called 'parliamentary system of government', the politics of patronage and the economy of favours that brought him into office take on a different appearance.

Through connections to the bureaucracy, MPs facilitate their business opportunities and may gain access to information that helps secure lucrative government contracts — particularly those that do not require calls for bids. A recent investigative report by news website Amman Net showed that MPs in the previous parliament (2012-2016) owned businesses worth JOD 1.5 billion (Euro 1.84 billion), either personally or through their kin. (13)

With economic privileges doled out in a way that blocked the emergence of independent entrepreneurs that might eventually challenge the autocrats' control, favoured firms were able to acquire virtual monopolies over entire liberalised economic sectors. (14)

In Egypt, for example, the firms of 32 businessmen closely connected with then-President Hosni Mubarak received in 2010 more than 80% of the credit that went to the formal private sector and earned 60% of the sector's overall profits, while employing only 11% of the country's labour force. In Tunisia, former President Zine El Abidine Ben Ali's cronies received 21% of all private-sector profits in 2010, though their firms employed only 1% of Tunisia's labour force. (15)

Unsurprisingly, this system generated only modest growth. Political loyalty does not translate into economic efficiency, and autocratic leaders' loyalists consistently failed to build competitive world-class corporations. With talented potential competitors at such a distinct disadvantage, nobody was motivated to innovate or adequately invest. (16)

Once politics becomes a potentially lucrative business and secure investment, then no doubt, a crony economy will emerge, and the negative consequences of a crony economy are severe and long-lasting for any society unless a drastic, meaningful and durable change takes hold.

Corruption is an efficient tool to consolidate the current political system in place in Arab countries. On one hand, it distributes rent-based revenues to its client base, 'it' being the factional system in power, whereas, on the other hand, such distribution exempts the factional system from accountability and responsibility. This is one reason why taxes in general and income taxes in particular, are marginalised as a source of government revenues, because with taxation the system must have representation and accountability on the use of public funds. Recently, a two-day seminar was held in Beirut about improving the control of public finance. Five country studies were undertaken as the first segment of a larger project encompassing the rest of the Arab countries. One major finding of such studies is that the political system in place interferes significantly with legislation and control systems in place to advance its political agenda. No improvement in control systems of public funds is to be expected if no political reform is undertaken. This goes to the root of the current problems plaguing Arab society, namely, its factionalism and the rent-based economy with which it is associated. Accordingly, with the marginalisation of taxation, accountability and responsibility wither away as the distribution of rent is considered as 'gifts' or unearned benefits to recipients who cannot, therefore, question their providers. Public expenditure policy undertaken in Arab countries to provide basic infrastructure and services to their countrymen is to assuage whatever claims the latter may have, so ruling elites would continue to pursue without accountability and responsibility their path of self-enrichment and gratification with public funds. (17)

Corruption and crony economies/capitalism that dominates the region is a system in which businesses realisation highly depends on personal ties to government officials, public bureaucrats and privileged access to economic opportunities rather than merit and value. This sort of economic mentality on the part of governments creates a lot of anger and popular dissatisfaction among the peoples of the region. To depict the picture simply is to say that the region has governments without people and people without governments.

Those economies are, almost without exception, crony economies, which marginalises or even distort a fair, honest and competitive market. It monopolises and controls the market in the hands of the few powerful elites, whose main intention is the self-prosperity and welfare of themselves and their acquaintances. It also creates big fractures and gaps between the haves and have nots, and the region, in general, is full of the latter. It leads to unnecessary delays and uncertainties to the business process and makes the task of setting up a manufacturing business or selling a service riskier and less predictable. Subsequently, these economies are considered; at least I consider them, as the economies of the few powerful, immoral and ruthless elite. What about the welfare of the rest of 'the people', well, they can go to hell? If the people in the mind and eyes of the state do not obey, do not submit and follow orders, or rebel in any way, simply and for sure, they will be targeted as traitors, as terrorists— which is the favourite nowadays— as trouble makers and you name it. And/or their reputations will be tarnished and humiliated or any other dirty means and tricks including covert assassinations, which the states of the region are experts on. Yes, the region has internal security branches that are much sophisticated than most advanced countries on the globe. When it comes to torching, humiliating and oppressing their people, the region, certainly, is awarded the gold medal.

Another vital point is the issue of sovereignty and independence of the 'countries' of the region as a whole. As their economies are rental and crony, their sovereignty is greatly diminished, and they become dependent on other big powers, 'their masters' for protection, a good example is Saudi Arabia. This is another consequence of the culture of rent. The dependency on the rest of the world, whether caused by the need to import goods and services that the local economy does not produce or the need to receive financial aid to finance the budget, diminishes the country's resistance to foreign hegemonic tendencies. That is why the culture of resistance is alien to the culture of rent.

Rentier state theory (RST) is a political economy theory that seeks to explain state-society relations in states that generate a large proportion of their income from rents, or externally-derived, unproductively earned payments. Rents are most commonly royalties or other payments for oil and gas exports, but other income such as fees and aid are typically considered rents as well. As its most basic assumption, RST holds that, since the state receives this external income and distributes it to society, it is relieved of having to impose taxation, which in turn means that it does not have to offer concessions to society such as a democratic bargain or a development strategy. (18)

Rentier states do not fight (they fight themselves, and the next chapter will deal with this point) and rent-based economies accept dictates from outside. The ruling elites have too much to lose by 'resisting' and that is one reason why foreign military occupation is seen as 'permissible'. The culture of rent also makes it easier to go into debt. Indebtedness, once frowned upon, has become 'legitimate'. Whether at the government level or the individual level, indebtedness allows for levels of consumption not proportionate with incomes.

In the Arab world, corruption is not exclusively the result of economic factors, but also the by-product of a crucially critical element with a deterministic impact: the political situation. In fact, the political aspect, in turn, incites corruption. Moreover, it is not easy in the Arabic universe to separate the political power and the economic one, as they must often converge into either a similar trend, a duly assumed long-lasting alliance, or into an objective consensus on a common ground of real interests. Even though the political situation which the Arab world is experiencing differs proportionately from one country to another, it remains overwhelmingly tyrannical in nature, even chaotic at certain times, owing to the triggered "Arab Spring"-related changes. Noteworthy, in this respect, the Arab political systems, marked by a democracy defect, helps to favour abuse of public power for personal-interest purposes, so public money misuse turns out to be normal practice conforming to the current trends and processes, or even necessary for the sake of guaranteeing the regime sustainability in the Arab countries. In such cases, corruption reveals an imperfection pertinent to the political system which had already been obscured and stained by public authorities. Structural corruption is, thus, a part of a systematic state policy. It is distinguishable from conventional corruption in which the author acts behind the administration's back, in fear of the law. Structural corruption is one of the main obstacles impeding reform in the Arab countries, given the fact that it is systematically used to sabotage political and civil activities and create classes, which take advantage from the status quo. Furthermore, by controlling the entire levers of power, the Arab countries' leaders can handle the judicial system to eliminate and put down their opponents and even dissidents. It is also worse noticing that the manipulation of law paves the way for the economic kind of corruption, as a natural outcome of political corruption. Those who falsify the results of elections, alter and distort law, acquire tentatively attractive instruments for forgery and for serving their own. Such a situation induces business entrepreneurs and undertakers to complain about the fact that persons in power monopolise the major economic domains, either directly or "jointly" with eminent businessmen (UNDP, 2004). All this highlights that the dominant political and legal structures underway in these countries make it difficult to distinguish between conventional corruption (abuse of public power for personal interest ends) and weaknesses inherent to the system. (19)

How can this endemic corruption, which is so highly prevailing in the region, be fought?

Many international and national reports and research articles regarding corruption in the region recommend certain actions for the 'governments' of the region to follow, such as, the heads of states of the region speak out immediately and publicly about their commitment to end corruption nationally and regionally, or 'governments' must prosecute grand corruption, no matter how low or high the level of the public official concerned, and so forth. Yet the main question arises in my mind, if these 'heads of states' are inherently corrupt and they are an utterly alien bunch of puppets in the eyes of the people and their wings of 'government'. And these puppets battle by their teeth against their peoples with an immense amount of repression and cruelty to stay in power. Therefore, my humble conclusion would say that these 'heads of governments', in no way are going to heed your recommendations or even heed to fifty per cent of them, as they are simply not going to impeach themselves.

The Corruption Perceptions Index 2018 presents a grim reality in the "Middle East and Northern Africa" where, despite some incremental progress by a select few, most countries are failing in the fight against corruption.

With a score of 70, United Arab Emirates (UAE) leads the region on the CPI, followed by Qatar (62). At the very bottom of the region, Syria scores 13, followed by Yemen (14) and Libya (17). Both Syria and Yemen are also in the bottom five of the entire index.

With an average score of 39, the "Middle East and Northern Africa" region falls behind both the Americas and Asia-Pacific regions (average score for both: 44) and does only slightly better than Eastern Europe and Central Asia (average score: 35) and Sub-Saharan Africa (average score: 32).

While the UAE and Qatar score higher on the index than other countries in the region, this has more to do with their level of stateness and human development, i.e., efficient public administration, and high levels of gross domestic product (GDP), health and education.

Arab governments do initiate anti-corruption drives from time to time but they tend to be patchy rather than systematic and are often part of a political game. Such campaigns rarely include measures that will make corruption less likely in the future and usually target those who have fallen out of favour for unrelated reasons. When so many of them benefit from ill-gotten gains, corruption charges provide a simple means to get rid of them if the need arises. Corrupt ministers and officials can also be turned into scapegoats for wider government failures. (20)

In many of the region's 'governments', powerful individuals have actively influenced government policies and diverted public funds and state assets for their self-interest and enrichment at the expense of citizens. This reduces anti-corruption efforts to merely ink on paper, where laws pass but are rarely enforced or implemented.

Corruption has become a self-reinforcing system that is an "integral feature" of regional regimes, according to one Egyptian academic. With the notable exception of Tunisia, Arab states possess a variety of autocratic features that are correlated with corruption. In authoritarian regimes, elites control all levers of power to some degree. Adequately addressing corruption in the region requires not only legal reforms, such as passing freedom of information and asset declaration laws, or technological solutions, such as e-government initiatives, but also a fundamental change in the political culture within which corruption thrives. In many places, such as the Gulf countries, Lebanon, and Morocco, tackling corruption would be detrimental to the ruling elites, who benefit from the status quo. But failure to address this problem can lead to instability that could do even more harm to the regime and elite interests. The elite often control key media outlets, the private sector, key industries, and, at times, even influential civil society organizations. Through these they can delay legislative decisions and judicial processes. (21)

For corruption to be eliminated or at least minimised and fought effectively, the rule of law and good governance must be established as both of these elements are the precondition for a legitimate state. Once the law itself is manipulated and the courts are bought by the highest bidder, subsequently, corruption and the ills associated with it will ultimately prevail in society and the major sufferers, at the end of the day, are the common people. As corruption in the region is widespread, and it's becoming more and more endemic, the common people are stuck in a vicious circle. And they are made to believe that their power and capacity to change the status quo is restricted by the ruthless machinery of the state, which in turn leads to complete silence which dominates the streets in the region.

The way out of this dilemma and this vicious circle can be categorised as (A) The region's intellectuals, academics, professionals and the region's media must expose and speak out and openly and constructively criticise the evils of corruption and its agents. (B) Unless the peoples of the region wake up and get their act together as one body and declare civil strife to force actions, which I will elaborate on in the final chapter of this book, unfortunately, the status quo will endure undefeated.

As a fact, and in practical terms, corruption has many harmful effects. It is intrinsically unfair; it undermines democratic processes, distorts free markets, denies people equality of opportunity and in general creates obstacles to progress. Though petty corruption (small payments to low-level officials) is often regarded as unimportant, evidence compiled by Transparency International shows that the poorest in all societies are the ones hit the hardest by bribery: "They face the most demands for bribes and they are more likely to pay. This, in turn, means that corruption acts as a regressive tax that increases income inequality. Denied their basic rights and free access to public services, the poor suffer most in corrupt environments."

The people of this region, for so many decades, have suffered a lot and endured a lot of adversities at the hands of colonists and now at the hands of their own "leaders". They deserve some respite, the youth of the region need to be given some hope for their ideas, abilities and goals. Citizens and non-citizens alike are eager to trust that their rights will always be protected and respected. All is possible, but only when we stand as one and we speak out and write the truth. Otherwise, the darkness will always prevail.

Corruption is worse than prostitution. The latter might endanger the morals of an individual; the former invariably endangers the morals of the entire country. Karl Kraus

References for Chapter 3: Plague Three: Corruption

1. Confidential letter to David Owen from the British embassy in Jeddah. ECO/121/3(E), 3 May 1977. http://www.guardian.co.uk/sys-files/Guardian/docum ents/2007/05/28/ch04doc04.pdf.

2. Corruption in the Arab countries, Poisoning the System, al-bab.com, https://al-bab.com/corruption-arab-countries

3. Arab Human Development Report 2004. P. 136.

4. Intissar Fakir, Governance and the Future of the Arab World, Carnegie Endowment for International Peace, https://carnegieendowment.org/2018/10/16/governanc e-and-future-of-arab-world-pub-77501

5. Oussama Romdhani, Why Not Estonia? Bureaucrats Drag in the Arab World, The Arab Weekly, August 2018, https://thearabweekly.com/why-not-estonia-bureaucratic-drag-arab-world

6. Ibid

7. Middle East Monitor, Minister: Egypt has 5m Civil Servants and not Enough Chairs, Dec. 2018, https://www.middleeastmonitor.com/20181212-minister-egypt-has-5m-civil-servants-and-not-enough-chairs/

8. Brian Whitaker, What's Really Wrong with the Middle East. Published by Saqi, London 2009, P. 162.

9. Ibid, P.163

10. Black Law Dictionary, http://thelawdictionary.org/corruption

11. Yazan Doughan, Corruption in the Middle East and the limits of Conventional Approaches, Giga German Institute of Global and Area Studies, www.giga-hamburg.de/giga-focus.

12. Ibid. P. 3.

13. Ibid P. 5.

14. Ishac Diwan, What Happened to Economic Growth After the Arab Spring, World Economic Forum, 7 March 2016, https://www.weforum.org/agenda/2016/03/what-happened-to-economic-growth-after-the-arab-spring/

15. Ibid

16. Ibid

17. Kamel Touati ,Determinants of Economic Corruption in the Arab Countries: Dangers and Remedies, Journal of Economics Studies and Research, 31 Dec. 2013 http://www.ibimapublishing.com/journals/JESR/jesr.html

18. Matthew Gray, A Theory of "Late Rentierism" in the Arab States of the Gulf, 2011, https://repository.library.georgetown.edu/bitstream/handle/10822/558291/CIRSOccasionalPaper7MatthewGray2011.pdf

19. Ziad Hafez (2009) The culture of rent, factionalism, and corruption: a political economy of rent in the Arab World, Contemporary Arab Affairs, 2:3, 458-480. https://doi.org/10.1080/17550910903034989.

20. Brian Whitaker, What's Really Wrong with the Middle East. Published by Saqi, London 2009, P.174.

21. Intissar Fakir, Governance and the Future of the Arab World, Carnegie Endowment for International Peace, https://carnegieendowment.org/2018/10/16/governanc e-and-future-of-arab-world-pub-77501

Chapter 4: Plague Four: Endless Wars, Endless Violence

"The most dangerous people in the world are not the tiny minority instigating evil acts, but those who do the acts for them. For example, when the British invaded India, many Indians accepted to work for the British to kill off Indians who resisted their occupation. So in other words, many Indians were hired to kill other Indians on behalf of the enemy for a paycheck. Today, we have mercenaries in Africa, corporate armies from the western world, and unemployed men throughout the Middle East killing their own people and people of other nations-for a paycheck. To act without a conscience, but for a paycheck, makes anyone a dangerous animal. The devil would be powerless if he couldn't entice people to do his work. So as long as money continues to seduce the hungry, the hopeless, the broken, the greedy, and the needy, there will always be war between brothers."

— Suzy Kassem

"It may well be that we will have to repent in this generation. Not merely for the vitriolic words and the violent actions of the bad people, but for the appalling silence and indifference of the good people who sit around and say, "Wait on time."

— Martin Luther King Jr.

Before I start this chapter, I just want to remind the readers that the black gold of the region is, unfortunately, the cause of the majority of problems it is facing. In particular, the endless wars and senseless human loss taking place and unfolding daily in front of our eyes. As I think, if we take oil out of the equation you'd get a "Middle East" that is willing to play the game, and the whole story would be completely different.

Competition between East and West is by no means solely responsible for the succession of the region's many crises. Deep-reaching influences at work among the countries and peoples of the region itself have put in motion a process of governmental, economic, and social change which naturally has stirred all kinds of conflict between old and new. It is a period of turbulence and instability made to order for designated foreign powers—but one which raises the fears of all other foreign powers with vital interests at stake.

Not since 1967 has the "Middle East" suffered so many simultaneous high-intensity crises. They are all linked by many threads, making partial solutions more difficult and dragging the region ever faster into the abyss.

Endless wars, endless violence, from Libya to Syria, from Palestine to Lebanon, from Yemen to Sudan and on and on and on, endless destruction, killings, agonies and endless cries. Lost hopes and dreams for so many millions of innocent people, lost belief on the part of the 423 or so million inhabitants on anything their so-called "leaders" represent or say...sadly, there are so many who are just lost and above all are very confused about how and why all this nonsense is happening. And why for so long a time, happening to them?

Maybe my answer here is very short, but as these brutal, power-hungry puppets rule the region, they will drive their societies into more civil wars and more destruction with the help of their big masters and their hidden agendas towards the region and its inhabitants. Yet, it also must be said that the peoples of the region are becoming extremely passive and more submissive than ever as if nothing is happening. We are becoming just like robots that are instructed and moved around and about with complete obedience and submission. And what is more concerning is the airy silence which is perpetuating the streets of the region, best described as a total capitulation, which is precisely the end aim of their watchful enemies.

Since the catastrophic year of 2003, when the US and Britain overthrew Saddam Hussein and the subsequent aftermath. And then Syria since 2011, when the uprising started against President Bashar al-Assad. So many conflicts were intertwined on the Iraqi and Syrian battlefields — Sunni against Shia, Arab against Kurd, Iran against Saudi Arabia, Saudi Arabia against Yemen, people against dictatorships, people against people, and the US against a variety of opponents — that the ending of these multiple crises was always going to be very messy indeed.

Regardless of the causes and the nature of the endless wars and conflicts in the region, the stakes are extremely high and very costly, particularly for the people throughout the region. The large scale destruction of the infrastructure in many parts of the region is beyond calculation, the mass and continuous daily killing of innocent people including countless children, the horrific lifelong disabilities (physical and mental) suffered by numerous young and old people alike, the devastation of people's livelihoods is immense, the health hazards and the environmental costs of the bloody and endless wars and violence is beyond anyone's imagination and the long-term socio-economic negative impact cannot be estimated.

The region's reputation has deeply plunged into and became synonymous with a region plagued with wars, conflicts and violence.

Every decade since the end of the Second World War, the region has seen at least one interstate conflict, in the 1990s has seen even two. In the same time frame 2.3 million (1) (and counting) of the region's population have been wiped from the earth as a result of meaningless political violence, which is 40 per cent of the global total of fight-related deaths, although the region accounts for only a mere 5 per cent of the world's population.

Leave the sad number of 2.3 million human deaths aside and look at what our so-called "United Nations" well, I call it "the United Five" has done to the Iraqi people and the civilisation of Iraq through their barbaric and inhumane prolonged sanctions against the defenceless Iraqi population and their "Weapons of Mass Destruction", and here I am quoting:

The war on Iraq did not begin in 2003, but in 1991 with the first Gulf War, which was followed by the UN sanctions regime "the hidden war against the Iraqis."

An early PSR study by Beth Daponte, then a US government Census Bureau demographer, found that Iraqi deaths caused by the direct and indirect impact of the first Gulf War amounted to around 200,000 Iraqis, mostly civilians. Meanwhile, her internal government study was suppressed.

After US-led forces pulled out, the war on Iraq continued in economic form through the US-UK imposed UN sanctions regime, on the pretext of denying Saddam Hussein the materials necessary to make weapons of mass destruction. Items banned from Iraq under this rationale included a vast number of items needed for everyday life.

Undisputed UN figures show that 1.7 million Iraqi civilians died due to the West's brutal sanctions regime, half of whom were children.

The mass deaths were seemingly intended. Among items banned by the UN sanctions were chemicals and equipment essential for Iraq's national water treatment system. A secret US Defence Intelligence Agency (DIA) document discovered by Professor Thomas Nagy of the School of Business at George Washington University amounted, he said, to "an early blueprint for genocide against the people of Iraq".

In his paper for the Association of Genocide Scholars at the University of Manitoba, Professor Nagi explained that the DIA document revealed, "minute details of a fully workable method to 'fully degrade the water treatment system' of an entire nation "over a period of a decade. The sanctions policy would create "the conditions for widespread disease, including full-scale epidemics," thus "liquidating a significant portion of the population of Iraq".

This means that in Iraq alone, the US-led war from 1991 to 2003 killed 1.9 million Iraqis; then from 2003 onwards around 1 million: totalling just under 3 million Iraqis dead over two decades. (2)

Even if these figures are remotely correct 'for the sake of argument', then how can any sane or moral person argue that they are a price worth paying for 'freedom and democracy'. Then I say, thank you very much, keep your freedom and democracy, I will settle for having all those people alive again.

Craig Unger in his book "America Armageddon" writes,

"How could one believe in the noble idea of democratising the Middle East when American soldiers — and even the Iraqi government itself — hide out in the Little America bubble of the Green Zone, the so-called Emerald City, with its discos, fast food, porno shops — and thousands of contractors from Halliburton? How could one see American soldiers as liberators after the reports of torture and horrifying abuses at Abu Ghraib that drove thousands of Iraqis not just to join the insurgency, but to cheer as the charred, mutilated bodies of dead Americans were dragged through the streets of Fallujah? How could one celebrate the rebuilding of Iraq's infrastructure when at least $12 billion in cash was flown to Baghdad, shrink-wrapped in plastic, and $9 billion of it vanished under highly suspicious circumstances? Or when untold billions went to virtually unregulated private firms, which brought in tens of thousands of mercenaries who were paid enormous sums." (3)

As a result of the ugly invasion of Iraq in 2003 and the subsequent barbaric events that took place thereafter Iraq, the "Crown Jewel of the Islamic civilisation" was destroyed beyond recognition. At one point in Iraq's modern history, the country was the most advanced country in the whole region including the education sector. Basically, that is exactly what the enemies of the region want to achieve 'destruction of the brain'. Once the brain is destroyed, nothing else can effectively function. And with agony, the puppets of the region are helping the enemies to achieve their goal with total submission and impunity.

Unfortunately, barbarism and low morality are evidently becoming obvious features amongst the region's societies. People fight each other, slaughter each other, destroy each other's cities and towns and with joy, they celebrate their barbarism on the streets of the victor. For example in 2005, the liquidation of Libyan opposition member Abdel Salam Akhchiba was horrific; he was dragged to his death without trial while dozens of soldiers beat and kicked him. It was not only the lawlessness that made these heinous public executions so horrific but also the forced participation of all those present — thus collectivising the crime. Yet, as I always say, history does not forgive or forget. Ironically, that is more or less how Muammar Gaddafi faced his last moments.

Yet barbarism has not remained confined to the state. It has long since infiltrated society and become a general feature of behaviour, marked by increased cruelty and a widespread lack of morality, or any modicum of human empathy and compassion.

This is simply madness, in any rational mind; it cannot be described as a victory and/or an event for joy. The logic does not say that slaughtering your own brothers, sisters, fathers, mothers and children of your own family can be seen or described as a victory; the mildest description of it is collective crime. But the important question is how did these societies sink so low? In the words of Morris Ayek, he writes:

I am convinced that one explanation lies in the relations between three specific elements — the state, society and law/morality. Before the advent of the modern state, the traditional system of rule saw to it that the "natural order" of things was preserved, embodied in morality and in the traditions common to all the state's inhabitants, which regulate their conduct. Morality and traditions were overlaid by religious laws, which were also part of the society. The role of the ruling system was therefore limited to maintaining the "natural order", as well as ensuring its survival and preservation. He continues:

With the onset of the Ottoman reforms, however, the state was increasingly empowered with legal authority in all possible matters, charged with wresting this authority from society and making the law its own exclusive domain.

This process reached its height after the end of colonial rule, which had itself previously snatched full legal authority from society until the state even ordered the seizure of the Waqf — the religious foundations — and their nationalisation. These very same Waqf had once guaranteed the independence of the religious institutions, which stood guard over all matters of religious and moral law and defended them from the incursion of the state. But the post-colonial state did not stop at merely seizing control over the law; it sought to attain a much more far-reaching goal — a revolution in ethics and morals and an abolition of all "reactionary" values and traditions. (4)

In addition to what Morris had written, which I fully agree with, I also would add to his analysis; that the post-colonial states that emerged had a strong determination to eliminate the education system by not allowing free thinking and analytical arguments. They have managed to ensure that their people are just subjects and are just like a herd led by the master without thinking. The type of the education system in the region, as a whole, has been dramatically reduced to a system of memorisation without questioning of logic which is very essential to building a strong and thoughtful society. Education, in my view, does not entail literacy only; it's far more than that, which I will elaborate on further in the next chapter.

In 1258 when the Mongols besieged Baghdad and then captured it from the then Abbasid Caliphate, they were savage and barbaric in killing the inhabitants and destroying the whole city, and they also destroyed the brain of the Islamic Empire at that time, and it seems that history has repeated itself in 2003 by very "civilised powers". I call them the new Mongols of the 21st century.

Many historical accounts detailed the cruelties of the Mongol conquerors. Baghdad was a depopulated, ruined city for several centuries and only gradually recovered some of its former glory.

The Mongols looted and then destroyed mosques, palaces, libraries and hospitals. Priceless books from Baghdad's thirty-six public libraries were torn apart, the looters using their leather covers as sandals. Grand buildings that had been the work of generations were burned to the ground. The House of Wisdom (the Grand Library of Baghdad), containing countless precious historical documents and books on subjects ranging from medicine to astronomy, was destroyed. Survivors said that the waters of the Tigris ran black with ink from the enormous quantities of books flung into the river and red from the blood of the scientists and philosophers killed. (5)

In complete contrast to the barbarisms committed by the Mongols against Baghdad in 1258, and the barbarism committed against the Muslims and Jews by the Crusaders in 1099 when capturing Jerusalem, which is illustrated beautifully by Conor Kostick in his book The siege of Jerusalem, and then the barbarism committed by the "civilised powers" and their puppets in 2003 against Iraq. Then, see that when Saladin entered Jerusalem in 1187, the scene is a complete reverse. When Saladin captured Jerusalem he restored it to Muslim rule. History tells us that he allowed all crusaders to leave peacefully without any kind of harassment by Muslims or looting, killing or destruction.

Jonathan Phillips, professor of history, University of London said "Saladin was famous throughout history for his generosity, his justice and his ability to inspire his people. This earned him respect on the Christian side and the Muslim side".

In another comparison in historical events which is relevant to today's region, Jonathon Lyons in his book "The House of Wisdom", states in relation to the capturing of Jerusalem: "not all Muslims were as indifferent to the arrival of the crusaders as the caliph and his court in distant Baghdad. Many Arabs had no doubt that the capture of Jerusalem and the creation of the crusader state along the Syrian coast were part of an ominous pattern of Christian expansionism that had to be resisted. Form the Umayyad Mosque in Damascus, the legal scholar and preacher Ali Ibn al-Sulami sounded the alarm. In his book Kitab al-jihad, or The Book of Holy War, published six years after the Muslims were first driven from Jerusalem, al-Sulami linked the coming of the crusaders to their earlier success against Muslim rule in Sicily. He saw the Christian campaign as a religious war against Islam. And he blamed the crusaders' successes on infighting among Muslims and their inability to adhere to faith, particularly their abject failure to unite to defend the lands of Islam from non-believers. (6)

I underlined the sentence above to draw attention to the vital issues of today's plagues in the region of continuous infighting and complete disunity. In terms of faith, I am not going to comment on this issue as I am not a preacher, nor an Islamic scholar or a theologian.

It has been more than a thousand years since these words were written, and yet, the similarity between then and now is remarkably striking (maybe the present situation is much worse). Unity in the region is as elusive as ever and worse is the infighting among the Arabs and Muslims in a broader sense, which have resulted in total chaos, poverty, more repression, widespread killings on an unimaginable scale and complete humiliation of souls and spirits of the innocent man in the streets of the Islamic civilisation. The region and its so-called leaders, "the puppets" are becoming the favourite joke and amusement to so many politicians in the West, as well as, to their so called intellectuals, especially in the US, who are more than happy to spread all kinds of nonsense, propaganda and smears against the people of the region and its history. Intellectuals such as Bernard Lewis or Samuel Huntington and so many others like them who do not even possess the skill of speaking the Arabic language, and yet they are called an expert on the region's history and its people. But I certainly do not blame them, simply because I believe that it's a very lucrative business for them to generate fame and above all generate more money. At the same time, they are more than glad to serve their neoconservative ideology and its destructive goals which is more prevalent since Bush's administration and now also prevailing in Trump's administration, in particular its support for a wider war against Iran, in which some puppets such as Saudi Arabia, Egypt and the UAE are more than glad to support, when the time is ripe enough to destroy the whole region for the sake of the eternal security of Israel and liquidation of the Palestinian cause.

Wars, whatever they are called, interstate or internationalised civil war etc., have ripped apart the whole region. And as a consequence, scores of people are brutally killed. But the consequences of war extend far beyond direct battlefield casualties. The strongest consequence of conflict in the region is political. Conflict increases human rights abuses, entrenches authoritarian rule, and exacerbates social fragility. And it fuels social, economic and political exclusion and above all armed conflicts enrich the seeds for more and more conflicts. In addition, wars and armed conflicts which, at the moment, are plaguing the region is a total opposite to development and has a damaging effect on, for example, infant mortality rates, GDP per capita, health, access to clean water and sanitation, as well as leaving inefficient regimes, which is already the highlight of the region. With agony, I say that the people of the region are deeply trapped yet, I believe that to end the conflicts, the only logical solution must come from within, and not to be imposed by aliens. Within means unity, coherence and sacrifice for the sake of a noble goal— an end to the madness.

This leads me to question who is benefiting from the madness of wars and proxy wars inflicted on the region. Well, in an era where the global system puts money, greed and profit over people's lives and welfare, it is no surprise that the weapons manufacturers and their killing machines are the main profiteers of the current situation in the region as a whole, and the miseries facing people day and night. And in terms of political ideologies, the profiteers are the neoconservatives in the US and their supporters, who are happy to infect people's minds with hatred, lies and degradations of the "others". Just to give the readers a flavour of the ugly mentality of the neoconservatives; Michael Ledeen one of the neoconservatives' ideologues, writes in the National Review Online, "It is what we do best. It comes naturally to us, for we are the one truly revolutionary country in the world, as we have been for more than 200 years. Creative destruction is our middle name." (7)

US Secretary of State Condoleezza Rice's speech on the "New Middle East" [2] had set the stage. The Israeli attacks on Lebanon – which had been fully endorsed by Washington and London – have further compromised and validated the existence of the geostrategic objectives of the United States, Britain and Israel. According to Professor Mark Levine the "neoliberal globalizers and neoconservatives, and ultimately the Bush Administration, would latch on to creative destruction as a way of describing the process by which they hoped to create their new world orders," and that "creative destruction [in] the United States was, in the words of neoconservative philosopher and Bush adviser Michael Ledeen, 'an awesome revolutionary force' for (...) creative destruction... (8)

This announcement was a confirmation of an Anglo-American-Israeli "military roadmap" in the Middle East. This project, which has been in the planning stages for several years, consists of creating an arc of instability, chaos and violence extending from Lebanon, Palestine and Syria to Iraq, the Persian Gulf, Iran and the borders of NATO-garrisoned Afghanistan. (9)

The "New Middle East" project was introduced publicly by Washington and Tel Aviv with the expectation that Lebanon would be the pressure point for realigning the whole Middle East and thereby unleashing the forces of "constructive chaos." This "constructive chaos" – which generates conditions of violence and warfare throughout the region – would, in turn, be used so that the United States, Britain and

---

[2]The term "New Middle East" was introduced to the world in June 2006 in Tel Aviv by US Secretary of State Condoleezza Rice (who was credited by the Western media for coining the term) in replacement of the older and more imposing term, the "Greater Middle East."

Israel could redraw the map of the Middle East in accordance with their geostrategic needs and objectives. (10)

Chas Freeman, former US ambassador to Saudi Arabia, said on May 2003, just after the invasion of Iraq, "The neoconservatives' intention in Iraq was never to truly build democracy there. Their intention was to flatten it, to remove Iraq as a regional threat to Israel." (11)

Yes, he is completely right. Iraq as a power in the region is unacceptable to Israel and its "security". The whole region must be flattened and destroyed for the sake of Israel's safety and its existence, irrespective of other people's lives or future. And I am quite sure Iran will be next when the right moment for the conspirators comes. But I wish I was wrong.

Military expenditure in the Middle East rose by 6.2 per cent in 2017, spending by Saudi Arabia increased by 9.2 per cent in 2017 following a fall in 2016. With spending of $69.4 billion, Saudi Arabia had the third-highest military expenditure in the world in 2017. Iran (19 per cent) and Iraq (22 per cent) also recorded significant increases in military spending in 2017. 'Despite low oil prices, armed conflict and rivalries throughout the Middle East are driving the rise in military spending in the region,' said Pieter Wezeman, Senior Researcher with the SIPRI AMEX programme. In 2017 military expenditure as a share of GDP (known as the 'military burden') was highest in the Middle East, at 5.2 per cent. No other region in the world allocated more than 1.8 per cent of GDP to military spending. (12)

Certainly, both the US and Russia, as the second-largest weapons exporter after the US, are extremely happy for this turmoil to continue. And their economies are prospering and expanding on the dead bodies, including countless children of the region. They have no intention whatsoever to see a peaceful region, as peace to them means no income, in particular, for their weapons contractors such as Lockheed Martin and Northrop Grumman. These corporates do not like us to know their true intentions, they prefer to be seen as good guys, that their aim is to defend the people from 'terrorists'.

Occasionally a weapon company executive will slip up and expose their true priorities. For example, in a call with investors around the time that the Iran nuclear deal was coming to fruition, an analyst from Deutsche Bank asked if the deal would hurt Lockheed Martin's bottom line by reducing conflict in the Middle East. Lockheed Martin CEO Marillyn Hewson's response was that there was still "a lot of volatility, a lot of things that are happening" in both the Middle East and Asia-Pacific regions that would make them "growth areas" for Lockheed Martin. In other words, war is good for business, but you would never know it if you only read the propaganda of the major weapons companies. (13)

In the same article, he continues to say:

The reality, of course, is that weapons produced by companies like Lockheed Martin, Northrop Grumman, Boeing and General Dynamics cause untold suffering.

For example, by a conservative estimate, since 2001 the wars in Iraq, Afghanistan, and Pakistan — waged in significant part with the US-supplied bombs, combat aircraft, drones, and armoured vehicles — have resulted in the deaths of over 370,000 people, including at least 200,000 civilians.

Or look at the war in Yemen, where US armed allies like Saudi Arabia have killed thousands of civilians in an indiscriminate bombing campaign, millions of people are on the brink of famine due to a blockade enforced with US arms, and hundreds of thousands of people have contracted cholera in part due to the bombing of civilian infrastructure by a Saudi-led intervention force. (14)

In another article which was published online in 2017 by Jonas Ecke, and I quote:

"Western weapons companies see the newly emerging proxy wars as momentous opportunities to increase revenues. During a 2015 conference of Lockheed Martin in Palm Beach Florida, its executive vice president Bruce Tanner predicted "indirect benefits" from the conflict in Syria. Similarly, as the Intercept reports, Raytheon chief executive Tom Kennedy spoke of "a significant uptick" for "defence solutions across the board in multiple countries in the Middle East." Referring to Saudi Arabia, Kennedy elaborates, "It's all the turmoil they have going on, whether the turmoil is occurring in Yemen, whether it's with Houthis, whether it's occurring in Syria or Iraq, with ISIS." And sure enough, stocks of arms have soared in recent years." (15)

In the next paragraph of his article, he writes: "But it is not only weapons but also oil which disincentives policymakers from de-escalating proxy wars. As Christopher Davidson, whom the Economist called "one of the most knowledgeable academics" writing about the Middle East, shows in his 688-page long tome "Shadow Wars: The Secret Struggle for the Middle East", how many covert operations in the Middle East were historically supported to advance the explicit geographical or economic interests of the funders. According to Davidson, the emergence of the US as a major oil producer has motivated US policymakers to let Saudi forces engage in exhausting proxy wars throughout the region so that a weakened Saudi Arabia is forced to sell its state assets." (16)

For so long a time this oil issue, as I consider it to be a curse for the region, has played an important role in shaping the US foreign policies towards the region, and the major modern powers have formulated their policies according to their strategic interests in the region accordingly; William Quandt, a leading mainstream "Middle East" scholar and former member of the National Security Council in the Nixon and Carter Administrations, observed that "three concerns—oil, Israel and the Soviet Union—were the driving forces behind American Middle East policy throughout most of the period from the 1950s through the 1980s." In terms of oil, it is common knowledge that the vast energy reserves (two-thirds of the world's total) located in the Saudi peninsula, in particular, are a major concern of the United States. The US State Department has described the region as "a stupendous source of strategic power, and one of the greatest material prizes in world history, probably the richest economic prize in the world in the field of foreign investment," or in President Eisenhower's words, the most "strategically important area in the world." While these quotes are from the 1940s and 1950s, they have been reaffirmed continuously by high-ranking American officials and by internal US government documents. Writing about the Middle East, Richard Nixon stated that "its oil is the lifeblood of modern industry, the Persian Gulf region is the heart that pumps it, and the sea routes around the Gulf are the jugular vein through which that lifeblood passes." In a subsequent book, Nixon argued that because the Middle East is likely to remain "the only source of significant exportable oil in the world for the next twenty-five years—we have no choice but to remain engaged in the area." Furthermore, in explaining the US rationale for maintaining a military presence in the Gulf, then-Secretary of Defence Cheney stated in 1991 that "given the enormous resources that exist in that part of the world, and given the fact that those resources are in decline elsewhere, the value of those resources is only going to rise in the years ahead, and the United States and our major partners cannot afford to have those resources controlled by somebody who is fundamentally hostile to our interests." (17)

The popular idea, of course, is that it's "all about oil", and oil is certainly a central factor, though not quite in the way that is often imagined. Wearing points out — perhaps surprisingly for many readers — that Britain doesn't actually depend heavily on the Gulf for its oil supplies. It does, however, have commercial interests in the Gulf's energy industry and, more crucially, large parts of the Gulf States' oil revenues are recycled back to Britain in the form of investments or arms purchases. The Gulf is a growing market and, partly as a result of arms sales, Britain has a trade surplus with the region. Its exports to the Gulf, worth around £14 billion a year, are roughly on a par with exports to China and India combined. (18)

Certainly, the UK government has a big stake in selling arms and killing machines to the region including Israel. For Israeli military apparatus to kill more Palestinians including children and inflict more damage and destructions upon livelihoods of occupied Palestine.

Since the ugly assault on Gaza by Israel in 2014, the value of the UK's weapons sales to Israel has increased tenfold. Weapons which include components for drones, combat aircraft and helicopters along with spare parts for sniper rifles among so many other killing machines, which are used predominantly to kill Palestinians. UK arms sales to Israel: 2015: £20m ($28m); 2016: £84m ($117m); 2017: £216m ($300m); Total: £320 ($445m).

Source: Dept. for Int. Trade

The map overleaf speaks louder than words.

Mapping Israel's suppliers

More than 100 companies supplying military and security equipment to Israel have bases in the UK. The map includes UK companies that sell arms or provide security services to Israel, UK sites of companies which sell arms to Israel and UK sites of Israeli arms companies. Find out more about the suppliers on your doorstep at caat.org.uk/map/israel

Elbit Systems (4 sites)

Elbit is an Israeli arms company with four subsidiaries in the UK. It produces military electronics and unmanned aircraft systems including the Hermes armed drone. Protest interrupted operations at its Shenstone site during Israel's 2014 bombardment of Gaza.

G4S (2 sites)

UK multinational G4S is the world's largest private security company. Its Israeli subsidiary provides services to prisons and detention centres where Palestinian political prisoners are held, and equipment and services to Israeli military checkpoints. In 2014, under pressure from campaigners, G4S announced an intention to end some aspects of involvement in illegal Israeli settlements, but campaigners have vowed to continue pressure on G4S until it entirely ends its role with all aspects of Israel's apartheid regime.

Boeing (6 sites)

Boeing is a US-headquartered company with locations in the UK. Boeing manufactures the Apache attack helicopter, regularly used in the Occupied Palestinian Territories, and its US arm markets Elbit's Hermes drones.

BAE Systems (50 sites)

BAE Systems is the world's third largest arms company, headquartered in the UK. BAE provided Head-Up Displays for Lockheed Martin F-16 fighters for delivery to Israel in 2003. The UK government approved the export arguing that it did not want to harm "the UK's defence relations with the United States". BAE is one of three main companies building the F-35 fighter, which will replace the F-16.

Schleifring (1 site)

Schleifring Systems Ltd is a subsidiary of a German engineering company. It has applied for UK arms export licences to Israel and has said that it supplies components for the Hermes drone made by Elbit Systems and the Merkava IV main battle tank.

Lockheed Martin (10 sites)

Lockheed Martin is the world's largest arms company. It is headquartered in the US, with offices in the UK and Israel. It makes the F-16 fighter aircraft, used by the Israeli Air Force since 1980. Israel has so far purchased 33 of its F-35s to replace the F-16s.

Dots refer to multiple sites of identified companies which produce or export arms or services to Israel.

Of course, not only arms manufacturers are benefiting from the endless wars waged against the region by different players and profiteers. Oil companies and their cronies, no doubt are also hidden players. In the build-up to the Iraq war in 2003, US administration spokesmen and neoconservative pundits asserted that Iraq's oil riches would make the war a cost-effective, even profitable, affair. "Iraq has tremendous resources..." said White House press secretary Ari Fleisher. "So there are a variety of means that Iraq has to be able to shoulder much of the burden for their own reconstruction." Promised neoconservative columnist Charles Krauthammer on WUSA-TV: "We will have a bonanza, a financial one, at the other end, if the war is successful." (19)

So, what I can gather from this statement is that we will destroy in every way, create chaos, loot your country's treasures and resources, spread killing and torture and at the end, you pay the bill and a bonus on top. How is this kind and moral?

Meaningless fighting and more fighting, has completely destroyed the already fragile social and economic cohesion in the entire region.

Yemen, one of the poorest nations in the entire globe, even before the war, is now just a country of destroyed bricks. Whatever was functioning before the start of the war is now dysfunctional and destroyed and its economy is a big zero. What is much more important than money and greed is the enduring suffering of its people. Thousands upon thousands of its people are killed indiscriminately, diseases such as cholera are spreading widely among the population, malnutrition is endemic, physical and mental disabilities are countless. If this whole madness stops now, the country will need generations to overcome the horrendous destruction it's facing now. All that thanks to their next of kin the so-called "Saudi Arabia", and its supplier of lethal weapons of mass destruction the US and its agents in the region.

Syria, one of the cradles of civilisation, destroyed beyond recognition in terms of heritage, buildings and infrastructure from hospitals, schools and universities to factories and everything else, all but destroyed. Again, money comes and goes, yet it's another human tragedy that has been unfolding for the past decade, caused mainly by the hands of their own so-called government, and fuelled further by their next of kin of the region and beyond. Saying beyond, I mean namely the US and Russia.

The war in Syria is tearing apart the social and economic fabric of the country, said Hafez Ghanem, World Bank Vice President for the Middle East and North Africa, "the number of causalities is devastating, but the war is also destroying the institutions and systems that societies need to function, and repairing them will be a greater challenge than rebuilding infrastructure — a challenge that will only grow as the war continues."

Saroj Kumar Jha, World Bank Director for the Mashreq says "the departure of five million refugees, combining with inadequate schooling and malnutrition leading to stunting, will cause long term deterioration of the country's most valuable asset, its human capital. In the future, when Syria needs it most, there will be a collective shortage of vital skills."

Syria has become the largest forced displacement crisis in the world since World War II. Over half of the country's pre-conflict population has been forcibly displaced. According to the United Nations High Commissioner for Refugees (UNHCR), the total number of Syrians presently registered as refugees outside the country in Lebanon, Turkey, Jordan, Iraq, Egypt and North Africa is 4.9 million. In addition, more than 800,000 Syrian nationals are estimated to have sought asylum in Europe in 2015 and 2016. Many of these individuals have moved more than once and have not been removed from registration lists in their first country of refuge. These numbers also do not include an estimated 0.4 million to 1.1 million unregistered Syrian refugees in Lebanon, Jordan, Turkey and Iraq. (20) And the more the conflict persists, the deeper will run the grievances and divisions in Syrian society, rendering it very difficult to reinstate efficient institutions and economic mechanisms.

The war in Syria and the atrocities and barbarism committed against the people is certainly not unique to Syria. It can be found in Libya, Iraq, occupied Palestine and other lands in the region.

Palestine, the cradle of ancient history, culture, religion and heritage. For almost a hundred years now the Palestinian people have been suffering and enduring so many hardships under Israeli military occupation. The longest and ugliest military occupation in modern history. Generations of Palestinian people, since 1948, have been condemned to the status of refugees living in cramped refugee camps, internally or in the surrounding countries, or scattered over the four corners of the globe.

Yet the occupier, for decades, has had a free hand to inflict barbaric acts against the Palestinians and their limited infrastructure with complete impunity. They act above any law, call it international law or international humanitarian law, it makes no difference. And the American policy towards the rights of the Palestinians is a shame, and it encourages the Jewish policymakers to perpetrate more open torture and destruction on the defenceless Palestinians. In the words of the Project for the New American Century think-tank, established in 1997 by neoconservatives, Daniel Pipes writes: "Israel must have a completely free hand in order to guarantee its security and define and fulfil its strategic interests; bartering territories for peace is out of the question, the objective is to ensure an armed peace. The Israelis must be allowed to do as they wish with the Palestinians, who are not yet approaching the point of giving up." (21)

In an analysis of the above statement, the magic words are free hand, security, armed peace, and giving up. Therefore, Daniel is telling the Israeli army to slaughter the Palestinians as they like with complete impunity. Security here means, build more and more walls and divide people and their families and do not bother about legality issues or civil behaviour as only the security of Israel is paramount above anything else, basically, he is asking (which is happening) to create big prisons and wide-ranging siege for the Palestinians. Armed peace, means imposing the will of the Israelis, by force, to destroy the spirits of the Palestinians by all means of terror, humiliation, subjugation and starvation to ensure the peace for Israel. Giving up implies that the Palestinians must willingly submit to their fate and surrender their legitimate rights of nationhood to the Israelis without question, further, it implies that their dream of humane existence is only subject to the dictates of the Israeli master and their security requirements.

If we go back in time, in the summer of 2005, on the massive and aggressive beyond comprehension assault on Gaza, a strip of land accommodating around 1.8 million people, one of the poorest and most populated on earth. Most of the human rights organisations which documented the war crimes committed during the so-called Operation Protective Edge by "Israel", equate and to a great extent exaggerate emphasis upon Palestinian resistance factions, namely "Hamas" pursued to represent or depict a state which places Hamas at an equivalence to Israel's power or military, in which these organisations, intentionally or otherwise, avoid the obvious distinctions between the civilians of the Palestinians and the Israelis. The latter having access to shelter, medical facilities and all kinds of assistance, yet the Palestinian civilians have to contend with murder and dismembered bodies of their children and their loved ones. I think the whole world has just gone mad for the sake of gold. I for definite, in modern international politics or even law, cannot find any, in practice, morality or justice beyond empty theories and rhetoric.

At the end of the day, Israel has all manner of lethal tools of destruction and a nuclear arsenal as well as weapons of mass destruction, which the civilised West is more than happy to ignore or overlook, for the happiness and security of Israel and its security prosperity and their civilians, as if the Palestinians have no civilians or children at all. They are all categorised as "tourists" including the unborn children in their mother's womb.

Gideon Levy in his book, The Punishment of Gaza writes:

"True, every few years a wave of violence erupts, but it usually happens in the country's outskirts and does not interest anyone in the centre. Qassam rockets in Sderot or Katyushas in Kiryat Shmona? Who cares? They will be followed by another period of quiet, like now. The separation fence, the media, our education system and political propaganda do a great job of creating an illusion to make us forget what we need to forget and hide what needs to be hidden. The troubles are there and we are here, and here life is a bowl of cherries, if not a blast. Like Switzerland? No, even better. (22)

"We always knew how to add a measure of significance to the pleasures of life. We practice the cult of security, society's true religion, and we perpetuate the memory of the Holocaust. You can enjoy yourself in Israel and also play a victim; party and gripe. Where else is there a place like this?

The Israelis don't pay any price for the injustice of the occupation, so the occupation will never end. It will end a moment before the Israelis understand the connection between the occupation and the price they will be forced to pay. They will never shake it off on their own initiative, and why should they?" (23)

Noam Chomsky, the West's most prominent political thinker and critic of US imperialism in his book who Rules the World? In relation to the Israeli bombing of the PLO headquarters in Tunis which killed 72 Tunisians and Palestinians he writes:

"The "terrorist attacks" that Shultz and Peres offered as the pretext for the bombing of Tunis were the killings of three Israelis in Larnaca, Cyprus. The killers, as Israel conceded, had nothing to do with Tunis, though they might have had Syrian connections. Tunis was a preferable target, however, it was defenceless, unlike Damascus. And there was an extra benefit: more exiled Palestinians could be killed there. (24)

"The Larnaca killings, in turn, were regarded as retaliation by the perpetrators. They were a response to regular Israeli hijackings in international waters in which many victims were killed and many more kidnapped, commonly to be held for long periods without charge in Israeli prisons. The most notorious of these prisons has been the secret prison/torture chamber facility 1391. A good deal can be learned about it from the Israeli and foreign press. Such regular Israeli crimes are, of course, known to editors of the national press in the United States, and occasionally receive some casual mention. (25)

"Klinghoffer's murder[3] was properly viewed with horror and is very famous. It was the topic of an acclaimed opera and a made-for-TV movie, as well as much shocked commentary deploring the savagery of Palestinians, who have variously been deemed "two-headed beasts" (Prime Minister Menachem Begin), "drugged roaches scurrying around in a bottle" (Israel Defence Forces Chief of Staff Raful Eitan), "like grasshoppers compared to us" whose heads should be "smashed against the boulders and walls" (Prime Minister Yitzhak Shamir) or, more commonly, just "Araboushim," the slang counterpart of "kiki" or "nigger." (26)

"Thus, after a particularly depraved display of settler-military terror and purposeful humiliation in the West Bank town of Halhul in December 1982, which even disgusted Israeli hawks, the well-known military/political analyst Yoram Peri wrote in dismay that one "task of the army today [is] to demolish the rights of innocent people just because they are Araboushim living in territories that God promised us," a task that became far more urgent, and was carried out with far more brutality, when the Araboushim began to "raise their heads" a few years later. (27)

"We can easily assess the sincerity of the sentiments expressed about the Klinghoffer murder. It is only necessary to investigate the reaction to comparable US-backed Israeli crimes. Take, for example, the murder in April 2002 of two crippled Palestinians, Kemal Zughayer and Jamal Rashid, by

---

[3]In 1985, Klinghoffer (then 69, retired, and in a wheelchair) was on a cruise on the *Achille Lauro* with his wife Marilyn to celebrate their 36th wedding anniversary. On October 7, four hijackers from the Palestine Liberation Front (PLF) took control of the liner off Egypt as it was sailing from Alexandria to Port Said, Egypt. Holding the passengers and crew hostage, they ordered the captain to sail to Tartus, Syria, and demanded the release of 50 Palestinians then in Israeli prisons, including the Lebanese prisoner Samir Kuntar. On 8 October, Kilinghoffer was shot dead by the hijackers.

Israeli forces rampaging through the refugee camp of Jenin in the West Bank. Zughayer's crushed body and the remains of his wheelchair were found by British reporters, along with the remains of the white flag he was holding when he was shot dead while seeking to flee the Israeli tanks which then drove over him, ripping his face in two and severing his arms and legs. Jamal Rashid was crushed in his wheelchair when one of Israel's huge US-supplied Caterpillar bulldozers demolished his home in Jenin with his family inside. The differential reaction, or rather non-reaction has become so routine and so easy to explain that no further commentary is necessary." (28)

Noam wrote, no further commentary is necessary, and I will stick to it.

The impunity of the so-called Israeli government in inflicting serious and continuous harms against the Palestinian people and their livelihood in whatever shape exceeds barbarism by miles. Albert Einstein once said, "It would be my greatest sadness to see Zionists (Jews) do to Palestinian Arabs much of what Nazis did to Jews." If you were still with us today, you would be very disappointed.

And the president of Turkey Recep Tayyip Erdogan, once rightly said "(Israelis) have no conscience, no honour, and no pride. They curse Hitler day and night, but they have surpassed Hitler in barbarism."

Of course, no one in the Western governments, and they call themselves civilised and humane, is willing to stand up with courage and morality to defend the Palestinians and their legitimate cause, apart from a very few indeed. They all are so scared of the propaganda machine and its media, claims of "anti-semitism" and the rest of it, and as a result, they also might lose their jobs and their career will be destroyed, therefore, they censor themselves. Whereas when it comes to people of the region including Palestinians, they will be automatically attacked as "anti-semitic" as well as "terrorists". And when it comes to the puppets of the region, they are just happy to talk the talk, reluctantly, to save a little face among the masses of the region. Yet in reality, as they have been doing for so many previous decades, they are playing with the Palestinian tragedy as a football game, or as pleasing speeches in front of their audience. Yet, behind the scenes, as honest and serious history books tell us, they take serious and sincere actions to starve and kill the Palestinian people and their aspirations. And I am pretty certain that as I am writing these words, some political entities in the region are discretely assisting the Zionist entity to liquidate the Palestinian cause.

Also, the Israeli propaganda machine puts huge pressure on journalists to report events on the ground according to the Israeli narrative and guidelines.

"You always come under particular pressure with [reporting on events in Israel and Palestine] because there is an intense and concerted Israeli media lobby—and there always was," said Sarah Helm, a former foreign correspondent for the UK's Independent newspaper. "And that includes a very intense Israeli political lobby working at every single level, which there always was too—and that was no secret and nor would they make a secret of it." (29)

David Cronin, for example, who had freelanced for The Guardian, wrote in 2015 about his frustrations with the newspaper in The Electronic Intifada, where he acts as an associate editor. Having reported about atrocities against Palestinians committed by Israel, the paper was later "not keen to have me writing from Gaza", he said, adding that one editor advised him to steer clear of covering the conflict altogether. (30)

The Western media narrative has been dominated by Israel during the entire 70-year conflict, according to Ilan Baruch, the former Israeli ambassador to South Africa;

"Israel was brilliantly successful in offering a narrative to the western hemisphere that was embraced with little or no objective judgement," said Baruch, who resigned from the Foreign Service in 2011 because he felt he could no longer represent the Israeli government's policies. (31)

"History has been allowed—and even recent history has been allowed—to disappear into a swamp," she said. "And everyone is so terrified of putting a foot wrong and being accused of being anti-semitic that they dare not even ask the [necessary] questions." (32)

As several critics of Israeli government policy find themselves accused of anti-Jewish racism, Baruch, the former Israeli ambassador to South Africa, said the debate needed to move past conflating these two notions. (33)

"Even criticising Zionism as the inspirational movement that created Israel is not anti-semitism," he said. "[The anti-semitism charge] is just a ploy to pull down criticism of Israel." (34)

Palestine, Syria and Yemen are only a few examples of the region's endless wars and violence.

Local violence and conflicts, social and political exclusion, civil wars, poverty and famines, illiteracy and unemployment, prevalence of contagious diseases, absence of real and honest systems of governance and basic human rights, absence of an equitable and independent judiciary, absence of security and equality, tyranny, despotism and greediness and so forth are all prevalent in the region's lands despite some variance between countries. Such circumstances and situations always provide—in any time and any place—a prime opportunity for outside intervention to exploit. I do not think that the region has been weaker and more mediocre; we have no institutions, no science, no co-ordination or co-operation, no strategies and counter-strategies, nothing. We just live on the fringes of history and pray that a miracle will turn our fortune. The only visible way to begin the process of change from the awful current status quo is to change the battlefield from the street to the mind.

States with thriving, stable economies and relatively equitable distribution of goods among their inhabitants are likely to be less shaky socially and politically than poor, highly in egalitarian and economically unstable ones. A dramatic increase in economic and social inequality within, as well as between, countries will reduce the chances of peace. The avoidance or control of internal armed violence depends even more immediately, however, on the powers and effective performance of national governments and their legitimacy in the eyes of the majority of their inhabitants. (35)

Dr Adib Nehmeh provided a very succinct comment that captured the important wider contexts that help explain why the Arab world in the past several decades has descended into its current state of violence and fragmentation. He noted: "The Arab region has for the most part not created stable, productive, and equitable civil states defined by modernity's benefits because for decades it has functioned under three simultaneous dominant contexts: neo-patrimonial states, neo-patriarchal societies, and neo-liberal peripheral economies." (36)

Any indigenous or foreign analysis of the conditions and trends in the Arab world that ignores these three critical factors will always come up short in both understanding why our region is in such a mess, and in suggesting appropriate policy responses by Arab or foreign governments. The three simultaneous defining realities of the contemporary Arab world that Dr Nehmeh points to have totally shattered any possibility of ordinary citizens drawing on their wellspring of decent values to shape productive, satisfying, and stable societies. Since the 1970s — when military-based families consolidated their hold over Arab power structures — citizens and states have never had the opportunity to negotiate a social contract that served their common rights and aspirations. (37)

The three power realities that Dr Nehmeh mentions provide as good a starting point as I know of for serious attempts to analyse or correct the threats that face our societies and that increasingly spill over into foreign countries. They provide critical clues to the underlying reasons for our tensions, violence, polarisation, sectarianism, fragmentation and other ailments. (38)

The bad news is that if these underlying drivers of citizen disenfranchisement and discontent are ignored — as they continue to be in prevailing Arab and foreign analyses and policies — we should only expect current trends to worsen. The good news is that all these problems have been caused by faulty policies implemented by human beings, and all of them can be corrected by more sensible and responsible human beings — but only people who dare to understand and then correct the distortions and constraints that are so well captured by Dr Nehmeh's succinct three-point summary. (39)

Wars, violence and civil wars have already inflicted immense pain, suffering, and destruction on the majority of people in war-torn nations and beyond. It is time to stop the violence and work towards morality, some sense and nation-building. And the region has forgotten its tender children who need love affection, shelter and education. Children and their potential to contribute to economic activity in the future. The economic damage associated with these unfortunate developments will be fully evident in the long term when today's children become active labour-market participants. In the short to medium term, the failure to educate young people of a vast region will translate into frustration and alienation and may have negative consequences for regional stability, which is already very unstable.

The above gloomy picture of the region as a whole does pose a serious question. But this question, I am going to direct it to the people of the region, to the intellectuals of the region, to their media, to their preachers and to the impotent different regional organisations and so on. What then? It might be a very short question, containing only two words, but I challenge them all to give us publicly an honest and courageous answer.

Morality is the basis of things and truth is the substance of all morality. Mahatma Gandhi

References for Chapter 4: Plague Four: Endless Wars, Endless Violence

1. Florence Gaub, Arab Wars: Calculating the Cost (online article), European Union Institute for Security Studies (EUISS) October 2017.
2. Nafeez Ahmed, Wednesday 8 April 2015,https://www.middleeasteye.net/columns/unworthy-victims-western-wars-have-killed-four-million-muslims-1990-3914939
3. Unger Craig, American Armageddon, Originally Published as the House of Bush, Scribner, 2007, P. 11.
4. Morris Ayek, Violence in the Arab World, Born of a Barbaric State, 2017. https://en.qantara.de/content/violence-in-the-world-born-of-a-barbaric-state.
5. https://en.wikipedia.org/wiki/Siege_of_Baghdad_(1258)
6. Lyons Jonathan, The House of Wisdom, How the Arabs Transferred Western Civilisation. Bloomsbury Publishing Plc, London, 2009.
7. Ledeen Micheal: "Creative destruction: How to wage a revolutionary war." National Review Online, 20 September2001. http://www.nationalreview.com/contributors/ledeeno92001.shtml.

8. Mahdi Nazemroaya, Plans for redrawing the Middle-East: The Project for a "New Middle-East", Nov. 2006, https://www.globalresearch.ca/author/mahdi-darius-nazemroaya

9. Ibid

10. Ibid

11. Robert Dreyfuss, Devil's Game: How the United States Helped Unleash Fundamentalist Islam (American Empire Project), October 13, 2005, PP. 330-337

12. Stockholm International Peace Research Institute, May 2018, https://www.sipri.org/media/press-release/2018/global-military-spending-remains-high-17-trillion

13. Patriots or War Profiteers? October 23, 2017. https//medium.com/@williamhartung55/corporate-patriots-or-war-profiteers-8eeb5f247142

14. Ibid.

15. Jonas Ecke, 19 May 2017, Whatever Happened to Peace? Arms, Oil and War by Proxy. opendemocracy.net/north-africa-west-asia/whatever-happened-peace-arms-oil-war-proxy-syria-middle-east-militray-industrial.

16. Ibid.

17. NADER HASHEMI, THE ARAB SPRING, US FOREIGN POLICY, AND THE QUESTION OF DEMOCRACY IN THE MIDDLE EAST, 15/12/2012,http://djilp.org/wp-content/uploads/2014/04/Hashemi_FinaltoPrinter.pdf

18. Brian Witaker, Oil, Money and Murder: Britain's Friends in the Gulf, al-bab.com, October 2018, https://al-bab.com/blog/2018/10/oil-money-and-murder-britains-friends-gulf

19. Unger Craig, American Armageddon, Originally Published as the House of Bush, Scribner, 2007, P. 289.

20. The Toll of War, The Economic and Social Consequences of the Conflict in Syria, file:///C:/Users/Set%20Up/Documents/The%20Toll%20of%20War.pdf

21. Daniel Pipes, New York Post, 25/February/2002

22. Levy Gideon, The Punishment of Gaza, Published by Verso 2010, P. 145

23. Ibid

24. Noam Chomsky, Who Rules the World? Hamish Hamilton, UK 2016, PP. 24-25

25. Ibid

26. Ibid

27. Ibid

28. Ibid

29. Alasdair Sossui, Why the Media Fail to Cover Palestine with accuracy and empathy, Al Jazeera English, https://www.aljazeera.com/indepth/features/media-fails-cover-palestine-accuracy-empathy-190316225136995.html

30. Ibid

31. Ibid

32. Ibid

33. Ibid

34. Ibid

35. Eric Hobsbawm, Globalisation, Democracy and Terrorism, Little, Brown, UK, 2007, P.29

36. Rami Khouri, Three Words that Capture the Arab World's Problems, Harvard Kennedy School, December 2015, https://www.belfercenter.org/publication/three-points-capture-arab-worlds-problems

37. Ibid

38. Ibid
39. Ibid

Chapter 5: Plague Five: The Age of Ignorance

The function of education is to teach one to think intensively and to think critically. Intelligence plus character—that is the goal of true education.

— *Martin Luther King, Jr.*

This is an age where the media is obsessed and filled with negative stereotypes of Arabs and the Islamic world, and supported by an army of so-called "experts" on the "Middle East" and its people's culture. One wonders when this is going to end. I think I should advise these so-called "experts", in particular the neoconservatives and their cronies, to read their own history first before spreading hatred and bigotry about the "Others".

For example, Anne Norton offers much anecdotal evidence of Straussian (and therefore neoconservative by association)

"Bigotry":

From the time I first came to Chicago to the present day, I have seen Arabs and Muslims made the targets of unrestrained persecution, especially among the Straussians. At school, students told me Arabs were dirty, they were animals, and they were vermin. Now I read in Straussian books and articles, in editorials and postings on websites that Arabs are violent, they are barbarous, they are the enemies of civilisation, and they are Nazis. (1)

Particular scorn is reserved for David Frum and Richard Perle's neoconservative manifesto: An end to evil: how to win the war on terror. Norton again:

Scholars familiar with the language of anti-semitism will find it reminiscent of old, long-dishonoured texts. The careful fabrication, the language of blood libel, the calls for violence in the name of defence, all are present here. Frum and Perle tell us that although others are too timid to say so, the enemy is Islam. (2)

But these people who preach hatred, bigotry and racism etc. against Arabs and Muslims in general have, totally and for the sake of their ugly ideology, forgotten intentionally or otherwise, to acknowledge that Islamic civilisation (Arabs and non-Arabs alike) for over a thousand years have massively contributed a great deal of knowledge in all fields of philosophy and science, from the knowledge of paper making and cartography to medicine and science. From the azimuth to the zenith, from algebra to the zero, so much came to the West and built their civilisation at the feet of the East and its civilisation. I just wonder how anyone would be able to build a computer without a zero.

The Arabs are old people, with an affluent past. It is the complex nature of their past which keeps the Arabs on different agendas, and a willingness to negotiate separately. The "Middle East" is where man first organised into a settled form of society, cultivating grain and raising livestock, establishing cities and promoting diverse skills and occupations. The "Middle East" is where the rich and complex cultures of the ancient Egypt, Sumer, Assyria, Babylonia and Phoenicia civilisations began and flourished.

The Arabic language developed during this time and spread through the centuries, until the appearance of Islam. This is where the language acquired the form in which it is known today. Arab poets of the pre-Islamic, or Jahiliyyah (the age of ignorance) period, had developed a language of amazing richness and flexibility, despite the fact that many were desert Bedouins (nomads) with little or no formal education. For the most part, their poetry was transmitted and preserved orally throughout the "Middle East". The Arabic language was then, as it is now, easily capable of creating new words and terminology in order to adapt to the demands of new scientific and artistic discoveries. The civilisations that thrived in the "Middle East" brought to the world discoveries about the human body and how blood flows. The study of astronomy was improved and many heavenly bodies were attributed to the Arab astronomers. The Arabs taught the world to navigate using the stars. The Arabs were very religious but progressive in their studies. Unfortunately, they were never to realise their renaissance and be credited with their discoveries.

Islam from its birth has placed a great deal of emphasis on education and learning. For example, the Holy Book of the Qur'an has more than 800 references to it. The first word revealed to the Prophet Muhammad, was not, for example, believe in Allah, or war or Jihad or anything else but learn. In addition to the so many references cited in the Qur'an stressing the importance of education and learning, there are also numerous sayings attributed to Prophet Muhammad also stressing and encouraging the believers to learn, think, analyse, and discover. That is why the Muslim scientists, in particular, during the Abbasid era never took anything that came to them from the Greeks or the Hindus etc. at face value. They looked at the theories, analysed them and took a great deal of work to prove their validity. They not only managed to translate and read, but to analyse, correct, and add numerous new discoveries. They themselves also created original works in different sciences, such as engineering. Irrigation systems they have built in so many cities around the Islamic empire at the time were just genius. Whereas the whole of the West, at the time, were fighting and killing each other with savagery as Western history books tell us. And now the picture is reversed, the region as a whole is fighting each other with savagery, yet the difference is the modern weaponry they use, mass killings on a massive scale.

Ignorance equates barbarism. When the Arabs and non-Arabs and the Muslim civilisation as a whole were immersing themselves, for long centuries, in research, in science, in discoveries and above all in logical and rational debates, they managed to rule almost half of the world known to man at the time. They managed and to grow the essential seeds and lay strong foundations of modern Western civilisation, without which even the computer, which we take for granted, wouldn't be available, as the computer's invention relied and was based on the zero, which was a discovery of Muslim mathematicians.

An interesting article written by a Yemeni Professor of Economics at Sana University said:

Americans have realised the importance of education in the international competition for progress, well-being and world leadership as evidenced in the report entitled "Nation at Risk" published in 1983 by the commission of education and edited by David Gardner. This report, written two decades ago, aimed to bring the attention of the American people — politicians, scientists, intellectuals, businessmen and the common people — to the harm the deterioration of education might cause. The writers of this report issued a call for help: "Our nation is losing a carelessness war". This carelessness was manifest, in the view of the authors, in the deteriorating level of education in the United States compared to the educational achievements of other advanced industrial countries. People who were in childcare in 1983 are after two decades of high school graduate students. Half of them are enrolled in universities and institutes or working in remunerative jobs, whereas the other half is either unqualified, working at low-wage jobs, unemployed, or depend upon governmental subsidies. Many of them are vagrants and many are involved in crime. All this happened because they did not get a good education. The danger warning sounded by the nation-at-risk report marks a relative danger to which the American nation, sitting at the peak of modern civilization, might be exposed. Hence, the type of danger which the report describes as only a relative danger, meaning that the American nation might lose its leading position in the international race of nations. It is not comparable to the threat that the Yemeni nation faces, a threat of destruction so complete that it will make such a great and deep-rooted civilization as Yemen's and its people no more than stories in a history textbook and CDs. (3)

Now the Arabs and Muslims, in general, all attacked and labelled left, right and centre by ignorant people who are called intellectuals such as Barbara Lerner, she writes in the National Review in relation to the Beslan attack on the 1st September 2004 in Russia the following:

"But in the end, these voices of blind bigotry and defeatism won't prevail, because millions of Russians have learned the same hard lessons most of us learned on September 11: That we are at war with a vicious global enemy, an Islamist enemy that hates Christians, Hindus and progressive Muslims as much as it hates Jews, an enemy that cannot be appeased, bought off, or safely sicced on others; an enemy we must unite to cut down wherever it rears its ugly head, or have our own heads and those of our children cut off by it." (4)

In no defence of any kind of atrocities committed against any innocent human beings from any side or any destruction of places of worship, safety or otherwise, would I question the above chilling statement. As if the souls and heads of the Muslim children who are, more or less, daily massacred by Western civilisation directly or indirectly are worthless and hardly mentioned by the international media and its barons, yet, when it comes to the people of the Christendom world and Jewish people, their human souls and properties are holy, full of worth and defendable?

Western media reports have too often fed us mythologies and half-truths about a vengeful Arab mentality. Commentators like neoconservative Michael Ledeen spoke of "the same kind of hate that we read every day in the newspapers about what the Saudi newspapers are printing: Kill the Jews, kill the Christians, be a martyr, go to heaven, 72 virgins, the usual. A Bernard Lewis piece in the Atlantic conjured up a unified Islamic anger predicated on historic injustices — neatly clumping together all adherents to a religion practised by nearly by one in five people on earth. More disturbing still is Lee Smith's sweeping and bigoted generalisation that "the Arabs hate us not because of what we do or who we are but because of what and who we are not: Arabs." (5)

Adding more petrol to fire, neoconservative 'intellectuals and policymakers' are more than eager to portray Islam and Muslims as just a bunch of 'terrorists' who do not think of anything but the destruction and killing of the West and its people, and the Muslims as a physical security threat to the United States. In a book called An End to Evil (Perle and Frum's), the authors highly embrace militancy against, as they describe:

Al-Qaeda, Hezbollah and Hamas

Mullahs

Terrorists

Iran

Baghdad

Imams

Misfits and thugs

Larger culture of incitements and hatred

Heavyweight of inertia

Bureaucracy's profound aversion to innovation

The ranks of the faint-hearted

Pessimism and defeatism

Gloom sayers

Middle East radicalism of all varieties (6)

Implicitly what they are trying to convey to the readers is one main point, Muslims everywhere must be killed and the survivors must be contained and impoverished more and more. The hidden message behind their book is to wage wars, endless wars, against anything called Islam, covering their message behind different terminologies. The idiocy of this book is grand. The authors' notions of good and evil are laughable and over-simplistic. Their logic is basically: "Neoconservatives and Capitalists GOOD, Islamists BAD". "Drones GOOD, radical Imams BAD". "Plundering nations in the name of nation building GOOD, Sharia law BAD". Their understanding of Islamist behaviour stops with the sweeping statement "they are evil". The result of this is that this fascist book is a formula for endless war. This leads me to conclude that they are basically ignorant. And in my view, the notion that the neoconservatives are trying hard to convey, that Muslims, if united are going to storm the West, makes no sense, on the contrary, what we are witnessing now, is an increased presence of Western military in Muslim lands, from Afghanistan to Iraq, primarily instigating Muslims against Muslims, Shia against Sunnis, and ultimately suffocating Iran of the privilege of a counter-balance to Israel and the West.

Irvin Kristol (one of the founding fathers of neoconservatism) notes philosophically that "insignificant nations, like insignificant people, can quickly experience delusions of significance....smaller nations are not going to behave reasonably with decent respect for the interests of others, including the great powers—unless it is costly to them to behave unreasonably." It is our duty to enforce this lesson. "In truth, the days of 'gunboat diplomacy' are never over....Gunboats are as necessary for international order as police cars are for domestic order." Because of "the legalistic-moralistic-'idealistic' mould into which American foreign policy was cast after World War II," we haven't been manning the gunboats as we should (witness our unwillingness to use force in Vietnam). But perhaps this moral flabbiness can be overcome and we can enforce standards of reasonableness on the insignificant nations. (7)

Irving here is sending a clear and loud message to all "insignificant nations" that: no one has the right of self-defence against US terrorist attack. The US is a terrorist state by right. That is the unchallengeable doctrine.

In his book After Jihad: America and the Struggle for Islamic Democracy, New York University professor Noah Feldman sets out this case with knowledge. "The alternative to this model is the "confrontation model," which has many characteristics of the "clash of civilisation." It posits that a clash between the West and Islam is inevitable, as differences are reflected in all aspects of life, from ideology to culture. Islam, in this model, is thought inflexible, intolerant, and resentful of Western advances. Islam is resistant to globalisation and instead reflects anger and resentment at the great disparity in wealth when compared with the West. Embattled and isolated, enraged Islamic calls to avenge loss of life have precluded productive contact with Western governments and instead, employed terrorism to great asymmetrical effect against Western "openness," exacerbating matters further. This is a model presented in effect by Princeton professor Bernard Lewis, the neoconservative's favourite Arabist, albeit more elegantly and with less bile than some of those, such as Daniel Pipes, who tread in his footprints. (8)

The concept of "knowledge ignorance" is defined as 'knowing a people, ideas, civilisations, religions or histories as something they are not, and could not possibly be, and maintaining these ideas even when the means exist to know differently.' (9)

This concept of 'knowledge ignorance' is a powerful phenomenon which is plaguing the minds of so many people around the world including intellectuals and policymakers, and which is adding more hatred and will cause irreversible damage for a long time to come. Knowledge ignorance does not stop on the shores of the intellectuals and thinkers; it also extends to young minds of a generation and the public of society in general. For example, in the United States, the majority of young American people are not able to locate Iraq on the world map, I am mentioning Iraq as the US fought two wars in that country in 1991 and 2003. To the extent that in 2006, three years after the barbaric invasion of

Iraq a survey was conducted and Andrew Buncombe wrote for the Independent the following:

"The US may be the world's only true superpower but global domination does not equal global knowledge. A new survey shows young Americans have what can only be described as shoddy geography skills, with six out of 10 unable to locate Iraq on a map and almost half incapable of pointing to the state of Mississippi." (10)

More than two-thirds of Americans don't know the year Israel declared its independence, and an equal amount wrongly believe Iran and Pakistan are Arab countries. (11)

Despite the fact that the so-called "Middle East" is central to the Americans and their own way of life, the region, its people, its culture remains completely ambiguous in the minds of the West.

In the Middle East Eye online, CJ Werleman writes:

Alarmingly, this collective breath-taking level of ignorance travels all the way to the nation's policymakers and law enforcement officials. A New York Times Op-Ed asked the question "Can You Tell a Sunni from a Shiite?" Jeff Stein writes, "Most American officials don't have a clue. That includes not just intelligence and law enforcement officials, but also members of Congress who have important roles overseeing our spy agencies. How can they do their jobs without knowing the basics?" He continues:

In a series of interviews with senior US political leaders, Stein asked a simple and straightforward question: "Do you know the difference between a Sunni and a Shiite? The responses were tragically comical. "One's in one location, another's in another location," said US Congressman Terry Everett (R-AL), a member of the House intelligence committee, before conceding: "No, to be honest with you, I don't know." When Stein asked Congressman Silvestre

Reyes (D-TX), chair of the House intelligence committee, whether al-Qaeda was Sunni or Shia, he answered: "Predominantly — probably Shia." Wrong! (12)

It is no surprise to me that the majority of the American public, as well as the majority of their political leaders and policymakers, have no real understanding or solid knowledge of the region and its inhabitants, due to, in my belief, lack of education in the American system, in particular schools. Their textbooks totally ignore the region, or when they hardly mention it, they deliver a naïve, meaningless, and even distorted image of the region and its peoples.

And of course, the neoconservatives like Peter King or Lindsey Graham, the Israel lobby, and much of the media and its arms continue to feed the American public with more ignorance and plant more dark seeds in the minds of the people to foster the false narratives of the fictional "clash of civilisation." They are seeding false fears, and fears cause one to panic, panic creates confusion, and confusion and misunderstanding create ignorance.

Prior to "Operation Iraqi Freedom", and certainly before the attacks on New York and Washington in September 2001, Americans lived mostly in ignorance of the Middle East. All these years later they remain ignorant but in a different way. Previously, Americans had simply been uninformed about the region. What little they knew tended to be shaped by the conflict between Israelis and Palestinians, the fading memory of the Iranian hostage crisis and the brief Persian Gulf War of 1991 to reverse Iraqi strongman Saddam Hussein's annexation of Kuwait. (13)

Today Americans remain ignorant about the Middle East not because they are unaware of the region, but because they are poorly educated about it. It was not long after the Twin

Towers fell and the smouldering fire at the Pentagon was extinguished that terms like Jihad, Salafi, Wahhabi, madrassa and al-Qaeda became part of the American political lexicon. It seemed that anyone who had attained the rank of a colonel, or could claim (legitimately or otherwise) one-time employment at the CIA, or was a columnist, who had visited an Arab country once or twice, was booked on television to shed light on "why they hate us." To be fair, this reflected a surge of genuine interest in the Middle East. Suddenly, University Arabic classes were oversubscribed, and books about the region that once reached tiny audiences did very well. (14)

As 9/11 became a distant memory and the Iraqi venture became a disaster, the laudable desire to learn more about the Middle East seemed to fall off even as the causalities returning home continued at a steady pace. Yet in some ways, the region continued to be an obsession — not just for policymakers and foreign policy analysts, but also for a network of groups and individuals that fostered mistrust and fear of Middle Easterners in general and Muslims in particular. (15) CJ Werleman continues:

Consider, for example, comedian and TV host Bill Maher. His Islamophobia is well-known. There are endless examples to pick from when it comes to Maher's anti-Muslim sentiments, but he outdid himself in an October 2010 episode of "Real Time with Bill Maher," his talk show on HBO. Maher confessed that he was afraid that so many babies with the name Muhammad were being born in Western countries. Addressing his panel, Maher asked, "Am I a racist to feel alarmed by that? Because I am. And it's not because of the race; it's because of the religion. I don't have to apologise, do I, for not wanting the Western world to be taken over by Islam in 300 years?" (16)

Stefan Halper and Jonathan Clarke, the authors of America Alone (p.19) write that "fully 80 per cent of the books (neoconservatives' books) deal with the "Middle East" or for a strong military." The same pattern is repeated elsewhere. In the same book, regarding the case for the war against Iraq they write:

"Empirical evidence shows that the media outlets (US media) were fundamental in this process (the process of misperception). From January to September 2003, seven different polls were conducted jointly by two polling networks that analysed the perception of the American public toward the war with Iraq. The data demonstrated that in the lead-up to the war and during the post-war period, a large section of the American public held a number of misperceptions that played a vital role in creating and sustaining support for the decision to go to war. For example: significant numbers of the US electorate believed Iraq to have been directly involved in the attacks of 9/11; that Iraq and al-Qaeda were linked; that weapons of mass destruction were found in Iraq after the war; that Iraq actually used weapons of mass destruction during the war; and that world opinion generally approved of America's going to war. The polls show that these data are derived, to a great extent, from how certain media outlets portrayed events. The results of the seven polls, which were fielded using a nationwide panel of some 10,000 randomly selected respondents, revealed that these misperceptions did not originate from a failure to pay attention, but rather from paying greater attention to particular news networks." (17)

I think the above speaks for itself but I must add, thanks to Robert Murdoch and his media empire.

The neoconservatives' propaganda machine went into action nearly as quickly as the Pentagon did. By 1:15 p.m., just four hours after the attacks (September 11), Michael Ledeen, the neoconservative operative who had won notoriety in the Iran-contra scandal, filed a dispatch on the National Review's website attacking the remaining realists in the US administration and urging someone to remind Bush that "we are still living with the consequences of Desert Storm (reference to Iraq war I), when his father and his father's advisers—most notably Colin Powell and Brent Scowcroft—advised against finishing the job and liberating Iraq." (18)

At 2:40 p.m., Secretary of Defence Donald Rumsfeld ordered the military to put together retaliatory plans to go after not just Bin Laden, but Saddam Hussein as well. According to notes taken by a Rumsfeld aide, the secretary of defence wanted "best info fast, judge whether good enough to hit Saddam Hussein at the same time, not only UBL," the initials used to identify Osama bin Laden. "Go massive, sweep it all up, things related or not", the notes said. (19)

Meanwhile, Laurie Mylorie, a darling of the neoconservatives who had falsely reported that Saddam Hussein was behind the 1993 World Trade Centre bombing, turned in an opinion piece that was published in the Wall Street Journal the next day, blaming the Iraqi dictator for 9/11 as well. Intelligence analysts had already begun to tell journalists that Iraq had nothing to do with it. Yet Mylroie's theory was cited by and given credence by the Washington Post, CBS News, ABC, Fox News, US News & World Report, CNN, The Times (London), the Dallas Morning and more than a hundred other media outlets—some of them repeatedly. "In my view, yesterday's events were the latest step in Saddam's war against the United States," Mylroie told CBS News. (20)

In addition, and with the Internet and social media exploiting the vulnerabilities, ignorance has become pandemic. Perhaps this is a logical evolutionary progression, but at no time in history has the public become so susceptible to the spread of wilful ignorance, intentionally deceitful lies, and blatant stupidity. As some elements of falsehoods are skilfully crafted on one hand, but gullibly accepted on the other, rumours prevail in a fact-free world in which even seemingly intelligent people frequently respond with the resonating, yet dangerous refrain: "I don't care!"

While observable ubiquitously, nowhere is this intellectual dilemma of the Age of Ignorance more perilous than in the current American political cycle. Rather than thoughtful discussions of issues, blows and counterpunching have devolved into a battlefield of tweets. Twitter, with a 140 (before it was increased to 280) character limit, so narrowly constrains content that important context is lost, and individuals are frequently left to interpret the meaning. The current progenitor of this manner of political parlance, Donald Trump, exploits the public vulnerability by seeming to assume that the audience will not delve more deeply into any given topic, but as sheeple, they will mentally embed the simplistic message and divest themselves of any further cognitive effort. (21)

When it comes to Europeans the situation is massively different as Andre Vltchek puts it: "The problem is also that intellectuals in the United States think that the people in Europe are better informed than those outside it, that they have a much wider sense of what can be discussed. I found out that this is maybe only the case in regard to issues that are directly related to the United States. Otherwise, there is a screaming ignorance in Europe. In general, I find educated people in Asia, Latin America and Africa better informed on current affairs than their European counterparts. I find Westerners in general, and Europeans in particular extremely indoctrinated and obsessed with the perceptions of their own uniqueness. Many see themselves as chosen people, after going through a one-sided education and after relying on their media outlets, without studying alternative sources." (22)

When speaking about education and knowledge, I certainly do not mean literacy and the statistics surrounding it. We find, or at least I found, when travelling and meeting people, that there are people who are illiterate (in terms of reading and writing), yet they have great knowledge and true wisdom when talking about different issues including current international affairs. And on the other side of the coin, I found people with the highest university degrees that can be only categorised and considered as 'knowledge ignorant'.

When I was a young boy at school (and this applies to colleges and universities) I attended in one of the lands in the region, I remember quite well that my education can simply be described as extremely passive. Meaning, in the classroom the activities consisted only of copying from the blackboard, writing, and listening to what the teachers said. There was no group work, creative thinking, or proactive learning. Individual investigations, analysing problems, and finding practical or theoretical solutions were not encouraged or even existed. We as a classroom of around 30–35 pupils were taught to memorise and retain answers already written in the books or told by the teacher. Therefore, we were just passive knowledge recipients without a meaningful context. So when I think back to my school days, I wonder what they have done for me as an individual. I come to the conclusion that they have managed to equip me to survive in an authoritarian regime/environment and turned my brain into a gullible recipient of ideas that would collapse under serious scrutiny. As far as I am aware, the situation in terms of education in the region did not change much even after three decades. The education system still relies heavily on the concept of memorising the teachers' words, rehearse them, avoid asking questions, and you will stay out of trouble.

An Israeli newspaper published a translation of a Muslim preacher (Abdelfattah Mourou) castigating Muslims and Arab culture for being unambitious, ignorant, and backward. "Where is your knowledge and lore today, o Muslims? Today, the Muslims are living in an era when everything they wear, from head to toe, is made by others. This cap was made in New Zealand. These glasses were made in Austria. This microphone was made in America. This watch was made in Switzerland and my shoes were made in Italy. The wool of this robe came from Britain. My brothers, we do not own anything in our lives. "Why do you raise your hands in prayer asking Allah to grant 'victory to Islam and the Muslims'? Victory over whom exactly? Why should you be victorious? Allah speaks of 'evil deeds out of ignorance'? 30% of Muslims cannot read or write. We cannot take pride in a single university in the (Muslim) world for producing minds that move the world forward. We are a nation that does not read or write. Today is the first day of the New Year; with all due respect, has anyone here read a single book (in the past year)? We do not read, and we do not teach our wives to read. Our sons do not read, either. On average, an Arab reads 0.79 books a year — that's three-quarters of a book, while in Japan, they read 80 books every two years. So how can we expect to be like the Japanese? How can I expect to be like the Americans, who have learned to read and plan their lives carefully? We, on the other hand, live our lives randomly, by whims and emotions." (23)

"Some researchers argue," the AHDR (Arab Human Development Report) noted, "that the curricula taught in Arab countries seem to encourage submission, obedience, subordination and compliance, rather than free critical thinking." The same can be said of teachers who adhere slavishly to the official textbook, in some cases even when it is wrong or allows only one answer to a question when other answers are equally valid. One researcher visiting a Moroccan primary school found children being taught that 4 x 3 = 11 because of a misprint in the textbook. The teacher had previously taught that the answer was 12 but, since the new book was issued, he felt it best to follow the approved text. That may be an extreme case but blogger/activist Hossam Hamalawy found similar rigidity at his school in Cairo: "In chemistry, an exam student wrote a formula that was right but he was crossed out because this was not what the government textbook said. You could get the same compound by two formulas." (24)

"At school," Hamalawy continued, "you memorise everything, even literary critique. When you are given a piece of poetry, you study the points of strength and the points of weakness. You do not move your brain, you do not use anything — you just memorise what the government textbook tells you." (25)

This is a massive difference between a knowledgeable Islamic civilisation built between the 8th and 13th centuries, and the current situation. The scientific advancements the Muslims created at the time were constructed mainly on logical thinking, on flexibility, on problem solving and theoretical or practical experiments. They did not just memorise or took for granted what other civilisations wrote and found, but instead, they analysed and examined the validity of the matters in question as well as adding magnificent discoveries which were the fruits of the current advancements in all different sciences and topics.

For several centuries the Muslim civilisation was socially, economically, and technologically advanced. One of the reasons for this was its people's appreciation of and openness to knowledge creation and dissemination. This trend lasted from the 8th to the 13th centuries. Knowledge became the most important and determining factor for economic growth. The impact and contribution of this wealth of knowledge were felt and appreciated across different sectors and disciplines and acknowledged beyond the region and around the world. However, things changed drastically in the 18th and 19th centuries following the Industrial Revolution. The situation now is turned upside down. The region is plagued with ignorance on a massive scale, conspiracy theories are rife and meaningful discussions and debates are hardly visible or even encouraged. People of the region are always looking for someone else to be blamed for their current ills and difficulties. The region's intellectuals, their policymakers and their media are all encouraging the masses to look outside their environments they live in, they are asking the masses to mend someone else's house while their own are broken. You hear so many people of the region talking about their glorious past history; how the people were united and lived peacefully, happily, with prosperity and pride, yet hardly hear people talk about how we can move forward. How we can mend the broken houses. It's no denial on my part that the recent history of the region and the colonisation of the region by alien imperial powers have created so many problems and disunity. But, the past is past and we seriously, every one of the regions, need to start thinking outside the box. The people of the region, as an example, are aware of the racial profiling when flying to the United States and they are disgusted by it, yet they don't debate the racial profiling committed in their own backyard. People of the region are more than happy to talk and criticise openly, even some preachers in Mosques, of the treatment and discrimination of black people in the United States, yet no one speaks and criticises the harsh treatment and discrimination the guest workers and housemaids are facing daily in their lands. People of the region are quite content to talk and criticise the barbaric tortures committed by the US and UK soldiers against Iraqi prisoners, yet hardly anyone speaks about the ugly and inhumane treatment and torture committed by the hands of their own next of kin in so many prisons around the region. This is hypocrisy and ignorance on a massive scale.

In the words of Jonathan Lyons, he writes:

"The arrival of Arab science and philosophy, the legacy of the pioneering Adelard and those who hurried to follow his example, transmuted the backward West into a scientific and technological superpower. Like the elusive "elixir" — from the alchemists' al-iksir — for changing base metal into gold, Arab science altered medieval Christendom beyond recognition. For the first time in centuries, Europe's eyes opened to the world around it. The encounter with Arab science even restored the art of telling time, lost to the western Christians of the early Middle Ages. Without accurate control over clock and calendar, the rational organisation of society was unthinkable. And so was the development of science, technology and industry, as well as the liberation of man from the thrall of nature. Arab science and philosophy helped rescue the Christian world from ignorance and made possible the very idea of the West". (26)

I am citing the above to convey three messages to the East:

1. There is an urgent need of re-organisation of society, as it is obvious that the region has lost track of time and time is running out fast.

2. There is also an urgent need for the East to liberate man, this time not from nature, but from the shekels and constant thoughts of being victims.

3. Without an open and meaningful system of education, real learning, analysing and problem-solving, ignorance will continue to thrive unrestrained.

Ignorance is the main enemy of good and honest thinking and it is plaguing the West, in particular the US, and it's also a major problem plaguing the region in question. And the issue I am raising here is not literacy or illiteracy, it is the question of real knowledge on wider grounds, take for an example think-tanks which can be defined: as research institute or a centre and organisation that performs research and advocacy concerning topics such as social policy, political strategy, economics, military, technology and culture. (27)

2017 Think Tank Statistics: Number of Think Tanks in the World in 2017

This chart reflects the number of think tanks in 2017 based on data collected as of December 2017.

Number of Think Tanks in the World in 2017

2017 Global Think Tank Total = 7,815

North America = 1,972

Central & South America = 979

Sub-Saharan Africa = 664

Europe = 2,045

Asia = 1,676
Middle East & North Africa = 479

Countries with the Largest Number of Think Tanks

The sequence is as follows: Rank of the country, name of the country and last is the number of the think tanks they possess:

1 United States 1,872
2 China 512
3 United Kingdom 444
4 India 293
5 Germany 225
6 France 197
7 Argentina 146
8 Japan 116
9 Russia 103
10 Canada 100
11 Brazil 93
12 South Africa 92
13 Sweden 89
(T)-14 Netherlands 76
(T)-14 Switzerland 76
16 Mexico 74
17 Austria 68
18 Israel 67
19 Bolivia 66
20 Iran 64
(T)-21 Spain 63
(T)-21 Chile 63
23 Belgium 61
24 Poland 60

25 Taiwan 58

Source - TTCSP Global Go To Think Tank Index Reports
Think Tank and Civil Societies Program (TTCSP) 1-30-2018
2017 Global Go To Think Tank Index Report

As the above clearly shows, out of the 25 top countries in the whole globe not a single Arab country is represented and the region's population is almost 423 million.

Think Tanks in the Region's Countries

Egypt: 36
Palestine: 34
Iraq: 30
Lebanon: 27
Jordan: 26
Libya: 2
Oman: 3
Tunisia: 20
Qatar: 14
UAE: 9
SaudiArabia: 8
Bahrain: 12
Algeria: 8
Kuwait: 15
Morocco: 14
Syria: 10
Yemen: 26

Please note that the report mentioned only 17 countries out of 22

It's obvious that research and development in the region as a whole is not a priority to the ruling parties. They rather import, particularly oil-producing countries, expertise from abroad instead of nurturing and developing their own workforce. As a consequence, the brightest brains of the region tend to move abroad as soon as their chances allow.

The underlying problem, though, is that "ingrained structural impediments" (as the Arab Human Development Report puts it) stand in the way of developing knowledge-based societies in the Arab countries. A knowledge-based society is essentially non-authoritarian and open to new ideas. It favours transparency and encourages a spirit of enquiry. It acknowledges unwelcome realities and addresses them. It is flexible and adapts quickly to changing circumstances. These are all traits that Arab societies, at home, at school, or in the workplace, actively discouraged — and the implications of this are far-reaching. Arab countries cannot develop knowledge-based societies without radical social and political change. They can, if they choose, try to stay on the side-lines, but self-imposed backwardness is an expensive luxury. (28)

Certainly, Islam as a religion did not and does not prevent acquiring of knowledge and scientific innovation, as some ignorant people are trying to convey. On the contrary, Islam and its teaching encourage logical thinking, discoveries and research, provided that important political and cultural factors are adhered to. Such factors include political freedom, freedom of rational and open debates, open and constructive self-criticism, listening to and respecting the thoughts of others without prejudice, and narrow-minded regional unity.

In the past, Islamic societies had negotiated between science and religion very successfully, creating and enabling one of the greatest periods of enlightenment of humankind. Yet, for the past centuries, we are lacking behind almost everyone in every field of philosophy, technology and science. When we nowadays speak, we only cite the past and how glorious our past was. It seems that the region and its people are stuck in the past as if there is no future for us or for our children. Without the prospect of real and positive change in attitude and thinking, for fighting the current ills of the region, without fighting the tyrannies imposed or self-imposed on us, I am certain, that the region will drift further and ever more downwards. History does not respect the weak.

Education here is the key variable in the formula of a modern strategic deterrent. There is no single country in the contemporary world that has achieved real development, welfare and security without effective, generous and planned investment in education. Investment in human resources will not only bring fruits in increasing individual ability to get or create a job and generate a household's income, to decrease poverty and increase aggregate economic resources of the nation, but also to enhance and strengthen the defensive capability of the nation in an effective and constructive manner. (29)

According to the World Bank, the quality of education in the region is falling behind other regions and needs urgent intervention and reform in order to address issues associated with unemployment. Although the knowledge ecosystem, including awareness, education, training and lifelong learning, represents a cornerstone for development and growth in the Middle East, there is still a lot that needs to be done before the education sector becomes a catalyst for economic production and development and a driver for societal growth. Moreover, higher education plays an invaluable role within society because it creates additional opportunities for development and provides knowledge transfer for students and other stakeholders, and promotes change, creativity, innovation and progress. (30)

The culture of rent which dominates the economic landscape of the region does not encourage innovation and risk-taking. Hence, scientific education and research in Arab countries is among the lowest in the world. The Second Arab Human Development Report (AHDR) sponsored by the United Nations Development Program (UNDP) and the Arab Fund for Social and Economic Development has clearly shown the low level of higher scientific education in the Arab World. Arab universities are subjected to the political will of ruling elites who see little benefit in associating larger segments of the population to access to knowledge and developing critical thinking. Universities are the laboratories where the youth first experiment in political and social interaction (UNDP 2004). Libraries are poorly endowed, classes small, and laboratories falling apart, and universities cannot absorb the growing number of student population. This leads to a widening gap between teachers and students (UNDP 2004). Ruling elites are more interested in showing larger statistics of student enrolment for political propaganda rather than the quality of education given. (31)

The enemy of bad governance is an informed, educated public able to think critically and be tolerant of different outlooks. That is why an area where serious reform is desperately needed in Arab countries is education—primarily the quality of education. What has been absent from many Arab educational systems are curricula that nurture the evolution of a healthy concept of citizenship and lead to proper state building by teaching values, including tolerance and appreciation for diversity. (32)

The crux of the matter is a meaningful and thinking based education, without which the region will slide more into disarray and backwardness. I cannot imagine for a moment that a nation can be built, prosper, be sovereign, and united without established sciences and innovations. How can a nation be sovereign if not able even to feed itself? How can they defend themselves from enemies if they do not know how to manufacture a weapon of any sort? How can a strong nation be built without solid and effective institutions? How can members of society trust justice if the judicial system is corrupt? How can a coherent nation be established without respect and without dignity? How can members of the nation sacrifice for a country when there is nothing to sacrifice for?

Investing in education helps people to unleash the creative capacities of all citizens irrespective of their background and effectively supports their drive to improve their lives and to build better societies. Meaningful education benefits all, individuals, organisations and society and leads to major positive transformations that could lead to further growth and development.

Now the question is whom to blame? — The blame game — shall we blame the Turks, the Mongols, the British, the French, the Americans, the Zionists and so on... as all the region's countries are ruled by impotent, oppressive and ineffective governments, this game of blame serves them very well indeed. They cannot explain to the peoples of the region why poverty is immense, why the region is held back in terms of knowledge and innovations, why unemployment is ridiculously high, why tyranny has recently intensified and so many other questions. They cannot answer so many questions, and to deflect the mounting anger and frustration among the people, they encourage and enrich the belief of blaming the other — an outsider. Yet, if anyone is to blame – we are.

References for Chapter 5: Plague Five: The Age of Ignorance

1. J. Lynch Timothy, Kristol Balls: Neoconservative Vision of Political Islam. Research Paper Presented at the European Consortium for Political Joint Sessions, Granada, Spain, April 2005. P. 13.

2. Ibid. P. 13

3. Mohammed al-Maitami, Education as a strategic deterrent in a backward society (Yemen as a case), al-bab.com, https://al-bab.com/education-strategic-deterrent-backward-society-yemen-case

4. BarbaraLerner,07/09/2004,NationalReview, https://www.nationalreview.com/2004/09/beslan-changed-russia-barbara-lerner/

5. Zogby James, Arab Voices, what they are saying to us, and why it matters, Palgrave Macmillan, 2010, P. 83

6. David Frum and Richard Perle, An End to Evil, Ballantine Books; Reprint edition (October 26, 2004), P. 4.

7. Noam Chomsky, Middle East Illusions, Rowman & Littlefield Publishers, UK 2003, P. 8

8. Noah Feldman, After jihad: American and the Struggle for Islamic Democracy, New York, Straus and Giroux, 2003, PP. 38/50

9. J. Lynch Timothy, Kristol Balls: Neoconservative Vision of Political Islam. Research Paper Presented at the European Consortium for Political Joint Sessions, Granada, Spain, April 2005. P. 30

10. Andrew Buncombe, The Independent, 03/May/2006, https://www.independent.co.uk/news/world/americ as/six-out-of-10-young-americans-cannot-find-iraq-on-a-map-5336161.html

11. National Geographic-Roper Survey of Geographic Litracyhttps://www.nationalgeographic.com/report2 006/findings.html

12. CJ Werleman, Middle East Eye online,http://www.middleeasteye.net/opinion.cluele ss-americas-ignorance-middle-east-will-shock-you

13. Council on Foreign Relations, Blog posted by Steven A. Cook, March 27, 2017, Bill Maher Makes Us Dumber: How Ignorance, Fear and Stupid Pop-Culture Clichés Shape Americans' View of the Middle East, https://www.cfr.org/blog/bill-maher-makes-us-dumber-how-ignorance-fear-and-stupid-pop-culture-cliches-shape-americans

14. Ibid

15. Ibid

16. Ibid

17. Stefan Halper & Jonathan Clarke, America Alone, The Neo-Conservatives and the Global Order, Cambridge University Press, Cambridge, UK, 2004, PP. 192/193.

18. Craig Unger, American Armageddon, Scribner, New York, 2007, P. 215-216.

19. Ibid

20. Ibid

21. John B. Alexander, Huffpost Online, https://www.huffingtonpost.com/john-b-alexander-phd/the-age-of-ignorance_b_11666646.html

22. Chomsky Noam and Vltchek Andre, On Western terrorism from Hiroshima to Drone Warfare, Pluto Press, London, 2013, P. 19/20.

23. Arutz Sheva Online, http://www.israelnationalnews.com/News/News.aspx/232606

24. Brian Whitaker, What's Really Wrong with the Middle East. Published by Saqi, London 2009, P. 24

25. Ibid

26. Lyons Jonathan, The House of Wisdom, How Arabs Transformed Western Civilisation, Bloombury Publishing Plc, Great Britain 2009, P.4.

27. https://en.wikipedia.org/wiki/Think_tank

28. Brian Whitaker, What's Really Wrong with the Middle East. Published by Saqi, London 2009, P. 34.

29. Mohammed al-Maitami, Education as a strategic deterrent in a backward society (Yemen as a case), al-bab.com, https://al-bab.com/education-strategic-deterrent-backward-society-yemen-case

30. Sherif Kamel, Education in the Middle East: Challenges and Opportunities, file:///C:/Users/Set%20Up/Documents/EducationintheMEChallengesandOpportunities.pdf

31. Ziad Hafez (2009) The culture of rent, factionalism, and corruption: a political economy of rent in the Arab World, Contemporary Arab Affairs, 2:3, 458-480. https://doi.org/10.1080/17550910903034989

32. Muhammad Faour and Marwan Muasher, "Education for Citizenship in the Arab World: Key to the Future," Carnegie Endowment for International Peace, October 26, 2011, http://carnegieendowment.org/files/citizenship_education.pdf.

Chapter 6: Plague Six: Discrimination

"O people! Your God is one and your forefather (Adam) is one. An Arab is not better than a non-Arab and a non-Arab is not better than an Arab, and a red (i.e. white tinged with red) person is not better than a black person and a black person is not better than a red person, except in piety" (Musnad Ahmad, 22978)

— Saying of Prophet Muhammad (Peace upon Him) (1)

It is often easier to become outraged by injustice half a world away than by oppression and discrimination half a block from home.

— Carl T. Rowan (2)

...any distinction, exclusion, restriction or preference based on race, colour, descent, or national or ethnic origin that has the purpose or effect of nullifying or impairing the recognition, enjoyment or exercise, on an equal footing, of human rights and fundamental freedoms in the political, economic, social, cultural or any other field of public life. (Part 1 of Article 1 of the U.N. International Convention on the Elimination of All Forms of Racial Discrimination). (3)

In 2001, the European Union explicitly banned racism, along with many other forms of social discrimination, in the

Charter of Fundamental Rights of the European Union, the legal effect of which, if any, would necessarily be limited to Institutions of the European Union: "Article 21 of the Charter prohibits discrimination on any ground such as race, colour, ethnic or social origin, genetic features, language, religion or belief, political or any other opinion, membership of a national minority, property, disability, age or sexual orientation and also discrimination on the grounds of nationality. (4)

Racism and discrimination in the region is a fact which too many people and their regimes deny. The irony is rather troubling, in a world where the region and its peoples have long been subjected to racism and discrimination at the hands of the imperial powers. Yet, we observe that the same people and societies are failing to consider how they treat, for example migrant workers, refugees, and even some of their own indigenous people who are in minority living among them.

For example, domestic migrant workers in Lebanon as in other parts of the region are badly and inhumanely treated and their basic rights are grossly violated. According to Human Rights Watch World Report 2019:

An estimated 250,000 migrant domestic workers, primarily from Sri Lanka, Ethiopia, the Philippines, Nepal and Bangladesh, are excluded from labour law protections.

The kafala (sponsorship) system subjects them to restrictive immigration rules under which they cannot leave or change employers without permission from their employer, placing them at risk of exploitation and abuse.

Civil society organisations frequently document complaints of non-payment or delayed payment of wages, forced confinement, refusal to provide time off, and verbal and physical abuse. Migrant domestic workers seeking accountability for abuse face legal obstacles and inadequate investigations, risking imprisonment and deportation due to the restrictive visa system. Migrant domestic workers in Lebanon have committed suicide, attempted to commit suicide, or have attempted dangerous escapes in 2018. (5)

According to a report published by the Open Society Foundations (OSF) in February, foreign domestic workers in Lebanon — of which there are around 200,000 live-in and a greater number beyond this — earn monthly salaries that begin at $100, a contradiction of the official Lebanese minimum wage of $500 per month. Their job description and working hours are dependent on the whim of their employers, and often subject to abuse.

The OSF report also said that three-quarters of surveyed domestic workers had had their passports confiscated, an illegal practice that is carried out to prevent workers from leaving without their employer's permission.

The report also highlighted that foreign domestic workers suffer from low salaries, lack of employment rights, physical abuse and isolation, all of which can lead to self-harming behaviour. (6)

As recently as 2018, a heart-breaking article was written under the title Racism and Kafala in Lebanon by Farah Salka, director of the Anti-Racism Movement (ARM) and of the Migrant Community Centre, and the following is just a snapshot:

Take a quick look at any conversational space online, comments on videos, or links or stories, and you'd cry your heart out in and from despair. Lebanese women (wives, mothers, employers) for instance, on the multiple support groups they communicate through on Facebook, have a lot to say. The 'Madame' discourse is real. They speak of domestic workers as the utmost threat to their families, husbands and children but they never refer to their utmost dependency on their daily (hourly?) labour and support. They encourage each other not to grant her any rights and confiscate papers and freedoms to the maximum of their ability from the beginning of the process so as not to lose control over her as time passes by. The language and rationale are so harsh you almost feel like they are speaking about a different species of people, non-humans, and machine robots. Many Lebanese employers do perceive themselves as the victims in this relationship and that's really scary. They constantly absolve themselves and this society and the systems in place of any responsibility in relation to the daily tragedies befalling workers. All they repeat are arguments on how stupid, lazy, slow and backwards Ethiopian women and others are. They categorise them in rigid boxes of racist stereotypes and believe the fallacies they say. They change their names, patronise them, treat them as Invisibles, and talk about them in their presence in mockery and sarcasm — while at the same time maintaining the belief that they treat her as family, and that's why they force her to go with them on Sundays to their own very Lebanese outings, where she knows no one, speaks to no one, sits on a separate table on her own and eats food that means nothing to her. If that's not a Sunday off well spent, then what is? (7)

In the same article, Farah continues to say in the fifth-last paragraph of the article:

I remember once going through the brochure of one of the 5-star private beach resorts in Beirut and it had two consecutive articles written down, one saying that dogs are not allowed and the one right below it, saying that nannies are not allowed. Right after each other. (8)

Discrimination and racism are not unique to Lebanon and how they treat their guest workers, Arabs or non-Arabs alike. In the Gulf States, Jordan and Lebanon, they have a unique system, which I call the slavery system, called the Kafala system. In practice, this system delegates the regulation and supervision of guest workers to civilians by giving them certain powers and privileges over these migrant workers, and that leads to open abuse.

A report published in Migrants-Rights.org states:

One of the biggest problems behind the kafala system is that it makes it so difficult for workers to contest or complain when any part of their contractual agreement is not upheld, when any of their legal rights are violated, or even when they face more serious forms of abuse. Complaining puts them in conflict with their sponsor, who has the power to cancel their residency visa and have them deported. A court order, or special permission from the Ministry of Interior, could allow workers legal permission to change jobs. But for many, this would take too long and cost too much in living expenses, transportation costs, and potentially legal or court fees, to be worth it.

Take, for example, the following case:

Gul Nawaz, an Indian expatriate living in Saudi Arabia, wrote of his plight to a Saudi newspaper columnist. When he tried to transfer jobs, his sponsor (kafeel) registered him as "huroob"—a "runaway" employee. In order to resolve the issue, his sponsor asked for 20,000 riyals (approximately US$5,300) in return. Gul Nawaz writes that he paid the money, but that when his new employer went to register his employment paperwork, he found that Nawaz's former sponsor had not approved the transfer and that the charge of "runaway" remained. Without the sponsor's cooperation, Nawaz was helpless. When he contacted his sponsor again, he says, the sponsor asked for more money and for his passport in order to resolve the issue. He paid, and again the issue was not resolved, nor did his sponsor return his passport. When he contacted him yet again, the sponsor asked for more money, which he again paid. After that, his sponsor stopped answering his calls. Nawaz writes:

Today my status is that I have become illegal through no fault of my own...I cannot move anywhere and cannot work. I have been without work for a year. I have not been able to send money to my family for a long time. I am the only breadwinner in my family...I have paid huge amounts to my sponsor, and I have borrowed from many friends, slept hungry many nights...(9)

The kafala system, in which foreign workers must be sponsored by an employer renders in particular, domestic workers unable to escape abusive situations until their contract expires, at risk of being reported to authorities and subsequently fined, jailed or deported. Workers whose employers cancel their residency visas often have to leave the country through deportation proceedings, and many have to spend time behind bars.

According to Human Trafficking Search:

Kafala, sponsorship, is an employment framework in the Gulf States — as well as Lebanon and Jordan — that requires sponsorship from a national for migrant workers to be employed and reside in the country. The sponsor, either an individual or a company, possesses substantial control over the worker. Without their employer's permission, a worker cannot leave the job, change jobs, or exit the country, and the sponsor is able to threaten deportation if a worker questions the terms of the contract. This system has created systemic abuse as employers are able to exploit and abuse workers with little recourse, leading many to argue that the kafala system facilitates exploitative and slave labour. (10)

The black people in the region, such as Sudanese, Somalis and other black Africans are also treated as second-class citizens and/or treated like animals. The majority of the region's countries regard the whites as human beings, but strip the black of their humanity, except when they are wearing shorts and scoring goals for football teams. They face a lot of hardships and ill-treatment on a massive scale from Egypt to Morocco to Algeria to the heart of the Arab lands. Despite all the horrific abuses and discriminations, the topic is shrouded with silence and ignorance in society's discussions and hardly mentioned or thoroughly debated in the region's media and the intellectuals.

One might hope that this issue will start to be eliminated as very recently Tunisia has taken the right and brave step of introducing a new law against all forms of racial discrimination.

On the 9th October 2018, Tunisia's parliament passed the "Elimination of All Forms of Racial Discrimination" Act. The law, which defines and criminalises racial discrimination, is an important step forward in defending the rights of the 10 to 15 per cent of Tunisians who identify as black, as well as the country's 60,000 sub-Saharan African immigrants.

The law originated in 2016 from the case of Sabrina, a black Tunisian who had been verbally abused on Habib Bourguiba Avenue in down-town Tunis. When attempting to report the crime, the police station turned her away due to "the lack of a specific law" against racism. Later, on the 25th December 2016, three Congolese students were stabbed in a train station in Tunis. Amid demonstrations by civil society organisations, Prime Minister Youssef Chahed expressed his support for the law the next day. (11)

Racism and discrimination are also very much thriving and alive against the Palestinian people under occupation.

The occupation continued without impediment, likewise the settlement enterprise. Gaza tried to resist forcefully from inside its wretched cage, using its paltry and limited powers and of course, the world averted its eyes from the occupation, as it has customarily done in recent years, and focused on other things entirely.

While Israel passed a "nation-state" law that further marginalises Palestinian citizens, such legislation is nothing new.

There are currently more than 65 Israeli laws that discriminate against Palestinian citizens in Israel and Palestinian residents of the Occupied Palestinian Territories, according to Adalah, The Legal Centre for Arab Minority Rights in Israel.

More than half of these laws were adopted since 2000. From 2009 to present elections have brought to power the most right-wing government coalitions in the history of Israel, led by Prime Minister Benjamin Netanyahu.

Adalah's database shows how Israel's laws — dating as far back as 1939 — discriminate against Palestinians. (12)

Right to acquire, lease land:

Basic Law: Israel Lands (1960) stipulates ownership of "Israel lands" — controlled by the state, Jewish National Fund (JNF) and the Development Authority — can only be transferred between the three entities, knowing that the JNF leases the land it owns to Jews only.

Ninety-three per cent of the land in Israel is public and belongs to the state, JNF or the Development Authority. 13 per cent is controlled by the JNF, which has a "hugely influential" role in Israeli land policies.

Palestinian citizens are blocked from leasing about 80 per cent of the land controlled by the state according to Adalah.

Right to return:

According to the Absentees' Property Law (1950), Palestinian refugees expelled after November 29, 1947, are "absentees" and are denied any rights. Their land, houses, apartments, and bank accounts (movable and immovable property) were confiscated by the state. Simultaneously, the Law of Return (1950) gave Jews from anywhere in the world the right to automatically become Israeli citizens.

Right to residency:

For Palestinians who have a "permanent" residency status to live in Jerusalem, entry into and residency in Jerusalem is "a revocable privilege, instead of an inherent right", according to human rights organisation Al-Haq.

Since 1967, nearly 15,000 Palestinians from East Jerusalem have had their residency rights revoked, according to the Interior Ministry.

Authorities justify most revocations on the basis of failing to prove that Jerusalem is their "centre of life". If Palestinians are away from Jerusalem for a prolonged period, they can lose their residency rights. The system pushes many Palestinians to leave their home city, amounting to forcible transfer, a violation of international law, according to Human Rights Watch.

In March 2018, Israel passed a law allowing the interior minister to revoke the residency rights of any Palestinian in Jerusalem on the grounds of a "breach of loyalty" to Israel. In recent years, Israeli officials have revoked status to punish Palestinians accused of attacking Israelis, as well as their relatives as collective punishment. The interior minister can strip the residency status of any Palestinian deemed to be a threat. These policies do not apply to the Jewish population.

Right to family life:

The Ban on Family Unification — introduced as an emergency regulation in 2003 following the outbreak of the

Second Intifada in 2000 — prevents family unification when one spouse is an Israeli citizen and the other is a resident of the occupied territories. Thousands of Palestinian families have been affected by the law, forced to split apart, move abroad, or live in Israel in fear of constant deportation.

In June 2008, Israel's parliament renewed the ban as part of the Citizenship and Entry into Israel Law for the 15th year, making it in effect a permanent law.

Right to commemorate Nakba "catastrophe":

Palestinians traditionally mark Israel's official Independence Day as Nakba Day, a day of mourning and commemoration marking the expulsion of more than 700,000 Palestinians in 1948 to make way for the creation of the state of Israel. The Nakba Law introduced in 2011 allows the finance minister to reduce funding or support to an institution if it holds an activity that commemorates Israel's Independence Day as a day of mourning.

"The law causes major harm to the principle of equality and the rights of Arab citizens to preserve their history and culture. The law deprives Arab citizens of their right to commemorate the Nakba, an important part of their history." Adalah wrote.

The Israeli Knesset (parliament) voted 62 to 55 on the 19th July 2018 to approve the Jewish Nation-State Basic Law that constitutionally enshrines Jewish supremacy and the identity of the State of Israel as the nation-state of the Jewish people. This law–which has distinct apartheid characteristics–guarantees the ethnic-religious character of Israel as exclusively Jewish and entrenches the privileges enjoyed by Jewish citizens, while simultaneously anchoring discrimination against Palestinian citizens and legitimising exclusion, racism and systemic inequality. (13)

Sarah Leah Whitson, Middle East director at Human Rights Watch wrote, "Israel today maintains an entrenched system of institutionalised discrimination against Palestinians in the occupied territory — repression that extends far beyond any security rationale." (14)

Israel continued to maintain its decade-long effective closure of Gaza, exacerbated by Egypt's keeping its own border with Gaza largely sealed, and to impose restrictions that limit the supply of electricity and water, restrict access to medical care and educational and economic opportunity, and perpetuate poverty. Approximately 70 per cent of Gaza's 1.9 million people rely on humanitarian assistance. (15)

In the Gaza Strip, Palestinians continue to suffer under an Israeli blockade that constitutes illegal collective punishment. When Israel is not conducting horrific large-scale attacks on the fenced-in territory, there are routine attacks on Palestinian farmers and fishermen. The majority of Palestinians in Gaza are actually refugees, whose lands are often a few miles away inside Israel's pre-1967 territory. It is a reminder of the fact that Israel's "Jewish majority" was only established by the expulsion of Palestinians and is maintained by their continued exclusion.

Also, Israel, which calls itself "an oasis of democracy", has thousands of Palestinian political prisoners subject to humiliation and torture on a wide scale, a lot of them have even been imprisoned without a trial, and when they are tried, it is just a show trial.

John Dugard — a South African professor of international law — has compared Israeli imprisonment of Palestinians to policies of apartheid-era South Africa, saying "Apartheid's security police practised torture on a large scale. So do the Israeli security forces. There were many political prisoners on Robben Island but there are more Palestinian political prisoners in Israeli jails." (16)

Racism and discrimination are not a new phenomenon, however in today's modern world which claims to be enlightened in so many ways, it's thriving amongst the communities of the region and encouraged by their puppets. While many people are happy to embrace diversity and appreciate the differences between those of different ethnic groups, religions and colours, there are many others who see those of other ethnic groups as a threat and this intolerance can have far-reaching consequences on our society. While racism on a personal level can cause disruption through offensive comments, poor attitudes and occasionally violent outbursts, when it happens on a governmental scale there can be major consequences. When racial discrimination occurs at a national level, we see atrocities such as ethnic cleansing, persecution, discrimination through the judicial system and detrimental segregation laws, for example, as in the case of the Palestinians. There is no denying that racism can be devastating to the culture and well-being of a country, causing economic and moral upheaval. If hatred is allowed to thrive within a society, its negative effects stretch through every part of everyday life.

A country with a racist mentality does not allow all of its citizens to contribute collectively to the nation, thus limiting its success and development in so many ways. If an entire class of people cannot enjoy the same privileges as the rest of society, they lack the educational and employment opportunities that would enable them to contribute to the overall economic well-being of their country or others, through essential sectors such as medicine, economics or technology. Also, by limiting one race's ability to participate fully in the culture of the country, the people as a whole are unable to appreciate and understand similarities and differences between them, leading to social stagnation and on-going perseverance of racism through future generations. On a more serious level, if racism is allowed to thrive within society as a whole, ultimately this will lead to aggression and even violence, either on a local or even a national scale. If the bad feeling is allowed to build up between community groups, over time this is sure to result first in low-level negativity, from name-calling and isolated incidents, and potentially on into a full-scale conflict. Fighting, rioting and even warfare can be the result of racial prejudice and intolerance.

No matter how much society tries to separate the different races and ethnic groups within it, it is important to realise that, in the end, people of all colours, religions and nationalities must interact at some level. The key, therefore, to encouraging development and a happy, peaceful future is to learn to develop tolerance and understanding for those who are different to us. By encouraging fellowship and participation between diverse communities, we regain our morality and forge new ways forward into a positive way of life where all members of society regardless of their race can be valued and make a difference for the better. For the better of their societies, communities, and for the region as a whole. Society as a whole must promote integration between its different communities, starting with the youngest members of the community in order to enrich a new generation of tolerant individuals who embrace diversity and value all members of society equally.

History has shown that immigrants, over the long term, assimilate to a large degree and also bring with them much-needed skills. Take New York City as a case in point. Throughout the 19th century, New York experienced wave after wave of immigration. Italians, Jews, Irish, Poles and Germans joined others who preceded them. Each of these groups at one point suffered from prejudices, some more than others. But by the time the second generation of their descendants came of age, they were almost fully assimilated as Americans, even if US civil rights laws had yet to catch up with the times. (17) Today, a credible and fair path to gaining Arab state citizenship away from nepotism simply does not exist. Furthermore, the mass emigration of minorities out of the region means that the Arab world is less diverse in 2016 than it was in 1916. Sectarianism, suspicion and distrust, fear and xenophobia are attributes that are common to a society that doesn't accept the other, not merely as a visitor but as one of its own. (18)

Arabs and non-Arabs of the region alike are today in desperate need of soul-searching and finding the right path.

It is strange that many "Muslims" are so apologetic that they rarely take the point about anti-racism and discrimination to its logical conclusion. Islam came to be a guide to ailing humanity, not to create venal poltroons cravenly APPEASING modern Pharaohs and Nimrods in their hubris. "Modern" Westphalia nationalism is just a variant of the ancient tribalism of the past. The worship of this idol is still strong and the resultant Machiavellian Realpolitik is harming billions.

If we really want to change the status quo, we need to mobilise moral outrage against the plague of racism and discrimination. We need a sense of outrage in the minds of the common man. Yet sadly, the common man is yet to exist because injustices and inequalities are massively widespread in the region.

References for Chapter 6: Plague Six: Discrimination

1. Annwar Amna, Iqra, April 3 2017,
    https://www.islamicfinder.org/iqra/race-discrimination-and-bigotry-in-islam/
2. https://www.brainyquote.com/topics/discrimination
3. Wikipedia, Racism,
    https://en.wikipedia.org/wiki/Racism#International_law_and_racial_discrimination
4. Ibid
5. Human Rights Watch, Lebanon Events of 2018,
    https://www.hrw.org/world-report/2019/country-chapters/lebanon
6. Labour Minister: Migrant workers are content in Lebanon, The Daily Star, June 2014
    http://www.rightsobserver.org/blog/labor-minister:-migrant-workers-are-content-in-lebanon
7. Farah Salka, Racism and Kafala in Lebanon
    https://thisislebanon.org/racism-and-kafala-in-lebanon/
7. Ibid
8. Migrants-Rights.Org, Understanding Kafala: An archaic law at cross purposes with modern development, 11/03/2015 https://www.migrant-

rights.org/2015/03/understanding-kafala-an-archaic-law-at-cross-purposes-with-modern-development/

9. Kane-Hartnett Liza, Kafala System – A Gateway to Slavery, Human Trafficking Search, 2018 http://humantraffickingsearch.org/kafala-system/

10. Sharan Grewa, In Another First, Tunisia Criminalises Racism, November 1 2018, LawFare, https://www.lawfareblog.com/another-first-tunisia-criminalizes-racism

11. Adalah, The Legal Centre for Arab Minority Rights in Israel, https://www.adalah.org/en/law/index

12. Adalah, The Legal Centre for Arab Minority Rights in Israel, https://www.adalah.org/en/content/view/9569

13. Israel: 50 Years of Occupation Abuses, Ramp Up Pressure for Accountability on all Sides, Human Rights Watch, June 4 2017, https://www.hrw.org/news/2017/06/04/israel-50-years-occupation-abuses

15. Israel and Palestine, Events 2017, Human Rights Watch, https://www.hrw.org/world-report/2018/country-chapters/israel/palestine

16. John Doguard, Apartheid and the Occupation of Palestine, April 2011, Al Jazeera, https://www.aljazeera.com/indepth/opinion/2011/11/201111395153781378.html

17. Sultan Sooud Al Qassemi, The Arab World's Other Migration Problem, March 2016, Middle East Institute, https://www.mei.edu/publications/arab-worlds-other-migration-problem

18. Ibid

Chapter 7: Plague Seven: Poverty and Inequality

"Overcoming poverty is not a gesture of charity. It is an act of justice. It is the protection of a fundamental human right, the right to dignity and a decent life."

— *Nelson Mandela, former President of South Africa.*

When King Idris of Libya was told in the 1960s that oil companies had found oil in his country, he is reputed to have replied: "I wish you people had found water. Water makes men work. Oil makes men dream." The quotation is a little too pat, but everything that has happened in the Middle East and North Africa over the last half-century has underlined the truth of his remark.

It must be pointed out, that not every country in the region is oil producing. Yet, one way or another most of them have benefited from the oil boom. Most Arab countries have not undertaken the course of establishing a production-based economy that generates wealth. To many Arab elites who would have hoped and expected to be quite ahead along the growth curve of nations. Some Asian countries whose GDP in the early 1950s were less than of many Arab countries are now leaders in growth rates and have achieved significant development and generated wealth. On the other hand, toward the end of the first decade of the 21st century, Arab countries are way behind such Asian countries. (1)

The region is currently facing a period of severe challenges at all levels. Armed conflict has resulted in a heavy humanitarian toll, reflected in unprecedented waves of refugees and displaced persons within the region and beyond, with over half of all refugees originating from the region. And one of the so many challenges facing the region and its peoples is the plague of grinding poverty which has so many negative impacts on people's physical and mental health. Endemic and persistent poverty combined with a lack of basic services such as health care and schools will generate a lasting crack in the fabric and the outlook of any society as a whole. Poverty, hunger, unemployment, misery, desperation and other social and political sicknesses prevailing in these countries are products of these political systems which are inherently corrupt.

In June of 1998, all heads of the U.N. agencies signed a statement defining the term "poverty." The statement read, "Fundamentally, poverty is a denial of choices and opportunities, a violation of human dignity... It means not having enough to feed and clothe a family, not having a school or clinic to go to... It means insecurity, powerlessness and exclusion of individuals, households and communities. It means susceptibility to violence, and it often implies living in marginal or fragile environments, without access to clean water or sanitation."

It's easy to believe that the region is flourishing and exotic—tall skyscrapers, the finest shopping retailers and wild animals riding shotgun in a Lamborghini. Yet with so much oil and so many other natural resources trading throughout the region, poverty is rising at extraordinary levels.

According to a recent UNICEF analysis covering 11 countries in the Middle East and North Africa, poverty continues to impact at least 29 million children — one in four children in the region. These children are deprived of the minimum requirements in two or more of the most basic life necessities including basic education, decent housing, nutritious food, quality health care, safe water, sanitation and access to information. (2)

The World Bank has recently updated its numbers on poverty from 2013 to 2015. The following provides a quick overview of what the latest datasets have to say about poverty in the Arab states:

First, according to the common measure of extreme poverty — the $1.9 per day international poverty line — the Arab region's poverty headcount ratio in 2015 was 6.7%. This may seem low, but it is the third highest among developing regions (after sub-Saharan Africa and South Asia). To put things in perspective, the global average was 10%.

Second, the Arab region fell short of reducing extreme poverty by half from 1990 (the first of the Millennium Development Goals), and it scored the second-lowest poverty reduction rate of 42% (after sub-Saharan Africa). The global average for poverty reduction was 72%, mainly driven by the massive fall in extreme poverty in East Asia (led by China) and to a lesser extent in South Asia.

Third, poverty reduction in Arab states took place independently of the choice of the poverty line. But it is worth noting that as a result of conflicts in some countries, the Arab region is the only one that has witnessed an increase in extreme poverty since 2013 when the $1.9 poverty headcount ratio was approximately 4%. This is an alarming indicator as it signals a new trend of reversing some progress in poverty reduction.

Fourth and more importantly, the Arab region's ranking vis-à-vis the global average varies significantly depending on the choice of the poverty line. Money metric poverty is low using the $1.9 line but not when we move beyond the $3.5 poverty line as the headcount rate for the 11 countries included in the Arab region (Algeria, Djibouti, Egypt, Iraq, Jordan, Libya, Morocco, Syria, Tunisia, West Bank and Gaza, and Yemen). Poverty is higher than the global average once we apply higher poverty lines — above $4.0 per day — which are closer to the level of national poverty lines in middle-income Arab countries. (3)

Before moving on, there is a point to mention, that some Western intellectuals and a great deal of literature available online are trying to suggest that Islam is the reason for the widespread poverty in the region. I totally and categorically oppose this line of enquiry which does not serve any intellectual purpose, yet it does serve the purpose of increasing the hatred and misinformation about a religion. Islam in various ways fights poverty:

For example, Muslims are required "by obligation" to pay 2.5 per cent of their annual income to the treasury of the state, which is called "Zakat" and must be used to help eradicate poverty in societies by distributing it to the needy or poor individuals. Also, Muslims are very much encouraged to spend their money in whichever amount on charitable causes and take care of the poor. And as illustrated in the previous chapter of this book, all forms of corruption have severe consequences in Islam so as to deter people and officials from participating in them, hence preventing their adverse effect on the economy and society as a whole. Prophet Mohammed (PBUH) said, "He is not a believer whose stomach is filled while the neighbour to his side goes hungry."

Poverty in the region is caused mainly by four main factors combined i.e. constant wars and instability which has plagued the region for decades, the ugly corruption and mismanagement which is also never-ending and unbeaten in the region, and third are the puppets and their cronies who are there just to fill their greedy stomachs as the Pharaohs did thousands of years ago. The fourth factor, I contribute to the constant brain-drain of the region's human resources. The best and the brightest, due to many reasons, are at different stages leaving, mainly to the West, with a one-way ticket. The issue of brain-drain will be discussed in the next chapter.

With the exasperating and continuous violence in the region, more and more people are driven to the brink of starvation. Lands such as Yemen, Syria, Iraq and Palestine are devastated by endless violence and misery. These conflicts pose the greatest challenge to poverty, as conflicts and wars will certainly push aside all efforts to alleviate hunger and poverty at the expense of winning a "victory".

It is an open secret that Palestine is unlikely to be free from the barbaric military occupation by Israel any time soon, however, I urge Fatah and Hamas to start uniting and work hand in hand towards reconciliation for the sake of the Palestinian people who are the end sufferers. It makes no sense whatsoever that Fatah and Hamas are fighting each other, divided and hence leaving the door wide open for more occupation and atrocities to be committed by Israel at will against the defenceless people of Palestine.

The vicious cycle of poverty means that lifelong barriers and troubles are passed on from one generation to the next. Unemployment and low incomes create an environment where children are unable to attend school. Children must often work to provide an income for their family. As for children who are able to go to school, many fail to see how hard work can improve their lives as they see their parents struggle at everyday tasks. Other plagues accompanying poverty include:

• Crippling accidents as a result of unsafe work environments.

• Poor housing—a long-lasting cause of diseases.

• Water and food-related diseases that occur simply because the poor cannot afford "safe" foods.

Ultimately, poverty is a major cause of social tensions and threatens to divide a nation because of income inequality. This occurs when the wealth of a country is poorly distributed among its citizens—when a tiny minority, as the puppet and their cronies, has a majority of the money. Wealthy or developed countries maintain stability because of the presence of a middle class. However, even Western countries are gradually losing their middle class. As a result, there has been an increased number of riots and clashes. For society, poverty is a very dangerous factor that can destabilise an entire country. The region's so-called "Arab Spring" is an example of how revolts can start because of few job opportunities and high poverty levels.

Even in oil-producing countries and very wealthy ones such as "Saudi Arabia" there is a grinding poverty problem, yet hardly anyone speaks about it, it is considered taboo. Take, for example, the case of Faras Boqna, Hussam Al-Drewesh and Khalid Al-Rasheed who posted a short film (less than ten minutes) on the dire poverty in Riyadh, "Saudi Arabia" and posted it on the internet. All of them were detained by the "Saudi" police for about two weeks for no crime committed. They were not charged with any specific crime but were held beyond the initial 24-hour period of questioning, which is against the Saudi police protocol.

According to Reporters Without Borders, the detention of the three bloggers was an attempt to intimidate them into censoring themselves.

Poverty and anger over corruption continue to grow. Vast sums of money end up in the pockets of the royal family through a web of nepotism, corruption and cosy government contracts, according to Saudi and US analysts. Basheer said some Saudi royals enrich themselves through corrupt schemes, such as confiscating land from often-poor private owners, then selling it to the government at exorbitant prices. (4)

Many international organisations find it very difficult to collect data on poverty in the region, as some lands do not collect data on poverty at all, and some other lands, if collected, are reluctant to share it. Adding to this, persistent conflicts make the matter much worse when it comes to data collection.

But according to the UN Development Programme (UNDP), between 2010 and 2012, the percentage of the population in the region making less than $1.25 a day increased from 4.1 per cent to 7.4 per cent. Previously, countries in the region had made progress in reducing poverty, but high levels of political unrest had reversed many of these improvements. (5)

In another report, "Arab Multidimensional Poverty Report" co-authored by the United Nations Economic and Social Commission for Western Asia (ESCWA), the United Nations Children's Fund (UNICEF), the Arab League, and the Oxford Poverty and Human Development Initiative, it says:

The present study reveals that across the 286 million people living in the 10 countries covered in this analysis, 116.1 million (40.6%) belong to poor households, of which 38.2 million (13.4%) live in acute poverty. It is also noted that the main deprivations requiring attention in the region are education — both schooling for children and lifelong learning activities for those who are past the school age. Whereas less than half of the region's population — 48%, — live in rural areas, these account for 83.4% of the acutely poor population and 67% of the poor population. (6) The same report also states that: "Arab countries face serious poverty reduction challenges since both the scale and depth of poverty are estimated to be extremely high. Multidimensional poverty among households and children is far more prevalent than commonly thought; tens of millions of households and children are vulnerable to fall into poverty and the intensity and severity of deprivation among the poor are alarmingly high in the LDCs (least developed countries). Although extreme poverty is relatively low in the region, poverty as a whole is widespread and is not confined to low-income Arab countries. The estimated number of people in poverty in the Arab region (the 10 countries surveyed) amounts to 116.1 million, or 40.6% of the total population. It is nearly double the poverty rate obtained by using the national money metric poverty lines. It is also worth emphasising that the definition of "poverty" employed here is still based on serious deprivations in terms of the needs for survival, such as having no electricity, not having access to drinking water within the dwelling unit and having more than 3 people sharing a room." (7)

It seems to me that the region has forgotten its moral obligation towards the needy people of our societies, not only that region is becoming blinded of this terrible plague, but the world as a whole is blinded by selfishness and greed. Toby Ord, Department of Philosophy, University of Oxford puts the picture of poverty around the globe as follows:

To put things into perspective, consider that of the 7,000 million people in the world today:

- 2,500 million live on less than $2 per day
- 1,300 million live on less than $1.25 per day
- 1,000 million lack clean drinking water
- 800 million go to bed hungry each day
- 100 million children don't get even a basic education
- 800 million adults cannot read or write
- 6 million children will die each year from preventable diseases

It is very difficult to really understand such a figure and the ongoing emergency it represents. Six million children per year are more than 16,000 deaths each day. This is equivalent to forty fully laden Boeing 747s crashing every day. If a single 747 crashed, it would be on the nightly news. Scenes of rescuers looking through the wreckage and doctors treating any survivors would fill our living rooms and it would — rightly — be seen as a moral emergency. Yet the much larger moral emergency of forty 747s worth of children dying each day from easily preventable diseases is left unsung. Even though tomorrow's deaths are not predetermined, even though it is part of a much more interesting and challenging story about who is responsible and how they should be brought to account. It is old news. It is an everyday emergency. (8)

Based on the above, I need to ask the region's so-called governments, how many Boeing 747s full of children are they crashing every day? If they have a bit of face left, they ought to answer this question and be accountable to it in front of their people.

In Islam as in other religions, poverty is a serious moral issue which needs to be tackled and eradicated from society as a matter of urgency. When poverty becomes impeded in societies, the social fabric and morality of individuals will eventually start to crack, and a massive negative impact will eventually lead to the destruction of family life, which is an essential part of a healthy society. Poverty can have a devastating impact on interpersonal and family relationships. The dangerous mix of stress about inadequate resources for the satisfaction of needs and the negative self-image formed from feelings of personal powerlessness can wreak havoc on interpersonal and social relationships. Patriarchal gender relations can become particularly strained when families suffer from poverty.

Children suffer many of the consequences poverty has on poor families. They are often part of unstable and broken families or live apart from one or both parents and are raised by people other than their parents. Lack of resources within household implies that children are often malnourished, poorly dressed, and without money for educational requirements. Children are often forced to work to generate income and are thus deprived of educational opportunities, despite the fact that parents might recognise the value of education as a method to escape poverty. The inability to continuously be a parent to one's children constitutes one form of neglect, besides others. When poor parents live with their children, they often do not have the energy to be involved in their children's lives to give spiritual, moral, emotional, or educational guidance. Although the parents might be physically present, they are emotionally or psychologically absent from their children's lives. Often the only way they are involved is either by getting rid of their frustrations through their children or by enforcing overly strict and cruel discipline. Tired parents sometimes discipline children through cruel physical abuse, as they are too tired to take proper care of children through more appropriate verbal communication. Frustration can be expressed through various forms of abuse and discipline is often arbitrarily enforced and accompanied by severe corporal punishment. At times poor adults vent their anger and release their negative emotions of failure, frustration and powerlessness through abusive and violent behaviour towards children. A poor mother in Armenia provides an example when she says: "They reproach me for beating my children. But what should I do when they cry when they are hungry? I beat them to make them stop crying." Children are often victims of interpersonal violence in poor communities. From a young age, children's bodies bear the scars of the inability of adults to cope with too few resources. Researchers use strong language to refer to these aspects of poor children's lives. Children in poor households are seen to be "massively vulnerable to violence of many kinds" and are said to face "appalling conditions". Although these conditions include deprivation of basic necessities of life, the abuse of poor children "in all forms, is pervasive". Besides being subject to violence from relatives, poor children are exposed to many negative experiences, such as violence against women and substance abuse. They cannot fail to observe such behaviour in the cramped conditions of overcrowded homes and residential areas. The impact of these negative experiences on their early childhood leaves scars that can hardly be erased in later years. (9)

If these are the facts, we cannot avoid concluding that by not giving more than we do, people in rich countries are allowing those in poor countries to suffer from absolute poverty, with consequent malnutrition, ill-health and death. This is not a conclusion that applies only to governments. It applies to each absolutely affluent individual, for each of us has the opportunity to do something about the situation; for instance, to give our time or money to voluntary organisations. If then, allowing someone to die is not intrinsically different from killing someone, it would seem that we are all murderers. (10)

In 2011, the region's people spoke loud and clear, voicing grievances crucial to their aspirations and well-being. Yet, unfortunately the uprisings did not deliver the change people hoped for and the situation deteriorated significantly in some countries as uprisings transformed into civil wars. Importantly, many of the factors that made people unhappy before the so-called "Arab Spring" are still present today. Economic reform stalled during the "Arab Spring" transitions so the structural impediments of the past have persisted. The civil wars in Syria, Iraq, Libya and Yemen have erased years of development progress and inflicted widespread suffering and displacement on a scale not seen since World War II. In several countries, the already fragile and modest state services have collapsed. Syria's case has been the most dramatic, with hundreds of thousands killed, disabled, and impoverished, millions driven away from their homes, and widespread infrastructure destruction.

The more people of the region are getting poorer and impoverished, the wider the gap of inequality broadens. The "World Inequality Report 2018" ranked the region as leading the world in economic inequality. The region, which is treated in the report as a bloc that includes Turkey and Iran, ranks just ahead of Brazil and South Africa in terms of income inequality among its citizens.

So how can one get a sense of wealth disparities in Arab countries? In the absence of income tax information, data on the net worth of billionaires offers a complementary perspective on wealth concentration. Forbes collects such data, although the list of world billionaires excludes monarchs and those heads of state that have accumulated assets as a result of their position. In the case of Arab countries, this omission seriously biases the numbers, so we have augmented the Forbes data with personal wealth data of Arab heads of state. This data reveals that in several Arab countries a few billionaires control a much greater share of wealth than billionaires in other countries at comparable levels of development (see Figure 1). Lebanon and Egypt stand out with a few individuals and their families controlling close to 30 per cent and 24 per cent of GDP. (11)

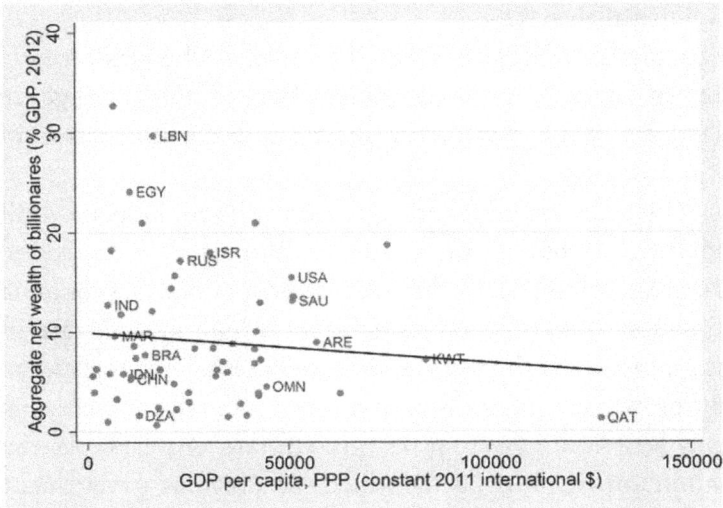

Figure 1: Share of National Wealth Held by Billionaires, 2012 (% GDP)

Still, this data underestimates the true concentration of wealth in Arab states. In general, it is unclear what share of rents, derived either from natural resources or political power or both, go to Arab ruling families. A recent paper by Andersen et al. (2013) argues that the rationale for holding political rents in foreign jurisdictions is that it provides secrecy and asset protection. According to their dataset on cross-border banking from the Bank for International Settlements, based on which they construct a measure of hidden wealth, oil-rich autocracies account for nearly eight per cent of global hidden wealth or almost seven per cent of their GDP. By contrast, oil-rich democracies and oil-poor autocracies account for one per cent and two per cent of global hidden wealth, equivalent to 0.5 per cent and two per cent of their GDPs, respectively. A large share of this hidden wealth belongs to Arab citizens with connections to the ruling elites, but data on the exact size of their hidden assets is not available. (12)

Jamal Khashoggi is a Saudi journalist who was recently assassinated by an ugly murky face of the intelligence service(s). He had written a short but interesting article in which he says:

There are money and opportunity even in poor Arab countries but bad administrations, monopolies, discrimination and corruption created an unusual economic situation. Macroeconomics achieves a high growth rate in some cases. But the truth is, this growth rate only represents the growth rate of Arabs of first world countries and citizens only benefit a little from this growth rate. For example, the minimum wage in Egypt, which the previous government considered as the most important of its achievements and which some say was the reason behind its ouster, is no more than $174 a month. This is the salary of millions of Egyptians. Meanwhile, the Egyptian elite live as per the standards of first world countries and if any government hints that it wants real economic reform in which the rich pay taxes and increase the wages of their employees, they'd say: "By doing that, you'd be killing the spirit of making initiatives. You'd force me to shut down my factory and leave to where I can be appreciated for my efforts." Don't ever believe an Egyptian or Saudi businessman when they say that, because if there was a country where they can make as much as they're making here, they would have left a long time ago. (13)

The more I read about the subject the more I get frustrated, disappointed and angry. The region is failing in almost every sphere, in technology, in science, in innovation and even its ability to feed itself sufficiently.

So what is it providing the world with? The hub of civilisation has been turned by the puppets and their cronies into beggars. In a recently published paper on the economic costs of the post "Arab Spring", it says "Estimates suggest that the poverty rates in Syria and Yemen surpassed 80% in 2015, but refugees, nearly half of them children, have also had to live in dire conditions. Poverty rates among refugees in Jordan and Lebanon were estimated at around 70% in 2014. Since many refugees have not been able to obtain work permits, they have to either remained unemployed and depend on aid or have been working in the informal sector with no protection and on an irregular basis at low wages. (14)

In a paper published by three scholars on the inequality in the region, they give us the following gloomy picture:

It is worth stressing that the origins of inequality are obviously very different in these different groups of countries. In the case of the Middle East, they are largely due to the geography of oil ownership and the transformation of oil revenues into permanent financial endowments. In contrast, extreme inequality in South Africa is intimately related to the legacy of the Apartheid system: until the early 1990s, only the white minority (about 10% of the population, which until today roughly corresponds to the top 10% income group) had full mobility and ownership rights. In Brazil, the legacy of racial inequality also plays an important role (it was the last major country to abolish slavery in 1887, at a time when slaves made up about 30% of the population), together with huge regional inequalities. It is striking to see that the Middle East, in spite of its much larger racial and ethno-cultural homogeneity, has reached inequality levels that are comparable to — or even higher than — those observed in South Africa or Brazil. (15)

In brief: according to our estimates, the Middle East appears to be the most unequal region in the world. This is true for the top docile income share, as well as for other inequality indicators; e.g. the top percentile income share is about 30% in the Middle East, vs. 12% in Western Europe, 20% in the USA, 28% in Brazil, 18% in South Africa, 14% in China and 21% in India. (16)

It should also be noted that the spread of extreme violence post Arab Spring in the region appears to be linked to high intergroup inequality and economic inequality. Although grievances alone do not lead to civil wars, grievance-motivated protests and uprisings can grow into civil wars if groups organised along sectarian and/or ethnic lines use the grievances to gain public support. In such highly polarised societies, the presence of natural resources and a high proportion of unemployed young men further increase the risks of conflict. Post Arab Spring, the region seemed primed to fall further into disarray.

The civil wars in Middle East and North Africa (MENA) have reversed years of development progress in Syria, Yemen, Iraq and Libya, undermining the health and skills of the Arab population and workforce. Millions of people are in need of humanitarian assistance in these four countries and the costs associated with meeting these needs have grown considerably as the wars have intensified during the past couple of years. (17)

The poor and vulnerable in other countries in the Levant have also suffered as the quality of public services has deteriorated, unemployment increased and real wages declined, especially for unskilled workers. The burden on poor communities in Lebanon and Jordan has been particularly heavy as the majority of refugees relocated to the poorest parts of these countries. (18) Starvation, disease and war-related disability have also affected the well-being of children and their potential to contribute to economic activity in the future. The economic damage associated with these unfortunate developments will be fully evident in the long term when today's children become active labour-market participants. In the short to medium term, the failure to educate young Arabs will translate into frustration and alienation and may have negative consequences for regional stability. (19)

The endemic poverty and the massive inequality in the region is the parent of revolution and crime and, much more to the point, is an example of human misery and social injustice that the nation's region cannot indefinitely countenance. Our poor today are mainly invisible, but we are being awakened now to see them. Poverty is unnecessarily massive, persistent, critical and very shameful—and its toll in human wastage and misery should be heart-breaking. This is the essential message, in a word, that a society which can marshal its resources to master unbelievable killings and destruction and keep wasting billions of dollars on killing machines, surely should have a bit of morality to marshal people's wealth and resources sufficiently to make available to all its people and provide the minimal contemporary requirements for civilised social living.

Arab underdevelopment has reached such proportions that one cannot expect spirits to lift straight away; the persistence of the West's hegemony, exacerbated by America's occupation of Iraq and Israel's ever-growing supremacy, precludes a swift Arab awakening. But nothing, neither foreign domination nor the economic structural flaws—let alone Arab cultural heritage—should prevent one seeking the possibility of some form of equilibrium, despite the terrible conditions at present. (20)

This will require many things, not all of which depend on the Arabs. But if we can't assemble them all, we can still force destiny's hand by starting with what is most urgent, what is indispensable to recovery; that we Arabs abandon our fantasy of a matchless past and finally see our real history, so that we can then be true to it. (21)

History will judge us all very harshly.

We just seem to have lost all our morals and principles and values these days.

— *Dolly Parton*

References for Chapter 7: Plague Seven: Poverty

1. Ziad Hafez, The culture of rent, factionalism, and corruption: a political economy of rent in the Arab World, Contemporary Arab Affairs, 11, Aug. 2009, http://www.tandfonline.com/loi/rcaa20
2. UNICEF, Rabat, 15/05/2017, https://www.unicef.org/press-releases/least-one-four-children-live-poverty-middle-east-and-north-africa
3. Khalid Abu-Ismail and Bilal Al-Kiswani, Extreme Poverty in Arab States: a Growing Cause for Concern, Economic Research Forum, October 16 2018, https://theforum.erf.org.eg/2018/10/16/extreme-poverty-arab-states-growing-cause-concern/
3. Kevin Sullivan, Saudi Arabia's conceal a growing problem of poverty, The Guardian, 1 Jan 2013, https://www.theguardian.com/world/2013/jan/01/saudi-arabia-riyadh-poverty-inequality
4. The Arab Millennium Development Goals Report, Facing Challenges and Looking Beyond 2015, http://www.undp.org/content/dam/rbas/doc/MDGS%20publications/Arab_MDGR_2013_English.pdf

5. Arab Multidimensional Poverty Report, http://www.ophi.org.uk/wp-content/uploads/ArabM PI-En-1.pdf

6. Ibid

7. Ibid

8. Ord Toby, Global Poverty and Demands of Morality, Department of Philosophy, University of Oxford, 2014, https://www.fhi.ox.ac.uk/wp-content/uploads/ Global-Poverty-and-the-Demands-of-Morality-1.pdf

9. H.P.P. (Hennie) Lotter, The Moral Challenge of Poverty's Impact on Individuals, Department of Philosophy, University of Johannesburg, http://www.koersjournal.org.za/index.php/koers/art icle/viewFile/202/168

10. Ibid

11. Elena Ianchovichina, Brookings, How Unequal Arab Countries, Feb. 4 2015, https://www.brookings.edu/blog/future-development/2015/02/04/how-unequal-are-arab-countries-2/

12. Ibid

13. GJamal Khashogi, Rich Arabs, Poor Arabs and the Ever-Widening Gap, Al Arabiya, 15 April 2014, http:// english.alarabiya.net/en/views/news/middle-east/20 14/04/15/Rich-Arabs-poor-Arabs-and-the-ever-widening-gap.html

14. Elena Ianchovichina, Economic Costs of Post-Arab-Spring Civil Wars in the Middle East and North Africa, https://www.iemed.org/observatori/arees-danalisi/arxius-adjunts/anuari/med.2016/ IEMed_MedYearBook2016_Economic%20Impact %20of%20Arab%20Spring %20Wars_Elena_Ianchovichina.pdf

15. Facundo Alvaredo ,Lydia Assouad, Thomas Piketty, Measuring Inequality in the Middle East 1990-2016: The World's Most Unequal Region? April 2018, World Inequality Lab. http://wid.world/wp-content/uploads/2017/12/WID_WORKING_PAPER_2017_15_MiddleEast_AAP.pdf

16. Ibid

17. Elena Ianchovichina, Economic Costs of Post-Arab-Spring Civil Wars in the Middle East and North Africa, https://www.iemed.org/observatori/arees-danalisi/arxius adjunts/anuari/med.2016/IEMed_MedYearBook2016_Economic%20Impact%20of%20Arab%20Spring%20Wars_Elena_Ianchovichina.pdf

18. Ibid

19. Ibid

20. Kassir Samir, Being an Arab, Paperback Edition published by Verso 2013, P.91-92.

21. Ibid

Chapter 8: Plague Eight: Brain Drain

"Self-discipline is often disguised as short-term pain, which often leads to long-term gains. The mistake many of us make is the need and want for short-term gains (immediate gratification), which often leads to long-term pain."

— *Charles F. Glassman*

According to the Cambridge English dictionary, brain drain is defined as the situation in which large numbers of educated and very skilled people leave their own country to live and work in another one where pay and conditions are better.

Brain drain can be also described as the process in which a country loses its most educated and talented workers to other countries through migration. This trend is considered a problem, because the most highly skilled and competent individuals leave the country, and contribute their expertise to the economy of other countries. The country they leave can suffer economic hardships because those who remain don't have the 'know-how' to make a difference. (1)

Brain drain can also be defined as the loss of the academic and technological labour force through the moving of human capital to more favourable geographic, economic or professional environments. More often than not, the movement occurs from developing countries to developed countries or areas. (2)

The term "brain drain" was coined by the Royal Society to describe the emigration of "scientists and technologists" to North America from post-war Europe. Another source indicates that this term was first used in the United Kingdom to describe the influx of Indian scientists and engineers. Although the term originally referred to technology workers leaving a nation, the meaning has broadened into "the departure of educated or professional people from one country, economic sector or field for another, usually for better pay or living conditions". (3)

There is no single, well-developed theory to explain the volume and direction of the migration movements. Economic as well as political and social factors play roles in the interpretation of empirical evidence about migration. On the supply side, the major reasons cited for international migration and for the wide variation in high-skilled migration rates among labour-exporting countries include income gaps between labour-importing and exporting countries, lack of employment opportunities in labour-exporting countries, political instability, internal conflicts, poor investment climates that limit the productive employment of high-skilled workers, and inadequate educational policies which have resulted in a large supply of university graduates for whom no suitable jobs exist. On the demand side, the need for migrant workers in many labour-importing countries has been stressed as one fundamental factor driving migration.

This growing phenomenon has existed as long as there has been an economic disparity between geographic areas, and its increase is one of the negative results of globalisation that has long favoured the developed world at the expense of the developing economies. Its negative impacts are numerous and long-lasting on the areas where the brains are removed, usually permanently, from the exporting lands. For example, the brain drain of health professionals impacts severely on the health systems of developing countries. These countries have invested in the education and training of young health professionals. This translates into a loss of considerable resources when these people migrate, with the direct benefit accruing to the recipient states who have not forked out the cost of educating them. The intellectuals of any country are some of the most expensive resources because of their training in terms of material cost and time, and most importantly, because of lost opportunity.

Nepotism and cronyism ensure opportunities stay within the confines of a small group of insiders. And as corruption, lack of opportunity, repression and violence are endemic in the region's lands, it forced many people to leave, draining away talent, skills and labour. Not only was the region losing its natural resources to the West, but its people were following suit. The opportunities offered outside the region were appealing and set off a brain drain, attracting the brightest, most innovative and industrious minds of the region.

Many Arab economies are likely to lose a good number of their most prized human resources. "The young folks that are most educated, most connected and most employed are the ones who want to emigrate more," said Ahmed Younis, a senior analyst at the Gallup Centre for Muslim Studies.

"Brain drain is the kind of phraseology that's used," said Mr Younis, who is also the director of strategic partnerships for Silatech. "But we're seeing an SME [small and medium enterprises] drain, an entrepreneurship drain, and there will be less innovation, less enterprise development and less ability for these economies to create an atmosphere that convinces ambitious young people to stay in the future."

Various are the reasons that drive the region's intellectuals to emigration. Some are attracted to the technological and scientific revolution in the West. Whereas, in their homelands, they are alienated by the absence of job opportunities and the fear of unemployment — a situation that breeds a feeling of frustration and despair. The political state of affairs is also a crucial element of brain drain, for most of the region suffers political turmoil and wars as witnessed in Palestine (under occupation), Iraq, Lebanon, Syria and others. It appears that this haemorrhage of skills is expected to increase with the continuation of turbulence. Customs, traditions and interference can also be strong deterrents for development which drive the learnt community to seek opportunities elsewhere. The brain drain inflicts massive losses on societies in general, losses that amount to billions of dollars.

The region, for decades, has seen the departure of its precious human capital and recently and due to continuous instabilities, this negative phenomenon has intensified greatly to a level which amounts to unprecedented catastrophe. The inescapable fears of the massive surge in departures by skilled professionals and young adults have turned into a nightmare. Particularly with the intensification of endless wars and endless violence, combined with poor economic conditions, severe income inequality and high unemployment rates around the region's lands.

The negative impacts of brain drain on the societies concerned, as long-term consequences are severe. These effects include but are not limited to:

- Loss of tax revenue
- Loss of potential future entrepreneurs
- A shortage of important, skilled workers
- The exodus may lead to loss of confidence in the economy, which will cause persons to desire to leave rather than stay
- Loss of innovative ideas
- Loss of the country's investment in education
- The loss of critical health and education service

This Arab demographic unravelling has not only weakened states and societies but also undermined, perhaps irreparably, cultural values of coexistence and pluralism. The creation of ethnic or sectarian entities could well further sow the seeds of conflict for decades to come, creating new claims for rights of return. (4)

According to the United Nations Development Project (UNDP), unemployment among youth in the Arab region (29.73 per cent) exceeded twice the global average (13.99 per cent), and according to estimates, the situation is expected to worsen in the near future. The report warns that Arab economies may not be able to generate the sixty million new jobs required by 2020 to absorb the number of workforce entrants in order to stabilise youth unemployment. (5)

The Middle East and North Africa witnessed a baby bulge in the 1980s and 1990s, as infant mortality rates rapidly dropped in societies that are characterised by large families. From 1980 until 2000, the region's population nearly doubled. Employment, however, failed to keep pace, and today the Middle East has the highest rate of youth unemployment in the world, according to the IMF, the World Bank and the Organization for Economic Cooperation and Development (OECD). (6)

Regional economies failed to keep pace with the rate of population growth for a variety of reasons. Some countries, such as Iraq, Libya and Syria, experienced war, conflict and sanctions, but in places that did not suffer such degradations, youth unemployment rose inexorably. Whether rich or poor, Sunni or Shiite, Arab or non-Arab, Middle Eastern states report more young people searching for work with every passing year. Hampering the youth's quest for jobs are a number of factors, including weak private sectors, mismatched skills and a region-wide over-reliance on the public sector. But beyond these commonalities, geopolitical issues unique to each country have driven youth unemployment, as local constraints and local problems have all conspired against youth trying their luck in the job market. (7)

Population Boom in the Middle East and North Africa
The declining infant mortality rate has contributed to the growing population in the Middle East and North Africa.

INFANT MORTALITY RATE

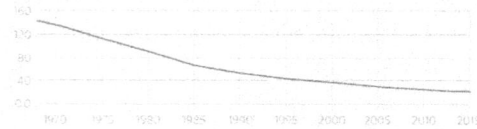

POPULATION

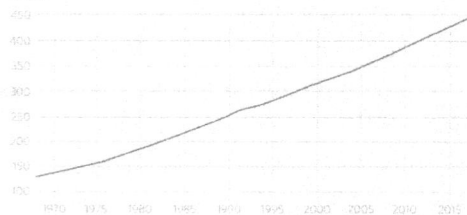

It is difficult to overstate the magnitude of the catastrophe. In 2015, it was estimated that more than 143 million Arabs were living in countries experiencing war or occupation, and around seventeen million had been forcibly displaced from their homes. Further, while Arabs constitute only five per cent of the world's population, they account for more than fifty per cent of its refugees. (8)

With more than 4.8 million people forced to flee the country and nearly 6.6 million displaced internally, one in five refugees globally is Syrian. Iraq, which has suffered through waves of displacement dating back to the 1980s, has also witnessed considerable internal displacement due to the ongoing conflict, with more than 3.3 million people fleeing territories held by the Islamic State. People in Libya, Sudan and Yemen are all facing forced displacement as well. Additionally, the Arab world has hosted significant numbers of Palestinian refugees—the oldest and largest refugee population in the world, numbering more than five million people—from the time of the Arab-Israeli wars of 1948 and 1967. (9)

A recent study, for example, found that eight-six per cent of Syrians who fled to Greece between April and September 2015 have secondary-level or university education. Further, more than 2.8 million Syrian children are not in school, which could have long-term consequences. (10)

The implications of brain drain are almost the opposite of those of brain gain. While the literature on brain drain argues that emigration deprives a country of its human capital, the literature on brain gain assumes that the arrival of high-skilled migrants may lead to an increase in the human capital level of a receiving country.

History has shown that massive and rapid outflows of high-skill people can generate economic damage which is hard to reverse. An interesting case is that of Iran, where pre-revolutionary economic development was rapid, although unevenly distributed among Iranians. The Iranian

202 | *The Region's Plagues*

brain drain started with the 1978–1979 revolution and was exacerbated in the early 1980s by the war with Iraq and the decision of the government to reform Iran's higher education system. The trend continued afterwards and is seen by many observers as one of the most important exoduses of talented academics, students and researchers. The pace of growth slowed dramatically after the revolution and Iran is still a lower-middle-income economy today. Since 2002, Iran's parliament has tried to reverse its brain drain but returns are still sporadic. A more recent example is the former Soviet states. Many scientists and academics went abroad after independence. Russian and Moldovan trade unions report that between half a million and a million scientists and professionals have left the country since 1991. This has worsened the economic situation and working conditions at origin; hence, almost none of the brain drain emigrants have returned. (11)

Brain drain can bring many disadvantages to the home countries. First, brain drain can weaken the employment structure; it is a major factor that inhibits the industry to move forward because it will affect the performance of the home countries in terms of economic growth. Second, the brain drain phenomenon is a vicious circle of underdevelopment, which brings a shortage of educated and skilled workers in home countries. The educated and skilled workers have left from the origin countries to find better opportunities in other countries. Third, it also widens the gap between rich and poor people. Fourth, it will waste the money of the origin countries, because they have spent a lot of money to educate the people to study. Fifth, the workers who emigrate will be replaced by expatriates with the same capabilities. But, they will ask for more expensive fees that lead to the inefficiency of the domestic economy. Sixth, the brain drain causes huge losses to human capital.

In the example of Iraq after the disastrous invasion of 2003 estimates of Iraqi exiles ranged from two to four million people, and since the US-led invasion, the country has not witnessed the return of these millions but instead the loss of more professionals, academics and artists, who are mostly from the middle class. (12)

Although there are no accurate statistics on the number of Iraqi academics and doctors who fled the country, one rough estimate suggested that there are 1,500 Iraqi academics living in Syria, Jordan and Egypt. Presumably, a number have also gone further afield. Estimates of the number of doctors who have left Iraq since 2003 vary widely, at anywhere from 3,000 to 17,000. What is clear, however, is that Iraq lost a large percentage of its specialists (some say 70%) and probably 25–35% of its overall medical staff. These are massive numbers considering that the majority of the exodus occurred over just eighteen months. With the departure of its professional elite, Iraq lost hundreds of years' worth of experience. (13)

The implications of this brain drain are reflected in Iraq's daily life: its health care system (among the best in the region until the 1980s) has crumbled and estimates indicate that almost 70% of critically injured people die in emergency rooms because of shortages of medical staff and essential supplies, the educational infrastructure has weakened significantly and education levels have dropped precipitously; and finally the bureaucratic machine of the government has deteriorated to the extent that it is affecting the execution of any capital or investment budget. (14)

The Iraq wars created the template for decades of conflict to come. Iraq was the first forever war. From oil, the reasons for being there shape-shifted effortlessly to containing Saddam via air power, to removing weapons of mass destruction, to freeing Iraq from an evil dictator, to destroying al Qaeda, to destroying the Islamic State, to now, a buttress against Iran. Over the years the media dutifully informed the American people what the new rationalisation was, reporting the changes as it might report the new trends in fashion. (15)

More insidiously, killing became mechanical, nearly sterile from our point of view (remember the war porn images of missiles blasting through windows in Iraq war 1.0, the high tech magic of drone kills, video game death dispensed from thousands of miles away). Our atrocities—Abu Ghraib is the best known, but there are more—were ritualistically labelled the work of a few bad apples. Meanwhile, the other side's atrocities were an evil genius, fanaticism, campaigns of horror. How many YouTube beheading videos were Americans shown until we all agreed the president could fight ISIS forever? (16)

The brain drain of the Palestinians is also immense. Palestinian people since 1948 have been scattered all over the globe, including in neighbouring lands, mostly in refugee camps. Yet here the brain drain of the Palestinians comes with differences. First, as the Palestinians were mainly forced to leave their homeland in 1948 and then 1967 by the Israeli military forces and the second is the continuous assassination of the Palestinian intellectuals and scientists by the Israeli intelligence services, namely Mossad.

The policy of Israeli blockade affects almost every aspect of people's lives in Gaza. Travelling, even for the purpose of medical treatment or education, is almost impossible. Every day that passes in Gaza under the blockade is haunting. Unlike war, where violence is visible as bombs are falling, the blockade is like a slow death. But siege and blockade take their toll. When people can't have access to decent nutrition, electricity, clean water and freedom of movement for political reasons, it's no less violent than war itself.

In an interview with the Times of Israel Ronen Bergman, the author of "Rise and Kill First, The Secret History of Israel's Targeted Assassinations", states:

I want to say, that from the very beginning of the state, Israeli leaders thought that secret operations and assassinations far beyond enemy lines were a useful tool to change history, or to do something to reality, without resorting to all-out war."

The statement is revelatory on several grounds. Apart from indicating Mossad's worldwide operations, it also closes in on two main issues which are central to the current context of Israel's resorting to targeted assassinations. The targeting of individuals, who, if allowed to work in the anti-colonial struggle, can embark upon building a resistance movement that goes beyond mere resilience, should dispel mainstream depiction of Israel's aggression on Gaza as "war". By Israel's admission and actions, there is no war, but rather a premeditated action against a population by targeting individuals who can contribute to Palestinian security and, as a result, the capacity to further their cause and their rights. (17)

Second, changing history and reality, as stated by Bergman, can also be applied to the Gaza context. It is not only the fact that Israel is choosing strategy over diplomacy, as Bergman says within the context of his research. Palestinians in the occupied West Bank and Gaza are actively involved in resistance. However, the periodical Israeli assaults upon Gaza and Hamas' attempts to defend the enclave have propelled the movement's visibility when it comes to armed struggle. The movement also prioritises education as a revolutionary goal. During Operation Protective Edge in 2014, Israel directly targeted higher educational facilities, prompting UNESCO to release a report documenting the damage done to infrastructure — 14 educational facilities were significantly damaged. In addition, 421 students were murdered during the operation, making up 27.4 per cent of Gaza's death toll. (18)

The UNESCO report document 2015 states:

The Israeli attacks "not only damaged vital infrastructure but destroyed human capital," thus "affecting specific subject specialisms (in particular, education and business subjects) and wiping out a generation of young scholars." A total of fourteen staff left their positions since the war, while 149 students were unable to return to their studies in the new academic year. (19)

Yet while Palestinian universities and students suffered serious losses, Israeli higher education institutions were busy supporting the offensive. Tel Aviv University offered its "thanks" to "those who did reserve service", and offered tuition stipends for soldiers, while the Hebrew University declared it was "joining the war effort to support its warrior students." (20)

I believe that Israel knows and understands quite well that knowledge is power, and for her power to continue and prosper the other side—namely the Palestinians—brainpower and knowledge must be eliminated by all means possible including long years of imprisonment or assassinations anywhere in the four corners of the world. For Israel to survive Palestine's possibilities must be wiped out, whether the means used are targeted assassinations, sniper fire or precision targeting of a civilian population, for them it makes no difference. Throughout the years and since the 1950s, Palestinian intellectuals and scientists in all fields of knowledge have been ruthlessly exterminated by Israel's brutal military forces or by their ugly intelligence services, with complete impunity. International law and international humanitarian law and any other international conventions apply only to Iraq and the other weaker nations who might pose a risk or potential risk to Israel. That is how it works.

Throughout the years of ruthless, harsh, and barbaric military occupation of Palestine, I did not read or recall a single killing/massacre that was thoroughly investigated, by the so-called Israeli democracy, with people convicted of wrongdoing. With shameless faces they say it's the only oasis of democracy in the "Middle East". Well, I say to hell with a democracy like yours which is equivalent to South Africa's apartheid system or even much worse.

On the 6th November, several news outlets reported that the widow of former Palestine Liberation Organisation (PLO) Chairman Yasser Arafat announced that the results of a Swiss investigation into her late husband's death concluded he was poisoned with polonium, a radioactive substance. In November 2012, Arafat's body was exhumed in order for medical examiners to take samples of his remains to test for polonium, part of a murder investigation launched by French authorities at the request of Suha Arafat following the discovery the previous summer of traces of the highly toxic substance on some of his personal effects. In October 2004, after enduring a two-year siege by the Israeli military in his West Bank headquarters, Arafat fell seriously ill. Two weeks later he was transported to a French military hospital where he died. Doctors concluded that he died from a stroke caused by a mysterious blood disorder. At the time, many Palestinians suspected that Arafat was murdered. Over the years, he had survived numerous assassination attempts by

Israel, and just six months before his death then-Israeli Prime Minister Ariel Sharon said that an agreement he had made with US President George W. Bush promising that Israel wouldn't kill Arafat was no longer valid, stating: "I released myself from the commitment in regard to Arafat." Two years prior to that statement, in an interview published in February 2002, Sharon told an Israeli journalist that he regretted not killing Arafat when he had the chance during Israel's invasion of Lebanon in 1982, stating: "I am sorry that we did not liquidate him." In 2002, current Israeli Prime Minister Benjamin Netanyahu, then in the opposition following his first term as prime minister (1996-1999), told the Likud Party Central Committee: "We must completely and totally eradicate Arafat's regime and remove him from the vicinity... This one thing must be understood: If we do not remove Arafat and his regime, the terror will return and increase. And only if we do remove them is there any chance of turning a new leaf in our relationship with the Palestinians." When Arafat died, Netanyahu was serving as Minister of Finance in Sharon's government. (21)

And the most recent assassination by Mossad was in April 2018 in Kuala Lumpur, Malaysia where they shot 35-year-old Fadi al-Batsh, an engineering lecturer described as an expert in electrical engineering and "rocket building".

Batsh's uncle Jamal al-Batsh, speaking to Reuters from the town of Jabalya in northern Gaza Strip, said he believed the killing was the work of Israel's Mossad espionage service. Officials in Israel declined to comment. When asked who he blamed, he replied: "The Israeli Mossad. The Israeli Mossad stood behind the assassination of educated people and intellectuals because Israel knows Palestine will be liberated by scientists.

Therefore, they tracked this young educated man." (22)

In December 2018, the World Bank said that the region needs to create 300 million new jobs by 2050.

One of the reports presented — "World Development 2019" — called for MENA (Middle East and North Africa) countries to invest in human capital, especially early childhood education, saying that: "If governments do not move now, invest in quality education, and improve learning, many of these young people will face a life full of frustration and disappointment, with impacts and implications not only for the region but also for the world." (23)

In another grim report about the region, recent Global Human Capital Development Index 2017, which illustrates how nations develop their human capital. This can be a more important determinant of their long-term success than virtually any other factor.

The Human Capital Index 2017 ranks 130 countries on how well they are developing their human capital on a scale from 0 (worst) to 100 (best) across four thematic sub-indexes —Capacity, Deployment, Development and Know-how—and five distinct age groups or generations—0–14 years; 15–24 years; 25–54 years; 55–64 years; and 65 years and over—to capture the full human capital potential profile of a country.

The top ten of this year's edition of the Human Capital Index is headed by smaller European countries Norway (1), Finland (2), Switzerland (3)—as well as large economies such as the United States (4) and Germany (6). Four countries from East Asia and the Pacific region, three countries from the Eastern Europe and Central Asia region and one country from the Middle East and North Africa region are also ranked in the Index top 20. (24)

The Middle East and North Africa region comprises 15 countries that had sufficient data for coverage in the Index.

Out of these, only one—Israel (18)—makes it into the top 20 of the overall Index. Three Gulf States—the United Arab Emirates (45), Bahrain (47) and Qatar (55)—outperform the rest of the region's Arab countries in terms of human capital development, benefiting significantly from the strong perceived quality of their education systems, and score in the mid-range of countries ranked in the Index overall. However, relative to their income levels these countries have additional opportunities to further boost their human capital performance, reporting some of the lowest skill diversity scores and tertiary and vocational enrolment rates in the Index. Turkey (75) crosses the 60% mark on the strength of its young generation's high tertiary and vocational education enrolment rates. Similar to other economies in the region it is held back, however, by low human capital outcomes across the Deployment sub-index, due in large part to significant employment gender gaps. The North African nations Algeria (112), Tunisia (115) and Morocco (118) make up the lower end of the regional rankings, ahead of Mauritania (129) and Yemen (129). Gender gaps in secondary school participation and youth unemployment continue to be widespread in a number of countries, risking a lasting impact on the workforce of the next generation. Saudi Arabia (82), the Middle East and North Africa region's largest economy, ranks ahead of Egypt (97), its most populous one. While Egypt scores ahead on the Know-how sub-index, as home to one of the regions most diversified economies and labour markets, Saudi Arabia's efforts to expand its future human capital potential are in better shape in terms of education quality and staff training, for which Egypt ranks near the bottom of the Index on both indicators. Both countries suffer from high unemployment rates among the young generation and have high employment gender gaps, pointing to both countries' additional untapped human capital potential. The Middle East and North Africa are one of the most disparate regions in the Index—spanning three income group levels and ranging in scores from those that are in line with high-income economies in Western Europe and elsewhere, to those more in line with the worst-performing countries in Sub-Saharan Africa. For example, Kuwait (96), whose GDP per capita is nearly eightfold higher, performs at a comparable level to Egypt, highlighting that economic factors alone are an inadequate measure of a country's ability to successfully develop their human capital. While the region's overall average score of 55.91 masks some of these significant differences in countries' circumstances, it also points to opportunities for countries to learn from one other across the region. (25)

Also, the launch of a civil society development programme in some countries in the region has pernicious effects that have not yet been analysed in detail. But what we have been able to observe in Central Asia also applies to the Middle East. (26)

"Civil society" is very often an artificial construct which has little impact, other than a harmful one, on society itself. Civil society is first and foremost a market: the sums of money brought into play destabilise the balance of microcosms (particularly that of the university) because its actors are placed directly on the market, with no state intervention. This leads to an internal brain drain. The most brilliant academics and even entrepreneurs become involved in the programme. When a bilingual taxi driver in Afghanistan or Tajikistan earns twenty times the salary of a university professor, the most competent leave academia to become taxi drivers. (27)

Every study I have read shows that investments in human capital are an essential element for sustaining economic growth. Take, for example, countries such as the United States, Japan and many European nations which have sustained economic growth over the past century due to heavy investment in the training of workers, and a better-educated labour force are given credit for much of the growth in per capita incomes and economic productivity.

If we are a nation whose population is eager to progress and develop and be stable, why are we not investing in them? We have so many millions of talented and skilled young people who are unfortunately wasted for no reason but due to the huge mismanagement, corruption, and misuse of the region's resources including the precious human capital.

"Funny how in a material world full of pundits and economists obsessed with assets and liabilities —personally, economically and globally—few speak about the greatest of all these... YOU."

— *Rasheed Ogunlaru*

References for Chapter 8: Plague Eight: Brain Drain

1. Jennifer Francis, What is Brain Drain in Economics? - Definition, Causes, Effects & Examples, https://study.com/academy/lesson/what-is-brain-drain-in-economics-definition-causes-effects-examples.html
2. Ibid
3. Human Capital Flight, Wikipedia, https://en.wikipedia.org/wiki/Human_capital_flight #Arab_world
4. Arab Fractures, Citizens, States, and Social Contracts, PERRY CAMMACK MICHELE DUNNE AMR HAMZAWY MARC LYNCH MARWAN MUASHER YEZID SAYIGH MAHA YAHYA , https://carnegieendowment.org/files/Arab_World_Horizons_Final.pdf
5. Arab Human Development Report 2016, https://www.undp.org/content/undp/en/home/pres scenter/pressreleases/2016/11/29/arab-human-development-report-2016-enabling-youth-to-shape-their-own-future-key-to-progress-on-development-and-stability-in-arab-region-.html

6. Youth Unemployment: The Middle Ester's Ticking Time Bomb, Feb. 2018, https://worldview.stratfor.com/article/youth-unemployment-middle-east-teen-jobless

7. Ibid

8. Arab Fractures, Citizens, States, and Social Contracts, PERRY CAMMACK MICHELE DUNNE AMR HAMZAWY MARC LYNCH MARWAN MUASHER YEZID SAYIGH MAHA YAHYA , https://carnegieendowment.org/files/Arab_World_Horizons_Final.pdf

9. Ibid

10. Ibid

11. David de la Croix and Fr´ed´eric Docquier, Do Brain Drain and Poverty Result from Coordination Failures? 2010, http://www.hec.unil.ch/documents/seminars/deep/309.pdf

12. Joseph Sassoon, Brain Drain and Return, Middle East Institute, July 2008, https://www.mei.edu/publications/brain-drain-and-return

13. Ibid

14. Ibid

15. Peter Van Buren, 2017: The Year the Iraq War Truly Ended, December 2017, The American Conservative, https://www.theamericanconservative.com/articles/this-year-the-iraq-wars-truly-came-to-an-end-iran-kurds-isis-is/

16. Ibid

17. Ramona Wadi, From Targeted Assassinations to Sniper Fire, How Israel Eliminates Palestinian Resistance, MPN News,

https://www.mintpressnews.com/from-targeted-assassinations-to-sniper-fire-israel-seeks-to-eliminate-palestinian-resistance/241717/

18. Ibid
19. Middle East Monitor, January 2015, https://www.middleeastmonitor.com/20150128-bds-and-israels-war-on-palestinian-higher-education/
20. Ibid
21. Israel's History of Assassinating Palestinian Leaders, Institute for Middle East Understanding, November 2013, https://imeu.org/article/israels-history-of-assassinating-palestinian-leaders
22. South China Morning Post, April 2018, https://www.scmp.com/news/asia/southeast-asia/article/2142754/assassinated-hand-treachery-hamas-says-man-gunned-down
23. World Bank: MENA Needs 300 Million Jobs by 2050, Middle East Monitor, Dec.2018, https://www.middleeastmonitor.com/20181222-world-bank-mena-needs-300-million-new-jobs-by-2050/
24. The Global Human Capital Index 2017, https://weforum.ent.box.com/s/dari4dktg4jt2g9x020 5pksjpatvawdb
25. Ibid
26. Olivier Roy, The Politics of Chaos in the Middle-East, Hurst & Company, London, 2007, P. 37
27. Ibid

Chapter 9: Plague Nine: Killing the Voices

"Once a government is committed to the principle of silencing the voice of opposition, it has only one way to go, and that is down the path of increasingly repressive measures, until it becomes a source of terror to all its citizens and creates a country where everyone lives in fear."

— *Harry S. Truman (Special Message to the Congress on the Internal Security of the United States, August 8, 1950)*

I believe that freedom of expression is the right of an individual (or group of individuals) to hold their own opinions and to express them freely without government interference. This includes the right to express your views aloud (for example through public protest and demonstrations) or through:
- published articles, books or leaflets
- Television or radio broadcasting
- Works of art
- The internet and social media

And also if we have freedom of expression, then we also have a duty to behave responsibly and to respect other people's rights.

Free speech and freedom of expression are something that we often, in the West generally, take for granted. It is also something that is widely debated and often controlled. There are many parts of the world where free speech and freedom of expression are not even something that people have. When words become controlled, it is a slippery slope to the controlling of other rights. This is what makes the right to free speech something that cannot be taken for granted, and when that right is imposed upon, it should also be taken seriously and fought against. Without freedom of voices, the masses are silenced. They are unable to speak out and spark change. They can't let others know what is happening within their country or their societies. They don't have the ability to make people aware of what is happening to them. This lets ruling dictators take complete control over the governing of a country and its resources without any kind of accountability to the nation who is supposed to be the watch-dog over the officials. I cannot stress enough that freedom of expression is a fundamental and basic human right. It also underpins most other rights and allows them to flourish and prosper. The right to speak your mind freely on important issues in society, access information and hold the powers that be to account, plays a vital role in the healthy development process of any society, whether in the East or West, it makes no difference.

Of course, the principle of freedom of speech indiscriminately allows bad free speech, ranging from the stupid to the malicious and maybe dangerous. If it is genuinely dangerous to life, as for example indirect provocation to murder, it invites a case-specific restriction. But by and large, the remedy for bad free speech is better free speech in consequence.

Internet use, including social media and online activism, played a prominent role in the 2011 Arab uprisings, allowing individual citizens — who long suffered from severe and prolonged restrictions on their freedoms of expression and assembly — to communicate on an unprecedented scale and ultimately to collectively challenge the autocratic regimes that corrupted their lives for decades. However, 2011 also saw autocratic regimes develop new countermeasures to block the online exchange of information and news and to harness the Internet to their own advantage, placing Internet freedoms at severe risk.

Strategies employed by governments of the region to limit the possibilities of Internet use include broad censorship and arbitrary blocking of websites critical of government policies and state brutality, in order to silence opposition and prevent critical information from reaching both domestic populations and international audiences; infiltration of opposition pages to gain information about members, sow dissent, and spread official narratives; harassment, arrest, prosecution, torture and even killing of online activists and bloggers and all other people who speak the truth; and abuse of repressive laws to facilitate the targeting of those who exercise their right to freedom of expression online as well as offline.

In reaction to what they label as "fundamentalist groups" and "terrorist groups" often relying on the Internet for propaganda and recruiting, several governments in the region have passed short-sighted cybercrime and counterterrorism laws apparently to combat these groups on the digital front. It is unclear what kind of motivation lies behind these laws; however, as it stands, national security appears to give these authorities a convenient excuse to crack down on the rights of the people to express themselves.

Unfortunately, there are so many people who been either eliminated such as the Saudi journalist Jamal Khashoggi or incarcerated in dark prison cells around the region's many entities.

In a note, the Washington Post's global opinions editor, Karen Attiah, explained the final column: "I received this column from Jamal Khashoggi's translator and assistant the day after Jamal was reported missing in Istanbul. The Post held off publishing it because we hoped Jamal would come back to us so that he and I could edit it together. Now I have to accept: That is not going to happen. This is the last piece of his I will edit for the Post. This column perfectly captures his commitment and passion for freedom in the Arab world. A freedom he apparently gave his life for. I will be forever grateful he chose the Post as his final journalistic home one year ago and gave us the chance to work together."

As a modest tribute to Jamal, I begin this chapter by quoting him; the column he wrote was published in the Washington Post two weeks after his barbaric murder.

Jamal Khashoggi extolled the need for a free press and free exchange of ideas in the region. As I have been following Jamal's writings for the past couple of years, I personally felt very much attached to his ideas, morality and great courage. He was a really passionate person who only wanted well for the region's people as a whole. My heart goes out to his family and all the families around the region whose loved ones have suffered the same fate.

"The Arab world needs a modern version of the old transnational media so citizens can be informed about global events. More importantly, we need to provide a platform for Arab voices," Khashoggi wrote. (1)

"We suffer from poverty, mismanagement and poor education," he continued. "Through the creation of an independent international forum, isolated from the influence of nationalist governments spreading hate through propaganda, ordinary people in the Arab world would be able to address the structural problems their societies face." The tepid international response, he warned, has empowered Arab governments to continue silencing their critics in the media. "These actions no longer carry the consequence of a backlash from the international community," Khashoggi wrote. "Instead, these actions may trigger condemnation quickly followed by silence." (2)

He was absolutely right, and not only the silence of the international community but what is worse is the silence of the majority in the region's streets.

A Website called Article 19 works to promote progressive legislative frameworks in countries open to reform, and holds governments accountable for violations of the right to free expression through advocacy, campaigning and support for local partners. It works to promote the use of the right to information, monitor freedom of expression and threats to safety online and promote policies for challenging hate speech through progressive legal frameworks and counter-speech. Article 19 says:

"The Middle East and North Africa hold some of the worst records of freedom of expression in the world. Many countries in the region lack legal protection for human rights and the rule of law is undermined by a lack of independent judiciaries. The 2011 Arab Spring popular protests brought hope for improvements but devastating wars, foreign intervention and instability have since made it an extremely dangerous environment for journalists, civil society and human rights defenders, forcing millions to leave in search of safety. As war and conflict tear apart infrastructure and cause huge regression in development indicators across Yemen, Syria, Libya and Iraq, elsewhere repressive governments in Saudi Arabia, Iran, Egypt and Bahrain have reinforced anti-human rights practices, often in the name of national security and countering terrorism." (3)

Also citing the Article 19 website in relation to an activist and blogger called activist Wael Abbas. Abbas was arrested after an early hours raid on his home on the 23rd May 2018 and has since been held without access to his lawyer at an unknown location. The arrest comes as part of an alarming rise in arrests of bloggers and journalists following the March elections, which saw the re-election of the repressive regime of President Abdel Fatah el-Sisi. (4)

Only the day before, journalist Ismail Alexandrani, also known for his anti-government writings and criticism of the army's role in Egyptian politics, was reportedly sentenced to ten years in prison by a military court on similarly trumped-up charges. (5)

And to make things much worse, these so-called governments of the region do not provide accurate or reliable data on the many arrests and imprisonment of activists, journalists, human being defenders or anyone that dares to speak against or criticise their policies. There are people we know about and undoubtedly many more other cases of prisoners of conscience that are kept entirely in the dark.

Using the pretext of "terrorism" to legitimise the crackdown on freedom of expression is a dangerous path. Journalists, political opponents, freedom of expression advocates and human rights defenders have been put on trial and some are detained without trial under the pretext of "terrorism".

For example:

The anti-terrorism law in Jordan allows the repression apparatus, composed of the country's intelligence agency and the State Security Court (SSC), to suppress any dissenting voice by means of systematic judicial harassment and torture. (6)

Vested with the investigation of "terrorist crimes", the General Intelligence Directorate (GID) — whose director is appointed by the King — operates without any oversight: its headquarters are used like a secret detention centre where torture — including beatings, stress positions, sleep deprivation and prolonged solitary confinement — are commonly used against detainees who are completely cut off from the outside world. Forced confessions are then used by the SSC prosecutor, a military officer who sits at the GID premises, to charge the suspect. (7)

In almost all the political entities of the region and in almost all cases related to political or social critics and dissidents, anti-terrorism laws drifted away from their supposed initial finality —fighting terrorism — tackling other issues such as the maintenance of public order or indirectly the control of dissidence and political opposition, with no or scarce legal checks and balances that could restrict possible police or judiciary abuses towards civil and political rights.

Look at another example:

Saudi Arabia has a long and ugly history of silencing any kind of opposition by all means possible including torture or even complete elimination and to the extent of even intimidating other countries and pressurising them to keep silent, such as the recent example with Canada when on August 2018, a routine tweet by Canada's Foreign Ministry calling for the release of Saudi women's rights defenders triggered a full-blown diplomatic crisis, with Saudi Arabia retaliating by expelling Canada's ambassador in Riyadh and freezing all new bilateral trade and investments.

Websites and social media pages belonging to human rights or political organisations, such as the Saudi Civil and Political Rights Organization (ACPRA) and the Arab Network for Human Rights Information (ANHRI), are blocked. Sites belonging to several Saudi religious scholars and dissidents are blocked, as well as some related to the Shiite religious minority, such as Yahosein, Awamia and Rasid, which has discontinued operations. Authorities have also blocked the website of the Islamic Umma Party, the country's only political party, which operates underground because political parties are illegal. The party has called for the royal family to step down.

Saudi courts have delivered some of the harshest prison sentences against internet users in the world, with numerous human rights defenders jailed for up to eleven years for their online activities. During the reporting period, both conservative and liberal social media users were arrested and prosecuted for criticising the government.

Saudi Arabia has no constitution. The Basic Law of Saudi Arabia contains language that calls for freedom of speech and Freedom of the Press, but only within certain boundaries. The 2000 Law of Print and Press also addresses freedom of expression issues, though it largely consists of restrictions on speech rather than protections. Online journalists employed at newspapers and other formal news outlets maintain the same rights and protections as print and broadcast journalists, and like their counterparts, are also subject to close government supervision. Similarly, laws designed to protect users from cybercrimes also contain clauses that limit freedom of expression. The 2007 Anti-Cyber Crime Law criminalizes "producing something that harms public order, religious values, public morals, the sanctity of private life, or authoring, sending, or storing it via an information network," and imposes penalties of up to five years in prison and a fine of up to SAR 3 million (US$800,000). (8)

In January 2016, the Communications and Information Technology Commission (CITC) required mobile network operators to register the fingerprints of new SIM card subscribers, and in August 2016, unregistered subscriptions were suspended. Subscribers were given a period of 90 days to document their fingerprints before the suspension became permanent. The CITC said that the new requirement was meant to "limit the negative effects and violations in the use of communication services." The new regulation built upon previous requirements to register subscribers' real names and identity numbers, even to recharge a prepaid mobile card, which was often circumvented in practice. (9)

Saudi Arabia has long invested in technologically sophisticated mass surveillance systems. In June 2017, a report by BBC Arabic and Danish newspaper Dagbladet presented evidence that UK aerospace and defence conglomerate BAE Systems sold Saudi Arabia and other countries in the region sophisticated surveillance systems. In January 2018, media reports surfaced that the government acquired a stake in Italian spyware technology company Hacking Team through intermediaries. (10)

According to Human Rights Watch and in relation to Saudi's anti-terrorism law, HRW says:

Saudi Arabia is misusing its broad anti-terrorism law to silence peaceful dissent and deny freedom of expression, imprisoning critics and allegedly subjecting some of them to torture. Saudi Arabia's new counterterrorism law (2017) includes vague and overly broad definitions of acts of terrorism, in some cases punishable by death, Human Rights Watch said today. (11)

The law replaces a widely criticised counterterrorism law promulgated in 2014, adding definitions of specific acts of terrorism and their corresponding sentencing guidelines. It includes criminal penalties of five to ten years in prison for portraying the king or crown prince, directly or indirectly, "in a manner that brings religion or justice into disrepute," and criminalises a wide range of peaceful acts that bear no relation to terrorism. (12)

The new law, however, does not restrict the definition of terrorism to violent acts. Other conduct it defines as terrorism includes "disturbing public order," "shaking the security of the community and the stability of the State," "exposing its national unity to danger," and "suspending the basic laws of governance," all of which are vague and have been used by Saudi authorities to punish peaceful dissidents and activists. Prominent human rights activists Abdullah al-Hamid and Mohammed al-Qahtani are serving eleven and ten year sentences respectively, based on charges that contain similar language. Human rights activist Essam Koshak is currently on trial on similar charges. (13)

In a recent report from September 2018 and published by the Middle East Monitor, it is claimed that the number of prisoners of conscience in Saudi Arabia has increased substantially.

The Twitter account of Prisoners of Conscience concerned with the detainees in Saudi Arabia stated in a tweet that: "the number of prisoners of conscience in Saudi Arabia has increased to 2,613 detainees." (14)

The Twitter account added that "prominent lawyers, judges, academics, Muslim scholars and media professionals" were among the detainees. (15)

It is noteworthy that there are detainees in the kingdom who have been imprisoned for more than ten years either under sentences approved by the court against them or without charges and judicial rulings. (16)

Numerous individuals report that they were tortured by police while held in custody, often to force confessions. Munir al-Adam, who was sentenced to death in 2016 for his role in anti-government protests in the Shiite-majority town of al-Qatif in 2011, said he was severely beaten by police and coerced into signing a confession. Among other accusations against him, police claimed he was "sending texts," although he denied owning a mobile phone. Raif Badawi, a writer and activist who founded the website Saudi Liberals, has so far received fifty lashes as part of his sentence on charges of contempt of religion. He was handed a total sentence of ten years imprisonment, a fine of SAR 1 million (US$266,500), and 1,000 lashes in May 2014. (17)

Authorities have allegedly physically and verbally abused detainees who were rounded up as part of the anti-corruption crackdown that began in November 2017. Notably, a number of sources claimed that Major General Ali al-Qahtani, who worked in the Saudi Arabian Royal Guard and managed the private office of Prince Turki Bin Abdullah, was tortured to death in December. (18)

The snow and freezing temperatures that struck Saudi Arabia unexpectedly in December 2013 were newsworthy in a desert kingdom better known for its extreme heat. But the fact that the ensuing power outages at a regional prison left prisoners without power or heat for nearly a week was apparently off-limits to reporters.

Mansour al-Mazhrm, a correspondent for the Saudi daily Al-Watan Online, reported on the outages on Twitter, only to find himself hauled into court for defamation on "information technology devices." Al-Mazhrm served seven days in prison and was forced to pay a fine for violating Article 3 of the country's Anti-Cyber Crime Law. (19)

In a new report[4], Amnesty International found that, since crown prince Mohammed Bin Salman took power, Saudi Arabia has seen mass detention of government critics and human rights defenders (HRDs). By the end of 2018, all Saudi Arabian HRDs were in detention or serving prison terms, or had been forced to flee the country.

In February 2018, Issa al-Nukheifi and Essam Koshak were sentenced to six and four years in prison respectively for their twitter posts criticising authorities and calling for human rights reforms.

The government also launched a wave of arrests targeting many prominent women's human rights defenders including Loujain al-Hathloul and Aziza al-Yousef who campaigned against the ban on women driving and the male guardianship system.

Human rights violations committed by Saudi Arabia also extend past their borders to Yemen where the coalition forces indiscriminately target civilian areas, committing serious violations of international human rights law. In one case, the Saudi Arabia coalition attacked a bus in Sa'da governorate, killing 29 children and injuring 30 others.

Despite the many violations in international law and human rights, the United States, United Kingdom, and France continue to export weapons, enabling the "Middle Eastern" governments to commit even more violations.

Is there any kind of human justice for all of these people, who have done nothing wrong but say the truth? I am just

---

[4]HUMAN RIGHTS IN THE MIDDLE EAST AND NORTH AFRICA: REVIEW OF 2018, 26 Feb. 2019, https://www.amnesty.org/en/documents/MDE01/9433/2019/en/

wondering as well as being perplexed as to how the so-called Kingdom of Saudi Arabia, with their endless propaganda of being a just country according to Islamic laws, can perpetuate and accommodate these injustices for such a long time for the sake of keeping themselves in an arrogant, greedy, and blind power!

And since President Abdel Fattah al-Sisi of Egypt secured a second term in a largely unfree and unfair presidential election in March, his security forces have escalated a campaign of intimidation, violence and arrests against political opponents, civil society activists and many others who have simply voiced criticism of the government. The Egyptian government and state media have framed this repression under the guise of combating "terrorism", and al-Sisi has increasingly invoked terrorism and the country's state of emergency law to silence peaceful activists. In addition to using the exceptional State Security Courts, for which court decisions cannot be appealed, authorities continue to prosecute thousands of civilians before military courts. Both court systems are inherently dreadful and abusive and do not even meet the minimum due process standards.

The hallmark of President Abdel Fattah el-Sisi's regime has been its brutal methods of shutting down protests, tactics that were established early on in response to the anti-coup sit-ins in Rabaa al-Adawiya Mosque in 2013 that resulted in 800–1,000 civilian deaths. Furthermore, since coming to power, the Sisi regime has reportedly imprisoned 60,000 Egyptians for various degrees of dissent, utilizing the most brutal forms of torture. This marks a shift from even former president Hosni Mubarak's rule—to say nothing of the post revolution era—during which, although crackdowns happened and constraints existed, activists were still able to mobilize. Public activism against the military or against Mubarak himself certainly inspired repression, but activists were generally aware of the redlines. Today, the redlines have shifted and are, at times, difficult to identify. Anyone, at any time, can face the ire of the state—as evidenced by stories of forced disappearances, unlawful arrests, and killings, notably the brutal murder of Italian doctoral student Giulio Regeni at the hands of Egyptian security services in 2016. (20)

According to Human Rights Watch Report 2019:

The Interior Ministry's National Security Agency (NSA) continues to operate with near-absolute impunity. Judicial authorities have investigated very few officers and even fewer have been prosecuted for abuses, including enforced disappearances and torture. Prosecutors continued to use detainee confessions despite credible allegations they were coerced through torture. Authorities announced in late 2017 that they were investigating Human Rights Watch claims of police and NSA forces' use of torture, but at time of writing, these investigations had not led to the prosecution of any alleged perpetrators. (21)

The Stop Enforced Disappearance campaign has documented 1,530 cases from July 2013 to August 2018. At least 230 of those occurred between August 2017 and August 2018. The whereabouts of at least 32 of those disappeared in 2018 remained unknown as of August 2018. (22)

According to Hafez Abu Seada, a member of the National Council for Human Rights, the Ministry of Interior acknowledged that 500 out of 700 people whose families reported their disappearance since 2015 remain in detention. Although he claimed enforced disappearances are not systemic in Egypt, he failed to explain why the Interior

Ministry did not report the whereabouts of 500 people to families who had submitted official complaints. (23)

Under Sisi, Egypt has been steadily restricting the space for online freedom, regularly targeting journalists, bloggers and media organisations. In May 2017, the government blocked access to twenty-one news websites, accusing them of supporting terrorism and spreading false news. Since then, according to the Association for Freedom of Thought and Expression (AFTE), Cairo has blocked access to almost five hundred websites, most of them belonging to media organisations. (24)

Cyber police in the UAE (United Arab Emirates) have been monitoring Internet usage for over three years, employing sophisticated filtering systems to block websites carrying dissenting political opinions, critical views of official Islam, or negative discussions of the society, economy or royal family. Social media sites are partially censored by topic; it is thought that over 500 keywords are blocked. The penal code broadly restricts speech, criminalising public criticism of government officials (Article 176) and allowing authorities to prosecute Internet activists. One affected blogger is Ahmed Mansoori, a member of Human Rights Watch's Middle East advisory committee, who was imprisoned from April 8–November 28 and who administered the online pro-democracy forum "Al-Hewar," which was banned by authorities. Mansoor received six death threats and was targeted by an online smear campaign prior to arrest. While in detention, he was reportedly mistreated and his family threatened. He and four other activists who were also detained, including online activists Fahad Salim Dalk, Hassan Ali al-Khamis, and Ahmed Abdul Khaleq, along with lecturer Nasser bin Ghaith, are popularly known as the "UAE 5." (25)

In March 2017, a United Arab Emirates court sentenced Nasser Bin Ghaith, a prominent economist who has advocated greater democracy and human rights, to ten years in prison. His alleged crimes largely consist of online posts, including some criticising the Emirates' ally Egypt for human-rights abuses. (26)

The economist was convicted of "communicating with secret organisations linked to the Muslim Brotherhood, by creating accounts on social media and publishing photos and articles that are offensive to the state's symbols and values, its internal and foreign policies and its relations with an Arab state." (27)

He was charged under a 2012 cybercrime law that provides for a maximum of fifteen years in prison for publishing material online with "sarcastic intent" or to "damage the reputation" of the state or its leaders; and under a 2014 counterterrorism law, which according to Human Rights Watch "enables the UAE authorities to prosecute those who express peaceful opposition to the government, whether in writing or verbally, as terrorists." (28)

Syria remains one of the most dangerous places in the world to use the internet. According to Reporters Without Borders, twelve citizen journalists were killed in 2017. In August 2017, it was confirmed that digital activist Bassel Khartabil Safadi was executed by the regime's security forces in 2015. He had been detained in 2012 for his democratic activism.

With the onset of the civil war, citizen journalism and social media provided the Syrian public with an alternative view of domestic events, especially as the perception of independence and credibility of state media outlets declined. In an environment of violence and arbitrary "red lines," self-censorship is widespread online and increased in recent

Palestinian inmates by type and year

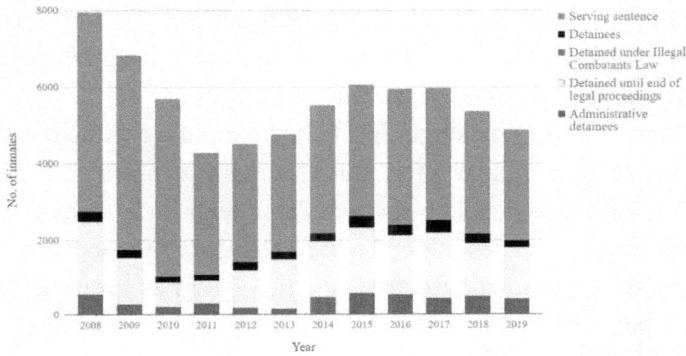

years amid growing threats and violent reprisals for critical content online. Sensitive topics include criticism of President Assad, his late father, the military, the ruling Ba'ath Party, or influential government officials. Covering religious and ethnic tensions or corruption allegations related to the ruling family are also off-limits. Most users are careful not only to avoid such sensitive topics but also to refrain from visiting blocked websites. (29)

Since anti-government protests broke out in 2011, the authorities have detained hundreds of internet users, including several well-known bloggers and citizen journalists. While it is difficult to obtain information on recent arrests, at least fifteen citizens remain in prison according to Reporters Without Borders, an international NGO. Bassel Khartabil, an open-source activist and recipient of the 2013 Index on Censorship Digital Freedom Award, was detained by the authorities in March 2012 and subsequently executed. (30)

When it comes to Palestine, as it is under military occupation the situation there is much worse for the people of intellect and political activists, as they suffer from two hammers instead of one. The first hammer is the Israeli security forces and their ugly intelligence service and the second hammer which is sadly occurring is from the so-called Palestinian authorities under the leadership of Mahmood Abass and his security apparatus.

The greatest challenge that Palestinians face while trying to use social media as a tool for freedom of expression is the change in Israeli policy toward those who dare to express themselves on Facebook or Twitter. Recently Facebook posts expressing political opinions have been used as grounds for possible imprisonment. Israel has sent dozens of Palestinians to jail for several months, asserting that they expressed extreme points of view on Facebook. Internationally, the discourse has always been that freedom of expression should be maintained on the Internet and that regulations should not allow digital expression to be used as a pretext to hunt down political activists. At the same time, many countries, including Israel, justify their control of the flow of Internet content by stating that this is done for national security and high-priority national interests. (31)

Activists say there is a growing crackdown on writers who criticise the Palestinian Government. According to Executive Director of Advancing Human Rights David Keyes, in 2013, Anas Awwad, a twenty-six year old Palestinian activist, was sentenced in absentia by a Palestinian court in Nablus, the West Bank, to one year in prison for "extending his tongue" against the Palestinian Authority's president, Mahmoud Abbas, on Facebook. Keyes also states that in 2012, Palestinian blogger Jamal Abu Rihan was arrested by the Palestinian Authority for starting a Facebook campaign called "The People Want an End to Corruption," he was indicted under the charges of "extending his tongue" against the Palestinian leadership. (32)

In 2017, violations against media freedom in Palestine escalated at a fast pace, compared to previous years. MADA (Palestinian Centre for Development and Media Freedom) documented a total of 530 violations against Palestinian journalists (around 38%) compared to 2016. (33)

Note that Israeli Occupation Forces committed a total of 375 violations, whereas Palestinian bodies committed a total of 154 violations (71% and 29% respectively of the overall documented violations for 2017). (34)

The first half of 2018 witnessed a serious deterioration since the Great Return Marches started in Gaza Strip. By the end of March 2018 two journalists had been killed and at least 80 journalists injured with explosive — live ammunition used by Israeli Occupation Forces. Whereas Palestinian security services attacked journalists while covering demonstrations in West Bank and Gaza Strip. Unfortunately, in the vast majority of violations, especially the serious ones, the aggressors are not held accountable. (35)

According to the Palestinian Centre for Development and Media Freedom, on January 2019, the first month of 2019 has witnessed an increase in the number of violations against media freedoms in Palestine. It is worth mentioning that most of the previous months have also witnessed high rates, which reflects the continued escalation of attacks against media freedoms, especially by the Israeli occupation, which commits the greatest part of these attacks. (36)

The Palestinian Centre for Development & Media Freedoms has monitored a total of fifty-seven attacks against media freedoms in Palestine during January 2019. Thirty-seven of these attacks were committed by the Israeli occupation, while twenty attacks were committed by the Palestinian authorities. It should be noted that January 2018 witnessed forty-seven attacks, thirty-two of which were committed by the occupation and fifteen by the Palestinian authorities. (37)

Apart from the continuing detentions and imprisonments as well as killings of Palestinian journalists and activists who dare to cover the daily events in the field or simply voice their opinions using the new platforms of the internet, there are also the hidden political Palestinian prisoners who are languishing behind Israeli iron bars and some of whom, unfortunately, may never see the light of sun again.

"Since the Israeli occupation of Palestinian territory in 1967, more than 800,000 Palestinians have been detained under Israeli military orders in the occupied Palestinian territory (oPt). This number constitutes approximately twenty per cent of the total Palestinian population in the oPt and as much as forty per cent of the total male Palestinian population... 8,000 Palestinian children have been arrested since 2000." As of August 2017, there are 6,279 Palestinian political prisoners in Israeli prisons and detention centres, including 465 administrative detainees, 65 women, and 300 children. (38)

And according to B'TSELEM, which is the Israeli Information Centre for Human Rights in the Occupied Territories:

At the end of January 2019, there were 5,298 Palestinian security detainees and prisoners being held in Israel Prison Service (IPS) facilities, including 293 from Gaza Strip. Another 657 Palestinians, 14 of them from the Gaza Strip, were in IPS prisons for being in Israel illegally. The IPS classifies these Palestinians — both detainees and prisoners — criminal offenders.

The figures from the military are received with a significant time delay and offer few details regarding inmates' legal standing. (39)

The following figures were provided by the military and the IPS, so responsibility for their accuracy lies with them. (40)

The sight of hundreds of thousands of Arabs and non-Arabs, Muslims and non-Muslims marching on the streets of a number of the region's countries in 2011/2012, demanding their dignity and rights, will remain among the iconic images of the twenty-first century or at least iconic in my mind. The willingness of so many people to take such tremendous risks to their own lives, with so many deaths and thousands injured for their freedom, stunned a world long accustomed to the image of the resigned, subordinate, cynical masses of the region. They marched through the streets of many so-called capitals and other cities of the region with utmost pride and humility and suffered a great deal at the hands of the thugs who represent the puppets and their cronies. Yet, with utmost sadness, more or less the whole region has plunged into complete disarray and anarchy with varying degrees. And as a consequence of the 2011/2012 events some countries such as Syria and Yemen are suffering from terrible and very costly civil wars or proxy wars and some others have even worse a dictator than before, the case of Sisi's Egypt being an obvious one. Yet, saying so, I also believe that history has taught us that transformational processes take time. The long-suppressed ideas and energies unleashed by events like the "Arab Spring" must mature before having their full effect on society. Consider the uprisings in Europe in 1848, in which citizens protested against authoritarian, feudal systems and the lack of economic opportunity. By the end of that year, the forces of the status quo managed to retake the reins of power, and the uprisings appeared to have been all but crushed.

Freedom of expression advances knowledge. It is easier for you to make new discoveries and gain new knowledge when you can suggest ideas and exchange information freely. Even if some ideas do not work, they provide a way of testing the truth of other ideas. Freedom of expression makes a peaceful change in society possible, peaceful change which the region desperately needs. If you are free to try to persuade others to change things, you are less likely to use violence. In societies where freedom of expression is respected, they have improved many things in their countries by using the right to freedom of expression. Freedom of speech and press, or freedom of expression, are "fundamental rights". Without these freedoms, a truly free society cannot exist. Free speech is not only about our ability to speak but the ability to listen to others and allow other views to be heard.

Across the Arab world, people are being suffocated, and we have had enough of our regimes' oppression. We are devoid of the right to freely express and share our opinions, let alone the right to participate in governing our own affairs. When the Arab Spring broke in 2010–2011, we were full of hope that a wave of change was finally coming our way. But as the world witnessed, this wave was either kept at bay (Egypt, Yemen) or put down with brutal crackdowns (Syria, Bahrain). Tunisia was the only success story. The Arab Spring and the revolutions it produced are one way in which change could happen within the political systems across the Middle East. The other way is a slow, guided and deliberate transformation. (41) For this transformation to happen, an essential element is to have informed participants, for in an ideal world, a true and just democracy that we all dream of is hinged on the inclusion of all citizens in the political process. However, this is not relevant for the current state of politics across the region where, democratically speaking, the standard falls below absolute zero. What is relevant is the importance of having informed citizens as a precursor to change. When most of the citizens are misinformed and controlled through the government narrative, it is easy for the dictator to control, and keep controlling, the population. (42)

It was painful for me several years ago when several friends were arrested. I said nothing. I didn't want to lose my job or my freedom. I worried about my family. I have made a different choice now. I have left my home, my family and my job, and I am raising my voice. To do otherwise would betray those who languish in prison. I can speak when so many cannot. I want you to know that Saudi Arabia has not always been as it is now. (43)

These were Jamal Kashoogi's last words.

References for Chapter 9: Plague Nine: Killing the Voices

1. Brett Samuels, Kashoggi Calls for Freedom of Expression in the Middle East in final Column Before Disappearance, 17/10/2018, The Hill, https://thehill.com/policy/international/411970-khashoggi-calls-for-freedom-of-expression-in-middle-east-in-final-column

2. Ibid

3. Article 19, Middle East and North Africa, In Focus, https://www.article19.org/regional-office/middle-east-north-africa/

4. Article 19, Crackdown Continues with Blogger Wael Abbas Arrested, May, 24, 2018, https://www.article19.org/resources/egypt-crackdown-continues-with-blogger-wael-abbas-arrested/

5. Ibid

6. Ines Osman, 10 years on: Jordan anti-terrorism law and the crackdown on dissent, Open Democracy, October 2016, https://www.opendemocracy.net/en/north-africa-west-asia/10-years-on-jordan-s-anti-terrorism-law-and-crackdown-on-dissent/

7. Ibid

8. Freedom on the Net, Saudi Arabia,
    https://freedomhouse.org/report/freedom-net/2018/
    saudi-arabia

9. Ibid

10. Ibid

11. Human rights watch, Saudi Arabia: New Counter-
    terrorism Law Enables Abuse, November 2017,
    https://www.hrw.org/news/2017/11/23/saudi-arabia-
    new-counterterrorism-law-enables-abuse

12. Ibid

13. Ibid

14. Middle East Monitor, Number of prisoners of
    conscience in Saudi Arabia has increased to 2,613,
    September 2018,
    https://www.middleeastmonitor.com/20180917-
    number-of-prisoners-of-conscience-in-saudi-arabia-
    increases-to-2613/

15. Ibid

16. Ibid

17. Freedom on the Net, Saudi Arabia,
    https://freedomhouse.org/report/freedom-net/2018/
    saudi-arabia

18. C. Radsch, Treating the Internet as the Enemy in the
    Middle East, April 2015, Committee to Protect
    Journalism, https://cpj.org/2015/04/attacks-on-the-
    press-treating-internet-as-enemy-in-middle-
    east.php

19. Ibid

20. Intissar Fakir, Governance and the Future of the
    Arab World, Carnegie Endowment for International
    Peace,

https://carnegieendowment.org/2018/10/16/governa
nce-and-future-of-arab-world-pub-77501

21. Human Rights Watch, Egypt Event of 2018,
    https://www.hrw.org/world-report/2019/country-
    chapters/egypt
22. Ibid
23. Ibid
24. Elissa Miller, Egypt Leads the Pack in Internet
    Censorship Across the Middle East, August 2018,
    Atlantic Council,
    https://www.atlanticcouncil.org/blogs/menasource/
    egypt-leads-the-pack-in-internet-censorship-across-
    the-middle-east
25. Ursula Lindsey, UAE Jails Economist: The Silence is
    Deafening, April 2017, Al-Fanar Media,
    https://www.al-fanarmedia.org/2017/04/uae-jails-
    economist-the-silence-is-deafening/
26. Ibid
27. Ibid
28. Cairo Institute For Human Rights Studies, Freedom
    of Expression and the Internet in the Middle East
    and North Africa,
    https://cihrs.org/wp-content/uploads/2012/02/Freed
    om-of-Expression-and-the-Internet-in-the-Middle-
    East-and-North-Africa.pdf
29. Freedom on the Net, Syria,
    https://freedomhouse.org/report/freedom-net/2018/
    syria
30. Ibid
31. Ziad Khalil AbuZayyad, Freedom of Expression and
    Social Media in Palestine, Palestine-Israel Journal,
    Vol. 21 No. 2, 2015

32. Wikipedia, Human Rights in the State of Palestine, https://en.wikipedia.org/wiki/Human_rights_in_the _State_of_Palestine

33. Palestine News Network, Moot court competition for the defence of freedom of expression in Palestine, http://english.pnn.ps/2018/09/04/moot-court-competition-for-the-defense-of-freedom-of-expression-in-palestine/

34. Ibid

35. Ibid

36. Palestinian Center for Development and Media Freedom, Monthly Report 2019, https://www.madacenter.org/report.php? lang=1&id=1856&category_id=13&year=2019

37. Ibid

38. Political Prisoners in Israel/Palestine, If Americans Knew, https://ifamericaknew.org/stat/prisoners.html

39. Statistics on Palestinians in the custody of the Israeli security forces, B'Teslem, 10 March 2019, https:// www.btselem.org/statistics/detainees_and_prisoner s

40. Ibid

41. Rasheed Alameer, Continuing Jamal Kashoogi's Fight for Free Expression in the Arab World, October 2018, Fair Observer, https://www.fairobserver.com/region/middle_east_ north_africa/freedom-of-expression-arab-world-jamal-khashoggi-news-65431/

42. Ibid

43. Jamal Khashoogi, Saudi Arabia wasn't always this repressive. Now it's Unbearable, The Washington Post, September 2017,

https://www.washingtonpost.com/news/global-opinions/wp/2017/09/18/saudi-arabia-wasnt-always-this-repressive-now-its-unbearable/?utm_term=.5013afcd551d

Chapter 10: Plague Ten: The Greatest Unity of Disunity

Today, the Muslim world is injured and corrupt. People who are the enemies of all Muslims are trying to cause disunity in the Islamic world by intensifying ethnic difference and separating people under names such as 'Shia and Sunni', 'Arabs and non-Arabs'.

— *Ali Khamenei*

"Our shouting is louder than our actions,
Our swords are taller than us,
This is our tragedy.
In short
We wear the cape of civilisation
But our souls live in the stone age"

— *Nizar Qabbani*

With the fall of Iraq to the barbarism of American and Allied forces and the possibility of a showdown between Christianity and Islam, as the theory of Samuel Huntington propagated in his book The Clash of Civilisation, is the region labelled as the "Middle East" on the brink of an abyss if it does not fulfil the promise of Arab unity?

Arab unity has been a dream and a promise, and for long a broken promise, since the fall of the Ottoman Empire, so why has this dream not been fulfilled in the past 100 years?

The Question of Arab Unity from the "Nahda", the Arab cultural renaissance of the 19th century, through to the turbulent and often disappointing and heart-breaking 20th century and today's bewildering array of dictatorships, political ideologies, teetering democracies and monarchies. The region's political entities are a loose, yet complex amalgam of 22 countries in which a pan-Arab identity is the ideal proclaimed by the puppet leaders.

A century after Prophet Mohammed's death, the Islamic empire stretched from India in the east to Spain in the west. But Arab unity was little in evidence. Even at this stage, British Middle East authority George E. Kirk has written, "The great social defect of the Arab character, its unreadiness to subordinate its overmastering self-will and self-interest, whether of an individual, of a family, or of a tribe, to the good of a larger group, was manifesting itself in incidents that boded ill for the future of the Arab Empire." This "great social defect" was in large measure responsible for the Arab decline which began as early as the 10th century. Mongol invasions further weakened Islamic power and in the 16th century, the Ottoman Turks brought almost the entire Arab-speaking world under their control. (1)

By the early 19th century, the Ottoman Empire had decayed from within and, following Napoleon's occupation of Egypt in 1798, European influence became increasingly important in the Arab world. The so-called "Arab awakening," of this period took many forms. "In the Arabian peninsula, Arab revival took the form of religious puritanism. In Egypt, it expressed itself as a movement for the liberation from Ottoman domination, for the founding of a nation state in the modern European sense and for socio-economic modernisation. In the Fertile Crescent [Iraq, Palestine, Jordan, Lebanon and Syria], it was mainly a cultural, literary and intellectual renaissance, drawing its sources from classical Arabic civilization, then recently discovered, and from the modern Western traditions of science, technology and literature, then recently rendered accessible to that sector of Arab society." (2)

In the early 20th century, an independent Arab world started to emerge from decades of colonial supremacy in the Middle East and North Africa region. In those days, the race for statehood among fledgling Arab countries was taken over by a hasty struggle for unity.

Although strong divisions existed among different Arab leaders, social movements and intellectuals, concerning what unity meant and what practical form it should take, the consensus was that an Arab unification of some sort was necessary for an Arab revival.

The mix of anticipated independence and Arab nationalism steered efforts among Arab states towards a new regional order; one which today we call the "Arab World". But was there ever any "unified" Arab world?

The Arab cultural renaissance, known as the Nahda, created and developed in response to the Ottoman Empire's constant efforts, in the late 19th century, to centralise Turkish control over the Arabs led to strong anti-Turkish feelings and revived in Arab people a sense of identity. But a looming World War was about to reveal the fragility of the intellectual renaissance on which the Arabs based their hopes of closing the gap between the dream and reality of unity. With the 1916 Arab Revolt against the Turks, it seemed that the dream was going to be fulfilled. However, European colonialism stopped the dream and divided the region. But were the Arabs really united in the first place?

The end of World War I left the Arabs feeling betrayed. Their dream of a new Arab Kingdom had not materialised; Britain and France had instead divided the region between them. As the promises of the past receded and their sense of fragmentation increased, Arabs began to turn to new political ideologies, charting a path for the Arab Nation in the hope of addressing the gap between the reality and dream of unity.

The 1920s and 30s saw the rise of a multitude of secular ideologies such as communism and socialism. And it was at this time that the importance of the idea of a secular Arab Nationalism began to emerge. for example, in Syria in 1947, Michel Aflaq and Salah Bitar founded the Baath party, a pan-Arabist party rooted in both socialism and nationalism which would eventually only have a genuine appeal in Syria and Iraq. Although ostensibly a secular party, Baathism differed from the Syrian Social Nationalist Party in positing religion, specifically Islam, as the greatest achievement of the Arabs and as the source of the Arab World's eventual regeneration.

World War II spurred efforts toward unification of the Arab world. The war removed the French from Syria and Lebanon and the Italians from Libya, leaving Imperial Britain the only colonial power in the so-called Middle East. Toward the end of the war, the Hashemite Arab leaders of Iraq, Jordan and Syria—all related as descendants of Prophet Mohammed, as they claim, through the house of Hashem—proposed plans to unite several Arab countries under their leadership. The plans were opposed by both the non-Hashemites, particularly by those in Egypt and Saudi Arabia, and by the British. The British and non-Hashemite preference for a non-binding alliance which would safeguard national sovereignties prevailed when the Arab League was established in March 1945. The original members were Egypt, Saudi Arabia, Yemen, Transjordan (now Jordan), Syria, Lebanon and Iraq. The Arab League, commonly known as the League of Arab States, was created to give political expression to the Arab nations. The British gave the original drive behind the league in 1942 hoping to rally the Arab nations against the Axis powers; but the league did not form until the final months of World War II.

According to its charter, the founding members of the Arab League (Egypt, Syria, Transjordan, Iraq, Saudi Arabia, Lebanon, and Yemen) agreed to seek "close cooperation" on matters of economics, communication, culture, nationality, social welfare, and health. They renounced violence for the settlement of conflicts between members and empowered League officers to mediate in such disputes, and in those with non-members. Signatories agreed to collaborate in military affairs; this accord was strengthened with a 1950 pact committing members to treat acts of aggression on any member state as an act against all. (3)

Countries Joining in Subsequent Years:

The Palestine Liberation Organization (PLO) was granted full membership in 1976. Other current members include Algeria (1962), Bahrain (1971), Comoros (1993), Djibouti (1977), Kuwait (1961), Libya (1953), Mauritania (1973), Morocco (1958), Oman (1971), Qatar (1971), Somalia (1974), Southern Yemen (1967), Sudan (1956), Tunisia (1958), and the United Arab Emirates (1971).

In assessing the past I consider it a big failure. The Arab League has failed to work together at almost every critical juncture in its history. Even shortly after Israel was founded, member states could not muster a unified or coordinated attack against it, which announced its statehood in 1948 after expelling Palestinians from their homes. The league officially was united in its opposition to the Zionist project in Palestine. While that remains its official stance today, member states have almost never agreed on how to address that conflict or others in the region.

Israel, the Arab League's official nemesis, is even reportedly dealing with Gulf nations behind the scenes. More telling, the boycott against Israel for occupying Palestinian lands has gained more support in Europe than in the Arab world. And Palestinians, of course, are treated either like a burden or a security threat in most Arab nations that host them. (4)

For example, in considering the response of the Arab League to the Iraq crises, the need for major reforms becomes apparent. The recent Iraq crises demonstrated, on a world stage, the weaknesses and disunity of the Arab League. As Qatar's foreign minister Sheikh Hammad bin Jassem remarked, "our meetings [the Arab League's] are ceremonial and we don't have a defined target." (5)

In the months leading up to the eventual war there was a distinct lack of unity among the nations of the Arab League. One notable confrontation evolved between Iraq and Kuwait. On December 7th, 2002, Iraq issued an apology to Kuwait for the events of a decade earlier, the invasion of Kuwait that precipitated the Gulf War. Saddam Hussein, the Iraqi leader, sent the following message to Kuwait: "We apologies for what happened to you in the past," while further proposing that the "devoted and holy warriors in Kuwait" join with Iraqi forces and their "common creator" against the "infidel armies of London, Washington and the Zionist entity." (6)

However Kuwait, instead of welcoming this apology and joining forces with Iraq as Saddam had hoped, instead labelled the apology as "efforts to create disorder amongst the leadership and people of Kuwait." Arab League chief Moussa declined any involvement in the Iraq-Kuwait issue, responding to questions about the confrontation by stating: "It is not obliged for the Arab League to make any statement on what Saddam is talking about. My stance is clear that it is imperative for Iraq to comply with the UN Security Council resolutions." This example illustrates the hesitation that the Arab League has shown in attempting to resolve any conflict within its member nations. By completely avoiding the issue, the Arab League let the hostility between the nations grow which led to further complications as the war approached. (7)

In an ironically named "Unity Summit" at the beginning of March 2003, the late Libyan President Muammar Gaddafi blamed Saudi Arabia, Kuwait, and others for involving the US in the area twelve years prior in the Gulf War, which he claimed was the source of the current Iraq conflict. Gaddafi had previously accused Saudi Arabia of entering into "a pact with the devil" by inviting US troops to defend its territory in 1990. Gaddafi's comments at the summit prompted the Saudi, Iraqi, and Syrian leaders to immediately leave the room and respond harshly to the comments, accusing the Libyan leader of ignorance. The Saudi representative further called Libya an "agent for colonizers." This series of insults prevented anything constructive from happening for the day at the conference, as the major issues were forgotten in a series of insults. Furthermore, the conference was broadcast live on Arab satellite television, making the disunity and arguments within the Arab League public for the whole Arab world to witness. In Saudi Arabia, Khaled al-Maeena, editor of the Arab News, said he was "shocked, appalled and saddened by the news." "I felt embarrassed," he said. "In front of the world we've become a laughing stock. The Arab people are disappointed and confused... The spat took the steam off the main thrust, which was the Iraq issue." (8)

Arab public opinion has long learnt that these Arab League summits are almost invariably disappointing. And the region's street know that these summits are just a waste of time and public resources as on so many occasions these gatherings have been scarred by public disputes which showcase Arab disunity rather than its intended opposite. And as usual, most summits have tended to conclude with the adoption of watered-down resolutions which the so-called leaders seem to forget the moment they walk out of the meeting hall.

The Arab League is very well illustrated by the prominent Saudi columnist Abdul Rahman al-Rashed. "The Arab League has become used to treating the patient's wounds only after his death," wrote Mr Rashed. "This elderly institution has been deaf to every big event because that is the best way of escaping responsibility. But it can also be said that the art of avoidance has killed the Arab League."

Interviews conducted by Al Jazeera in 2009 illustrated the Arab public's frustration with the organisation. "If we are to measure competence in terms of results and achievements," said a twenty-four-year-old Syrian, "then the Arab League is not competent simply because they have not achieved anything." Even the League's secretary-general, Nabil al-Araby, joined the chorus of criticism in September 2011, describing the organisation as "impotent." (9)

Many Middle East experts say the Arab League is likely to improve a little on its record of collective action until members agree to sacrifice some sovereignty and comply with resolutions. And until democracy is the mainstay of the Arab world, the League will continue to struggle with issues of legitimacy. (10)

In summit after summit they are unable to come up with any solutions for the many woes facing the region. So why do Arab League summits usually end up paying nothing but lip service to Arab issues? The Arab League, in a sense, cannot move ahead of the nature of the current Arab entities themselves. The problem of the Arab political entities are the nature of their regimes, centralised systems, with no accountability, so the regimes can fail repeatedly and remain in power and in control. Disunity and dysfunction are common themes within the League. Countless intra-Arab wars, endless infighting and bloody conflict bear testament to this fact. That is why Arab League summits generally lead to nothing but trivia and a collection of empty, banal pronouncements proclaiming unity and solidarity and boring repetition of the usual clichés, and their summits are infamous for being 'talking shops' that come up with long lists of resolutions which are almost never implemented and are regularly plagued by verbal and sometimes even physical assaults involving the participants.

Neither the Arab League nor the oft-stated desire for unity was effective in bringing about pan-Arab solidarity. The only agreement among league members was their opposition to Jewish claims in Palestine. After years of strife in Palestine, the United Nations partitioned it in 1947 into Jewish and Arab areas. The following year came Israel's declaration of independence and, immediately, an invasion by extremely dis-organised "armies" of Arab neighbours. But instead of coordinating their efforts, the Arab countries acted on their own and sought to prevent their rivals from achieving any advantage. The result was an Arab defeat in the first Arab-Israeli war, bitter feuds among the Arab political entities, assassinations and upheavals in several countries, Jordan's unpopular annexation of part of Palestine and the influx of unwanted Palestinian refugees into neighbouring Arab lands.

Arab regimes' exploitation and undermining of the Palestinian cause, and their secret cooperation with Israel and its strategic interests, date back to when Israel was first created in 1949 and even before. And in my view, the whole affair of the Arab-Israeli war of 1948 is just a big joke. They, according to many history books dealing with this issue, had no intention whatsoever to prevent the creation of Israel. Their main intention was to accumulate more land for themselves.

Avi Shlaim in his article The Debate About 1948 states: "in a book published by Colonel Abdullah al-Tall who had served as a messenger between King Abdullah and the Jews, following Tall's abortive coup and defection to Egypt. A similar charge was levelled against Ben-Gurion by Lieutenant-Colonel Israel Baer in the book he wrote in his prison cell, following his conviction of spying for the Soviet Union. Tall condemned King Abdullah for betraying his fellow Arabs and selling the Palestinians down the river. Baer condemned Ben-Gurion for forming an unholy alliance with Arab reaction and British imperialism." and he continues to say: "His objective (King Abdullah's) in sending his army into Palestine was not to prevent the establishment of a Jewish state, but to make himself master of the Arab part of Palestine which meant preventing the establishment of an independent Palestinian state. The one purpose which the Arab invasion did not serve was the ostensible one of coming to the rescue of the embattled Palestinians. Nowhere was the disparity between pan-Arab rhetoric and the reality greater than in relation to the Palestinian Arabs. The reality was one of national selfishness with each Arab state looking after its own interests. What was supposed to be a holy war against the Jews, quickly turned into a general land grab. Division and discord within the ranks of the ramshackle Arab coalition deepened with every successive defeat. Israel's leaders knew about these divisions and exploited them to the full. Thus they launched an offensive against the Egyptian army in October and again in December 1948 in the confident expectation that their old friend in Amman would keep out." (11)

There was no love lost between Abdullah and the other Arab rulers who suspected him of being in cahoots with the enemy. Abdullah had always been something of a pariah in the rest of the Arab world, not least because of his friendship with the Jews. Syria and Lebanon felt threatened by his long-standing ambition to make himself master of Greater Syria. Egypt, the leader of the anti-Hashemite bloc within the Arab League, also felt threatened by Abdullah's plans for territorial aggrandisement in Palestine. King Farouk made his decision to intervene in Palestine at the last moment, and against the advice of his civilian and military experts, at least in part to check the growth of his rival's power. There were thus rather mixed motives behind the invasion of Palestine. And there was no single Arab plan of action during the 1948 war. On the contrary, it was the inability of the Arabs to coordinate their diplomatic and military plans that was in large measure responsible for the disaster that overwhelmed them. (12)

The revised military history of Transjordan's British-led 'Arab Legion' army in the 1948–49 Arab-Israeli war, connected military imperatives — the conduct of operations — to the politics of the war. Such a history re-imagines significant debates and reveals new facts about the Legion's military effectiveness, the role of its British commander General Sir John Bagot Glubb 'Pasha', and on the relationship of policy to military operations.

When asked in 1978 on BBC Radio's Desert Island Discs programme what he would be happiest to escape on his desert island, Glubb retorted, "politicians, all the time". Glubb may have had "a soldier's aversion to politics — and to politicians" but he was party to political discussions on the treaty status of Transjordan with the UK and on the future of Palestine prior to war in May 1948, most recently in February 1948 when he accompanied a Transjordanian delegation visiting London. He was a central figure in talks between London and Amman and in discussions with the Jews and Abdullah, and he knew that political imperatives would complicate the Legion's deployment, commenting later that the fighting in 1948 "was a curious imitation of a war, artificially limited by political consideration". Britain hoped to restrict Legion operations in any war with Israel to the Arab areas allotted by the November 1947 United Nations Palestine partition plan, and Glubb — while Abdullah's "great friend" and "very fond" of the Arabs, recalled Desmond Goldie[5], whom Glubb sent to negotiate secretly with the Zionists before the war — had his part in this plan. As Glubb wrote to Norman Lash on 9th July 1948, "All of this is really going back to the original scheme before May 15th of holding the Arab areas and doing nothing." (13)

---

[5]In May 1948, the four mechanized regiments were formed into two brigades (1st and the 3rd) commanded respectively by British colonels Desmond Goldie and 'Teal' Ashton in the 1st Division. British Brigadier Norman Lash led this division, to which was also attached a four-company strong dummy 4th Brigade based nominally in Ramallah, there to deceive the Israelis, and commanded by Jordanian Colonel Ahmad Sidqi al-Jundi.

Another shameful example of Arab regimes' complicity is when on 5th June 1982 Israel besieged and invaded Beirut (Lebanon) when Prime Minister Begin and his Defence Minister Ariel Sharon launched "Operation Peace for Galilee", killing around 15,000–20,000 Lebanese and Palestinians to try and eliminate the Palestinian resistance, and the subsequent massacre of Palestinians in the Sabra and Chatila camps in Beirut by Israel's Lebanese militia allies a few months later. Ariel Sharon, who was held personally responsible by Israel's own court of enquiry, is an unindicted war criminal. For a month, the Palestine Liberation Organization sat with its 5,000 to 6,000 fighters in West Beirut, surrounded by Israeli forces, manoeuvring desperately to save its political life. Yet it received virtually no assistance from any Arab state. After the Syrians withdrew from combat, following several days of disastrous fighting in early June, no other state offered to help the PLO. Not a single regime of the whole region did even the bare minimum to assist. No cuts in oil sales to the West, no withdrawals of funds from the US, no breaking of diplomatic relations, no demonstrations in Arab capitals. Ironically, the only public rally calling for an Israeli withdrawal took place in Tel Aviv! No Arab state offered to take in the PLO fighters; and the late Libya's Gaddafi suggested that they commit mass suicide. The silence has been sicking and deafening. I believe that they were busy watching the 1982 Football World Cup. I think these so-called Arab governments should bury their heads in the sand of Arabia's desert.

As one American official with long experience in the region said: "The lack of any Arab governmental response to what took place in Lebanon this summer has exposed the inadequacy of practically every Arab regime, in a way that is wider in its revolutionary potential than the war of 1948, which led to the downfall of almost every important Arab leader." (14)

Hani Fares, a Lebanese political science professor at Kuwait University who is studying the effect of the Lebanese war on the Arab public, said: "The man in the street had more intense feelings about this war than any other war in Arab-Israeli history. (15)

"For the first time, an Arab capital was being besieged, and the resistance was being mounted not by an Arab army, but a popular movement. People tried to volunteer, they tried to demonstrate, but in almost every case they were prevented from doing so by their governments." (16)

"The 1982 defeat was a defeat for all Arab governments, just like the one in 1948," remarked Dr Ahmed Katib, a Kuwaiti who helped found the Arab Nationalist Movement and is now an editor of the well-known magazine Al Taliah, published in Kuwait. (17)

"We had an Arab capital occupied and none of them moved a finger. They didn't even want to meet to discuss it. Their attitude was, 'Let the Palestinians take it in the neck and we can spare our own regimes.' The only solution is to get rid of all these governments." (18)

And the Arab tragedies do not end here. Among the so many tragedies that happened that year and due to the shameful impotency of the so-called Arab governments. Professor Khalil Hawi (1919–1982) was one of the most famous Lebanese poets of the 20th century. Hawi committed suicide with a rifle in his apartment near the American University of Beirut. He was outraged by Lebanon's inability to stand up to the Israeli army when the latter invaded, and he deeply resented the other Arab governments' silence about the Israeli invasion.

Hawi's suicide created a controversy among intellectuals in the Arab world. What kind of disappointment had he suffered to lead him to a decision not familiar in that culture? Following his poetic impulse might give us an answer to that question. Searching Hawi's poetical journey one can find that he stopped writing after his poem "Lazarus", which was a reflection of the state of depression and disappointment that overcame the Arab world after the fall of the Arab union in 1961. The poet broke his silence after the 1967 Arab-Israeli war and the bitter defeat he sensed pushed him to write "The Mourning Mother", which was a depiction of the impotence and nothingness where the face of the creator turned to a deadly desert; the whole world had died by the death of its creator. The poem does not see, in the June defeat, a mere martial or political or cultural downfall, but a complete death and an end of life. He compared the mourning of Virgin Mary to the Arab situation and declared that the Arabic state is worse. The Virgin had sent one, and only one son to the grave while the Arab nation sent thousands and thousands of Messiah... darkness, despair, depression, smears the poem from the very beginning to the last word: "nothing in the horizon, but a coal soot/from ocean to gulf" After this sardonic poem, Hawi submerged again in silence. In 1971, he broke his silence and wrote "Lighting and Fogs". The deep sadness that characterised his previous works had been replaced by sarcasm towards himself and the surroundings. He also predicted that a new enlightenment was about to shine from within the deep heart of darkness and fog, but due to consecutive disappointments he had experienced before, he was cautious not to attain high expectations. In the Israeli invasion of Lebanon, disaster had struck to devastate the poet and all his promising dreams. Amidst fatal despair and disappointment, Hawi decided to put an end to his life. While his response to the defeat of June 1967 was a sardonic poem "The Mourning Virgin", the unbearably harsh situation of June 1982 led him to a bullet to the head in order to relieve the heart of all its sufferings and disappointments. (19)

> *Leave me alone! All lanterns died in my eyes*
> *Let me go to where I don't know*
> *I will not be seduced by the far harbors*
> *Most of them are but heated mud*
> *Oh! How many times I was burnt in the heated mud*
> *I will not be seduced by the far harbors*
> *Leave me for the sea, for the wind, for death*
> *Spreading blue shrouds over the drowned*
> *Sailing, died in his eye, lantern of the road*
> *Died that light in his eyes, died*
> *Neither heroism saves him, nor the humble prayers*
> *(Khalil Hawi)*

And in a very recent example when the US's Trump administration in December 2017, recognised Jerusalem as the capital of Israel, more or less nothing really happened apart from the usual rhetoric on the part of the puppets. Professor Efraim Inbar, president of the Jerusalem Institute for Strategic Studies, told Arutz Sheva, an Israeli newspaper:

"All in all, the interruption of the routine is relatively small, and there is also a thunderous silence on the part of the Arab world. It is important to note that even if the Palestinians act violently, and I doubt that they will do so, it will not help them." (20)

The timing of the embassy's move to Jerusalem from Tel Aviv on the 70th anniversary of the creation of Israel, a day Palestinians regard as their "nakba" or "catastrophe", when they lost their homeland, added insult to injury. Yet, the deafening silence of the Arab regimes and their resignations are extremely scary, and unbelievable.

"We look at our shattered world where we accuse each other of betrayal and of abandoning Palestine, while the truth is we have all abandoned it," tweeted the late Jamal Khashoggi.

Pan-Arabism, at least in relation to the Palestinians, is a figment of the Arab regimes' imagination, and the plight of the Palestinian people is invoked by Arab regimes only when it can further their own political ends.

Supposed champions of the Palestinian cause, Arab states have refused to criticise one another as well as take responsibility for their deceptive treatment of Palestinians. This apathy is revealed not in their mundane and routine condemnations of Israel, but rather in the deafening silence of these regimes when the plight of the Palestinians no longer suits their needs. The Arab antagonism towards integrating Palestinian refugees into their societies has led to the denial of basic Palestinian rights to work and live, and in some cases has culminated in the outright violent expulsion of Palestinian families (such as in Kuwait in 1991). More recently, the Egyptian cooperation on the Gaza blockade, the perpetual squalid conditions of Palestinian refugee camps in the Arab states, and the notable silence during Operation Cast Lead of Arab governments who feel threatened by the Hamas regime are just some of the manifestations of a trend that has not changed since 1948. (21)

And the irony is whereas Arab leaders before would make repeated hint to the great Muslim leader Salahuddin al-Ayoubi who defeated the Crusaders and recaptured Jerusalem in 1187; they never lived up to his legacy. In attempting to claim leadership of the Arab world, they would often use and abuse the Palestinian cause, while rarely taking their Palestinian brothers into account. In fact, Arab puppets had less in common with Salahuddin, and more in common with Abu Jahal — a man renowned for his staggering ignorance and rudeness who lived in Arabia at the birth of Islam.

Between 1952 and 1967, the drive for Arab Unity was at its strongest. This period gave new meaning to Arab nationalism. It was an age of solidarity and pursuing of unity through mass political movements. It was an era dominated by a leader the likes of whom the Arabs had not seen in a long time, in the name of Gamal Abdel Nasser of Egypt. The high point of Arab unity came in 1958 when Nasser proclaimed political unity between Egypt and Syria. Nasser was a very charismatic leader who was passionate about the idea of Arab unity. Certainly, he made mistakes, yet he was forgiven because he was loved so much by the whole masses of the region. The United Arab Republic lasted only until 1961, falling apart amid Syrian accusations of Egyptian arrogance and high-handedness. This is the only example of Arab Unity and seen as a dark time by the Syrians.

Less than a fortnight after Egypt and Syria united in February 1958, the Hashemite kingdoms of Iraq and Jordan announced that they were forming a less centralised and pro-Western federation called the Arab Union. Predictably, Nasser denounced the Jordanian-Iraqi venture as a tool of imperialism and "a false federation" which would be "dispersed like dry leaves in the wind." The Arab Union came to an abrupt end in July 1958, after a successful coup by Nasser's supporters in Iraq. But Nasser's relations with the new leader, Abdul Karim Kassim, deteriorated quickly.

Kassim arrested Nasser's followers in Iraq and allied himself with Iraqi Communists rather than the Arab nationalists. Nasser reacted by condemning Kassim as a tool of Soviet imperialism. (22)

The Arab Defence Pact was put to the test in 1967, in what became known as the Six Day War. In a pre-emptive strike on the 5th June, Israel destroyed most of Egypt's air force on the ground. Arabs refer to the Six Day War as the Naksa — the Defeat. The Arab Defence Pact failed, Jerusalem and the rest of Palestine were occupied, and Syria lost the Golan Heights as well as the strategic Sinai desert of Egypt. Nasser was humiliated and did not recover thereafter. The military defeat of 1967 showed a lack of coordination among Arab entities, Arab land was lost, the common enemy was triumphant and this defeat served a big blow to Arab self-confidence and worked its way deep into the collective Arab psyche.

The biggest tragedy of that war was that its defeat did not end when the ceasefire was signed on 11th June 1967. Instead, the defeat has been drip fed to the Arabs on and on until the present day, leading to many parallels between the situation of the Arabs back then, and their situation now. (23)

It may be difficult for the Arabs of today to seriously reflect on the meaning of the defeat they suffered fifty years ago, given their current calamitous predicament. A half-century ago in the free sanctuary of Beirut, Arabs engaged in introspection and self-criticism, seeking to answer the central questions of their political life: What went wrong, and how did we reach this nadir? That unique moment of guarded hope and promise lasted but a few years. (24)

Fifty years later, there is no equivalent to Beirut in which to ask the hard questions about why and how the moment of enthusiasm that followed the 2011 Arab uprisings lasted for only a few months before the peaceful protest movements gave way to violence and civil wars. And in the last half-century, the Palestinian movement — along with its numerous Arab allies — has failed to become a transformational force, just as the uprisings of recent years never became transformational revolutions. (25)

On the morning after the war's end, Arab novelist and Nobel Prize laureate, Naguib Mahfouz, expressed commonly-held sentiments: "Never before or after in my life had I ever experienced such a shattering of consciousness as I felt at that moment." (26)

Arab disunity, which the 1967 war had prompted, or perhaps illuminated, depending on which way you look it, would be further exacerbated. As Anwar Sadat took power in Egypt following Nasser's death in 1970, the new leader began directing Egypt in a different direction. Pan-Arabism, although greatly weakened by the Arab 1967 defeat, still "remained a force among the Arab masses", was put under further pressure by Sadat's peace treaty with Israel which was signed in 1979.

The collapse of Nasserism as a uniting force and the inability to regain the territories lost in wars with Israel, led to the questioning of the secular ideologies that had dominated regional politics since World War II. With many political entities in the region finding it increasingly difficult to fulfil their promises of prosperity and national strength in the face of globalisation and increased foreign intervention, Islamist movements, long suppressed started to gain political ground and mass public support. And in recent years nothing symbolises the sorry state of Arab politics more than the march of ISIS or Daesh as they are called in the "Arab World". "The Arab World" appears to be fast descending into a political quagmire, only a few years after the euphoria of the so-called Arab Spring. The unravelling of old dictatorships in Libya, Tunisia, Egypt and Syria has opened up a Pandora's box of sectarian, ethnic and tribal divisions, old fault-lines that have persisted under the heavy hand of police states for the last century. The situation then, as now, is that the many Arab dictators are so busy fighting and killing each other they are not attending to the real social challenges which are causing real social harm: disunity, unemployment, poverty, corruption, and social inequality. It also must be mentioned that "With the exception of the Nasser military coup in Egypt that sought to establish a national pan-Arabic project on the basis of the Arab Nahda (renaissance), which ended with defeat in the Six-Day War in 1967, all other Arab coups have resulted in a reproduction of autocratic, family-centred, tribal and denominational power, albeit in different guises, deploying different slogans and built on different ideologies," writes Faraj Alasha. (27)

I think that, and it might be easier said than done, as Adam Roberts said; "getting rid of a dictatorial and corrupt ruler is not enough. Building democratic institutions, and restoring confidence in a flawed state, are much harder tasks. It was a failure to understand this that led the US and Britain into their disastrous Iraq adventure in 2003. However, it is not only the neoconservatives and their friends who need to learn this lesson. So do advocates and practitioners of non-violent civil resistance, who have often concentrated on the task of getting rid of dictators with less thought and planning about what comes after." (28)

For too long, the question of social policy in the Arab countries has been sidelined by raging political disputes, and these states badly need to start using policy to articulate a lost sense of the common good. An essential dimension of this governance reform would require Arab countries renegotiating their place within the wider political economy and being less hostage to outside political influence of ally states (both within the Middle East and the West) and more receptive to the will of their people. Until that happens, the reign of terror will prevail. (29)

The "Arab world" is in a dilemma and is in a big mess. Never before have internal dissension and the ills facing it been so numerous and so challenging. Arab unity has never been more distant either. Contradictions and discord have plagued the Arab League, almost since its inception in 1945. Countries are collapsing and brothers are fighting, killing and humiliating each other. Despite its massive natural resources, you only find pockets of wealth and the wealth found is usually mismanaged and misused. There are more refugees in the "Arab World" than anywhere else in the world and I am not even referring to Palestinian refugees. Basic human freedoms are virtually absent. There are always parameters to what you can and cannot say or do.

Nowadays, Arab commentators scoff at the concept of Arab nationalism as being naïve then or way past its sell-by date today. The cynics are wrong because they ignore the fundamental principle of strength in numbers. They dismiss the thought that Iraq, Syria, Yemen and Libya are all in intensive care while tomorrow it could be our own homeland that is the new target. Then they will be yelling for help, but there will be no one left to hear them. (30)

It seems to me that these regimes are just concentrating on one goal, which is a holy goal for them, to keep the status quo for their own survival and nothing else. Deep chaos and the crisis of political instability has currently engulfed the major parts of West Asia and North Africa following the short-lived Arab Spring. Certainly the major part of West

Asia is suffering from deep ethnic and religious conflicts, civil war and national conflicts, which are fuelled by Western as well as non-Western players, but this does not explain why Saudi and Iranian regimes, which primarily derive their legitimacy from Islam and are in competition to lead the Muslim world, would not organise a protest at home, which they have done regularly on such an occasion. It seems that as Islam has re-centred itself in the political discourse of the region, the governments are wary of mobilising people around such Islamic symbols, particularly in the context where Islamic political mobilisation carries an anti-status quo tone. This partly explains the fear of the Arab puppet governments of organising protest rallies on issues that carry universal Islamic symbols which might endanger the security and stability of their so-called governments.

I have reached the conclusion that the majority of Arab States are their own worst enemy. The Arab nation of which we were once so proud has disintegrated. Great swathes have descended into violent trouble spots. Millions have been killed, millions more rendered refugees, while our leadership, with few exceptions, have morphed into do-nothing spectators keen only to preserve their own patch. Big mistake! (31)

One by one, our countries will go down like nine-pins unless we stand together, united and strong. The all-for-one, one-for-all spirit has all but died. This attitude has to change for our very survival over the coming years and decades. We continually pile blame on interfering foreign powers for our woes, and they have a lot to answer for. But the time has come to put our own actions — or lack of them — under a microscope. (32)

This is our part of the world and ultimately we must take responsibility for fixing it. To be sure, that is easier said than done. I do not minimise the challenges and obstacles in our path. But if we cannot bring ourselves to put our hands together and take a leap of faith towards mutual trust, not only our territories but our very identity as Arabs will exist only in history books. (33)

Our security cannot be left to the whims of foreign presidents who would sell us down the river when it suits, which is exactly what US President Barack Obama did when he sealed an empowering deal with the greatest state sponsor of terrorism on the planet, with which he 'instructed' us to share the neighbourhood. That alone should have been a wake-up call to all Arab governments unwilling or unable to see "danger" flashing in neon. (34)

With few exceptions, the Arabs present a pathetic picture of oppression, poverty and waste. In foreign affairs they stand disunited, powerless, dependent and unable to influence the international community on behalf of Arab causes. It is depressing indeed, that despite its strategic and economic advantages, this Arab world which borders the Indian Ocean, the Red Sea, the Gulf, the Mediterranean Sea, the Suez Canal and the Atlantic Ocean; this Arab world which is so rich in natural and human resources; yes, this Arab world which stretches over two continents, Asia and Africa, and which borders Europe, seems so marginalised and so impotent both on the regional and international scenes.

What the Arab political leadership has tragically failed to understand is that the best assurance of Arab rights and common good is Arab unity, political coordination and collective action. After Egypt went ahead with an Egypt-first policy and signed a separate peace with Israel at the behest of the United States, it was isolated in the Arab world and expelled from the Arab League. Having lost Arab leadership and financial backing, Egypt lost its international prestige and became hostage to the two billion dollars it receives annually from the US. Without the leadership of Egypt, the other Arab states suffered more disarray and moved from one crisis to another such as the wasteful eight-year Iran-Iraq War, the Israeli invasion of Lebanon and its dire consequences on Lebanese and Palestinians alike, and the destruction of Iraq. (35) Taking history as a guide, I do not believe that some one hundred and fifty million — now many more — Arabs can be written off for good and relegated to the dustbin of history. The Arabs, however, must do their homework. They must reread their history and draw the right conclusions. History tells us that foreign occupation, past and present, direct or indirect, entered the Arab world largely through holes provided by the Arabs themselves. The Western Crusaders succeeded, at the end of the eleventh century, in occupying the Syrian coastline and Jerusalem, not because of their numbers or advanced technology but because of the division of the Arab Camp into two hostile states, an Abbasid one based in Baghdad, and a Fatimid one based in Cairo. Similarly, the Arabs would not have lost Palestine in 1948 had they not been divided into selfish rival regimes, each looking out for its own regional interest and placing trust in the West! (36)

But history tells us that the West cannot be trusted and will not be trusted at least by the masses of the region's streets, especially the US. The US is hell-bent on aiding and abetting inter-Arab conflicts and crises. Drawing strength from history, America is confident of dealing with the Arab puppets. And the US knows that the Arab puppets' reaction will be confined to rhetoric and rhetoric only. Alas, the Arabs have many a strategic weapon in their hands, and if only they had used them properly, the situation would have been completely different now.

If we look at a very recent example involving Qatar, the US instigated the embargo on Qatar and now somehow is trying to mediate to solve the crisis between the rest of the Gulf States, led by Saudi Arabia, and Qatar. So far, however, the crisis continues, along with references to "mad dogs" in the Arab League, and new sets of mutual accusations. The end result is, as Anthony Cordesman puts it: "The end result has done little more than revive the long history of self-destructive divisiveness among the Arab states. Once again, Saudi Arabia and the UAE are bickering with Qatar. Egypt is putting repression and counterterrorism before stability and development. Bahrain is reviving its own tensions with Qatar while deepening its internal divisions between Sunni and Shi'ite. Qatar is turning to Iran, Oman, and Turkey. Oman is increasing ties to Iran, increasing its tensions with Saudi Arabia and the UAE, and—at least to some extent— quietly allowing support to Saleh and the Houthi in Yemen to flow through Oman." (37) And he continues to say: "Divisiveness has always proved easier to achieve than unity. The end result is that the Arab world has developed its own peculiar approach to game theory. It seems to love playing games where every player loses regardless of who is playing and what moves they make: It is locked into what might be termed 'N-player, constant common loss', games." (38)

It's understandable that America has proven their military dominance during the Gulf wars, and also shown economic and political dominance through obtaining an economic stronghold in the region. With the recent struggles in the US economy, we've seen how dependent America has become on the global market. Therefore with the ability of large numbers of Arabs and sympathisers' of

Arab causes to influence worldwide opinion, the Arabs if unified, would have the power to severely affect the US's position in the global hierarchy, and become a body which demands the respect of both its own people and the rest of the world. Yet again, alas, they do not look beyond the narrow self-interest and their regime's survival.

The Arab countries share more bonds and common denominators together than did the German or Italian states in the 1860s. Why could Germany and Italy unite and the Arab states cannot? Why could the fifty diverse American states forge a strong federation and the twenty-two Arab states cannot? Why can the countries of Western Europe forget their bloody past and forge political and economic unity and the Arabs cannot? It seems to me that what Germany, Italy and the US had, but the Arabs have so far lacked, is capable, enlightened leadership. (39)

References for Chapter 10: The Greatest Unity of Disunity

1. CQ Researcher, Arab Disunity, Contention Among Arab Countries, https://library.cqpress.com/cqresearcher/document.php?id=cqresrre1976102900#NOTE[13]

2. Ibid

3. Jonathan Masters and Mohammed Aly Sergie, The Arab League, Council on Foreign Relations, October 2014, https://www.cfr.org/backgrounder/arab-league

4. The Demise of the Arab League, Fanack.com March 2018, https://fanack.com/international-affairs/league-arab-states/demise-of-arab-league/?gclid=CjoKCQjw7YblBRDFARIsAKkK-dLfzo2zwragSbwt3GcbR-gft8333yx6FvBUwmCoLx6urCoSQm8cdpAaAjPXEALw_wcB

5. CQ Researcher, Arab Disunity, Contention Among Arab Countries, https://library.cqpress.com/cqresearcher/document.php?id=cqresrre1976102900#NOTE[13]

6. Jeremy Marcus and Julia Kung, The Arab League, 6/9/2003, https://web.stanford.edu/class/e297a/Arab%20League.doc

7. Ibid
8. Ibid
9. Jonathan Masters and Mohammed Aly Sergie, The Arab League, Council on Foreign Relations, October 2014, https://wwdebate w.cfr.org/backgrounder/arab-league
10. Ibid
11. Avi Shlaim, The Debate About 1948, International Journal of Middle East Studies, 1995, http://users.ox.ac.uk/~ssfc0005/The%20Debate%20About%201948.html
12. Ibid
13. Matthew Hughes, The Conduct of Operations: Glubb Pasha, the Arab Legion, and the First Arab–Israeli War, 1948–49, Sage Journals, March 2018, https://journals.sagepub.com/doi/full/10.1177/0968344517725541
14. Thomas L. Friedman, After Lebanon: The Arab World in Crisis, The New York Times, Nov. 22 1982, https://www.nytimes.com/1982/11/22/world/after-lebanon-the-arab-world-in-crisis.html
15. Ibid
16. Ibid
17. Ibid
18. Ibid
19. Nejmeh Habib, Khalil Hawi (1919 – 1982) A trip of depression and suicide, Sydney 1/16/2001, http://www.nobleworld.biz/images/hawi.pdf
20. Prof. Efraim Inbar, Thunderous Silence in the Arab World, Arutz Sheva, 20/12/2017, *http://www.israelnationalnews.com/News/News.aspx/239558*

21. Gabriel Kohan, Silence Over Arab Betrayal of Palestinians is Deafening, Nov. 1 2010, MIC.com, *https://mic.com/articles/42/silence-over-arab-betrayal-of-palestinians-is-deafening#.AnwhzcOxj*

22. Jeremy Marcus and Julia Kung, The Arab League, 6/9/2003, https://web.stanford.edu/class/e297a/Arab%20League.doc

23. Tallha Abdurazaq, Isreali Dominance over Palestinian Destiny is Fueled by Arab Weakness, TRT World, June 2017, https://www.trtworld.com/opinion/the-main-beneficiary-of-arab-disunity-and-corruption-is-israel-373331

24. Hisham Melhem, The Arab World Never Recovered From the Loss of 1967, Foreign Policy, June 2017, https://foreignpolicy.com/2017/06/05/the-arab-world-has-never-recovered-from-the-loss-of-1967/

25. Ibid

26. David Sousa, The 1967 and 1973 Arab-Israeli wars: Causes of Triumphs and Failures, May 2014, https://www.e-ir.info/2014/05/26/the-1967-and-1973-arab-israeli-wars-causes-of-triumphs-and-failures/

27. Faraj Alasha, Ternary in the Islamic World: Keeping the tribe alive, Qantara.de, 2018, *https://en.qantara.de/content/tyranny-in-the-islamic-world-keeping-the-tribe-alive?nopaging=1*

28. Khalaf Ahmad Al Habtoor, Disunity: A grave threat to the Arab World, Al Arabiya, Oct. 2016, http://english.alarabiya.net/en/views/news/middle-east/2016/10/13/Disunity-A-grave-threat-to-the-Arab-world.html

29. Adam Roberts, The Arab Spring: Why did things go so badly wrong, The Guardian, Jan.2016,

https://www.theguardian.com/commentisfree/2016/
jan/15/arab-spring-badly-wrong-five-years-on-
people-power

30. Rena Jawad, Bad social policy, not ideology, is to
blame for the Arab world's downward spiral, The
Conversation, July 2014, http://theconversation.com/
bad-social-policy-not-ideology-is-to-blame-for-the-
arab-worlds-downward-spiral-28632

31. Khalaf Ahmad Al Habtoor, Disunity: A Grave Threat
to the Arab World, Middle East Policy Council,
https://www.mepc.org/commentary/disunity-grave-
threat-arab-world

32. Ibid

33. Ibid

34. Ibid

35. Philip Saliba, The Future of the Arab World: A
Vision,
http://www.alhewar.com/MetropolitanPhilip.html

36. Ibid

37. Anthony Cordesman, 100 Days and Counting of
Pointless Arab Self-Destruction, Real Clear World,
September 2017,
https://www.realclearworld.com/articles/2017/09/20
/100_days_and_counting_of_pointless_arab_self-
destruction_112552.html

38. Ibid

39. Philip Saliba, The Future of the Arab World: A
Vision,
http://www.alhewar.com/MetropolitanPhilip.html

Chapter 11: Plague Eleven: Killing the Spring

"We're going to fight this battle with everything we have, and we will probably lose. But then we will fight it again, and we will lose a little less, for this battle will win us many supporters. And then we'll lose *again*. And *again*. And we will fight on. Because as hard as it is to win by fighting, it's impossible to win by doing nothing."

— Cory Doctorow

"If Syria is to rise from the ashes it needs a united Arab world which has one thing on its agenda, not the falling of a dictator for we have seen many of those fall, but the re-emergence of a prosperous Arab nation, one that is not reliant on foreign aid but is self-sustained and set on its way to become powerful once again."

— Aysha Taryam

For the first time in history, the "Arab world" became a mobilising source of inspiration for dissident movements worldwide. To start this chapter, it's worth mentioning that any democratic transition isn't about whom you can overthrow or whom you replace them with. It's about whether or how you can change the vast network of institutions underneath that person.

The "Arab Spring" designation harks back to the term "Spring of Nations", used by some historians to describe the European revolutions of 1848. Despite its Eurocentric character, the term could however prove useful when comparing the European revolutions of 1848 and those in the Arab world between 2011 and 2013. (1)

Just as in the Arab Spring, the revolutionary aspirations of 19th century Europe didn't stop at national borders. They gradually took hold in France, Germany and Hungary and ultimately gave fresh impetus to the protests that had previously erupted in Italy. In the same way, in the wake of its initial beginnings in Tunisia, the Arab Spring spread to Egypt, Syria, Libya, Bahrain and Yemen.(2)

The revolutions of 1848 were motivated by a profound sense of the urgent need to overhaul the status quo — even if Republicanism, as in the case of France, wasn't the only alternative up for debate. The definitive form of the political systems that the 1848 revolutions hoped to install may not have been entirely clear. Nevertheless, the bolstering of democratic institutions and the integration of broad swathes of the populace into the political process were fundamentals on everyone's list of goals. (3) What the "Spring of Nations" and the Arab Spring also have in common is that the romantic ideas that underpinned their designation would very soon turn out to be just that. Neither was destined to succeed and the "Spring of Nations" quickly turned into a long and icy winter. Shortly after the outbreak of the European revolutions in February 1848, repressive monarchies succeeded in reasserting their control after realising that not only were the revolutionaries unable to pose a serious threat to the state apparatus, they were also unable to count on support from the military.(4)

Following the self-immolation of the Tunisian vegetable seller Mohammed Bouazizi on the 17th December 2010, the demonstrations had spread rapidly, culminating in a large rally outside the interior ministry in Tunis on the 14th January 2011. On that day, facing huge opposition and a planned general strike, the president of Tunisia, Zine al-Abidine Ben Ali, who served from 1987 until his ousting in 2011, fled the country. He has been holed up in Saudi Arabia ever since.

The Tunisian success in getting rid of Ben Ali was followed in Egypt by the resignation of president Hosni Mubarak in February 2011, by Colonel Muammar Gaddafi's death in Libya the following October, and by the departure of president Ali Abdullah Saleh from Yemen in February 2012. Four autocrats gone in just over a year.

Why was the apparent success of the Tunisian revolution followed by so many disasters ever since? Can it really be true that a largely peaceful development, which inspired millions around the world, contributed to the situation faced today: internationalised civil wars in both Syria and Yemen, the rise of Islamic State, authoritarian rule in Egypt, the collapse of central government in Libya, and migrants risking all to flee these horrors?

In my view, and it's the view of some commentators of the region, the so-called Arab Spring emerged as a result of decades of repressions and lack of real developments, multiplied by endemic corruption and mismanagement of resources. After all, all Arab regimes had failed to provide minimum levels of developmental progress and stability. Moreover, they weren't even able to defend their territory themselves, despite the massive but wasteful increase in recent years on defence spending and arms purchases. The Arab Spring was, however, a blessing for arms producers.

The sales of arms to Arab countries has greatly increased since the beginning of the protests. This has helped some countries, including Russia and China, to have access to the Middle East market. The Arab Spring has brought Russia back to the region through its two military bases in Syria: Tartus and Hmeimim. The security and stability of Middle Eastern countries and the continuation of their regimes depend on regional and international alliances, particularly in Syria, where the regime was heavily reliant on the Russian intervention that helped turn the balance of power toward the regime forces (5).

Yet its failure is very much debatable. Many murky hands — internal as well as external — have played their role to ensure that the status quo remains, there was an unknown player who was deliberately working on instigating chaos to affect the state and national unity by encouraging extremists from all over the world. They seized border crossings to facilitate the task and destroyed state-owned social and economic institutions. Noam Chomsky in his book Who Rules the World? writes:

"The United States and its allies have tried hard to prevent that outcome (the outcome of democracy) so far, with considerable success. Their policy toward the popular uprisings has kept closely to the standard guidelines: support the forces most amenable to US influence and control. (6)

Favoured dictators must be supported as long as they can maintain control (as in the major oil states). When that is no longer possible, discard them and try to restore the old regime as fully as possible (as in Tunisia and Egypt). The general pattern is familiar from elsewhere in the world: Somoza, Marcos, Duvalier, Mobutu, Suharto, and many others. In the case of Libya, the three traditional imperial powers, violating the UN Security Council resolution they had just sponsored, became the air force of the rebels, sharply increasing civilian casualties and creating a humanitarian disaster and political chaos as the country descended into civil war and weapons poured out to the jihadis in western Africa and elsewhere. (7)

The United States in particular has played a profoundly negative role since 2011. Former president Barack Obama was always someone more fearful of disorder and commitment than he was supportive of democracy. This was particularly true in Syria, where behind periodical assurances that Mr Al Assad's rule had ended, Mr Obama did nothing to change the balance to the rebels' advantage, even before the arrival of radical Islamic groups such as the Nusra Front and ISIL.(8) Donald Trump has, similarly, had little concern for what happens in Syria. His administration has made contradictory statements about its desired political outcome for the country but has been largely absent from the diplomatic tracks on Syria, whether in Geneva or Astana. Given his narrow nationalistic agenda, Mr Trump has no interest in spreading human rights, democracy and good governance, which are all motivated by a universalist approach to foreign affairs. (9)

In the case of internal factors, the Arab Spring counter-revolutions were for the most part successful because the Gulf monarchies supported the reactionary powers that had come under pressure from the revolutions. A clear illustration of this support is the fact that in March 2011, the Gulf Cooperation Council sent troops to Bahrain, led by Saudi Arabia to tackle the revolution there.

In Egypt too, the counter-revolution under the leadership of Abdul Fattah al-Sisi would not have been possible without generous financial support from Saudi Arabia and the

Emirates, as well as the backing of Israel's intelligence services.

In an interview, Tawakkul Karman, the first Arab woman to be awarded the Nobel Peace Prize, she said:

"The revolutionary forces of the Arab Spring and the counter-revolutionary powers are currently locked in a fierce struggle. The ignominy of the latter is clear to the world. The conflict is fuelling further wars and instability. And behind it all is a conspiracy led by Saudi Arabia and the United Arab Emirates (UAE). They are the ones leading the counter-revolution. Riyadh, Abu Dhabi, not to mention Tehran, saw the Arab Spring as a direct threat to their interests. So they attempted to use their money to foment coups, war and chaos in the capitals of the Arab world — in Cairo, Tripoli, Damascus and Sanaa." (10) She continued to say:

"The Arab peoples are currently struggling to find their way out of this dire situation. We will neither give up, nor renounce democracy, freedom and human rights. We will not accept a return to dictatorship, oppression and corruption. Our peoples will one day enjoy democracy and freedom. That much is certain." (11)

Research done by Isabel Bramsen examines the interactive dimensions between movements and their opponents to explain why civil resistance is successful or silenced, and analysed by Molly Wallace. I find this interesting:

Through her analysis she finds the following: In Tunisia, the violent repression of the uprising in late 2010 and early 2011 only further unified and energised the protest movement across the country, providing it with greater momentum that eventually contributed to a deterioration of regime cohesion; therefore, when the movement escalated with a massive demonstration on a major street outside the

Ministry of the Interior, it was from a position of strength and momentum for the movement and at a moment of division and uncertainty for the regime, leading to Ben Ali's departure.(12)

In Bahrain, the initial violent repression of the movement in early 2011 had a similar unifying and energising effect, with activists of different stripes, as well as Sunnis and Shias, coming together against a common enemy. The regime's shift in tactics after a few days, however, pulling out of the Pearl Roundabout (the centre of protest activity) and generally allowing the demonstrations to proceed, allowed divisions within the movement to emerge, both between revolutionary and reformist contingents and along sectarian lines — despite some concerted effort on the part of the movement to be decidedly non-sectarian. (13)

A few weeks later, when some segments of the movement decided to escalate with a blockade of the financial district, it was from a position of disunity, without widespread Sunni participation and without the participation of the biggest opposition party. The entrance of Saudi forces the next day and the regime's crackdown against the movement and clearing of the Pearl Roundabout within the next two days had an important psychological effect on the movement in this context, "emotionally dominat[ing] the protesters."(14)

Bramsen argues more generally, therefore, that the success of a civil resistance movement depends on the movement's maintenance of "unity and coherence" while "challeng[ing] the cohesion of the opponent" — where these are influenced by the regime's "repressive strategies" and the timing of the movement's escalation, namely whether or not it is undertaken while the movement has momentum. Based on these findings, she urges activists to consider the timing of escalatory activities carefully, planning them for moments of "cohesion and momentum."(15)

Nine long and agonising years have passed since the revolutions broke out across the region in a number of countries. Widely considered a rebellion against bad autocratic regimes, many international observers and media outlets optimistically called this movement the "Arab Spring," seeing it as the beginning of a new era of democracy for the region. Yet, researchers at the New England Complex Systems Institute (NECSI), predicted otherwise.

Their analysis pointed to a low success rate for fledgling democracies that might result from these revolutions. They also predicted problems with power vacuums and the use of force to re-establish order. Today, nine years after the original report was published, events have proven them correct.

Time is a key factor. After a government has been overthrown, a replacement must be established quickly to restore basic order and essential services. Under this deadline, military rule or another autocracy are quicker and easier to put in place than a new democracy. Violent revolutions in particular are likely to damage basic societal institutions and infrastructure, further reducing the baseline complexity of society and placing a successful democracy even further out of reach. (16)

So how have the countries of the Arab Spring fared in the past six years? Using data on democratic and autocratic ratings, NECSI researchers assessed the outcomes for 16 states in the Levant and North Africa. Among them, Tunisia is the only clear success story with a marked increase in democratic measures. Somalia established a government after years of lacking one, a success arguably not attributed to the Arab Spring. Other countries were not so successful. (17)

Revolts in three other countries resulted in full-scale civil wars: Syria, Libya, and Yemen have become failed states filled with violence and terrorism, spurring a mass refugee crisis. Despite initial efforts toward democracy, Egypt and Bahrain have ultimately shifted towards more autocracy. The balance of states, Algeria, Djibouti, Jordan, Kuwait, Lebanon, Mauritania, Morocco, Oman and Saudi Arabia, have experienced only minor changes, returning to or retaining a pre-Arab Spring status quo.(18)

The outcomes of the Arab Spring may have disappointed many of those who were involved and outside observers, but the reasons can be understood and this information has implications for the future. "A functioning democracy is a very complex system," says NECSI President Yaneer Bar-Yam. "Achieving a higher level of complexity of governance is much more likely to come about through peaceful processes that replace rather than destroy existing societal structures."(19)

For me as a Palestinian and as an Arab who believes in Arab-Islamic solidarity and unity, it's extremely hard and to some extent painful to evaluate the so-called "Arab Spring". My argument is quite simple, is what is taking place nowadays worth it? Hundreds of thousands of innocent lives have been lost, an unimaginable number of people injured and so many have been disabled for life. Countless infrastructures has been destroyed or damaged beyond repair. Aimless and senseless tragedies occurred to millions of children. Millions of souls have been rendered as refugees and displaced, and the count is mounting by the day. In addition, there is hardly any entity in the entire region strong enough to counter balance the strength of Israel. All the power houses, if you like to call them that, of the region have been completely eliminated, and the only counter balance left is Iran, which is under severe restrictions and embargo from Israel's friends in the West and some of their puppets in the East. Therefore, the sad story of Iraq, more or less, is repeating itself. Eight years on, it is tragic to see how little has been gained despite all the efforts and sacrifices for dignity and justice. Except maybe for Tunisia, Arab autocrats all over the region adjusted their seats, rolled back the few concessions they were forced to make and returned to business as usual, and the usual has been ongoing for so many decades.

The failure of the Arab Spring is not just a story about frustrated aspirations or authoritarian survival. The deeply troubling story here is the region's weak support for modern democracy beyond the promise of majority rule and social justice. Only weeks after the overthrow of the dictators, the creative artistic energy, progressive principles and forward-looking cultural ethos that animated young men and women in Tunis, Cairo and Sanaa were already forgotten. (20)

The people are realising that they are further than ever from their aims. The killings they suffered, the fascist phase when they colluded in the killing of others — all count for nothing. The grand projects touted by the government — even if they are real — will have no effect on the lives of the poor. The number of ordinary citizens detained and ill-treated by the security services is higher than ever. (21)

But there are also differences between now and then. The euphoric hope generated by Ben Ali's swift departure from Tunis has been replaced by horror at the spectacle of Libya, Syria and Yemen. People feel they have tried what is available — revolution, political Islam — and nothing has worked. Where is the alternative, they ask. (22)

Today, many see "hope" and "optimism" as obscene words. But there are two reasons to feel encouraged. One: the physical causes of the revolution on the 25th January 2011 — corruption, tyranny and poverty — still exist, and have an uglier face. The situation is so dire that it is not sustainable; the revolution is still possible because nothing else is. Two: for the millions of Egyptians who experienced that glorious moment and passed through its pain and joy, the discovery of their potential, self-esteem and courage will not be easily lost — the fact that they did it once is proof that they can do it again.(23)

There has long been talk, especially by the neoconservatives, of a new Middle East fragmented not into the multi-confessional states that arose after the first world war but rather reduced to fragments on ethno/religious grounds. Instead of an Iraq there would be three state-lets: one Sunni, one Shia and one Kurdish. And likewise with Syria and Lebanon. In this exclusivist Middle East, Israel as a Jewish state would not stand out as the only state organised on religious grounds. There is no doubt that many among those now fighting in the Middle East deploy terror with devastating consequences for civilians. But the failure to distinguish between the freedom fighter, with a legitimate cause who should be supported by those countries claiming to support democracy, and the criminal terrorist, has resulted in deepening the chaos in the region. US law gives terrorism too wide a definition, rendering legitimate resistance to occupation and oppression illegal. The same goes for many other Western powers whose laws also prejudice the cause of law whether municipal or international, as a vehicle for peaceful change and transformation. The criminalisation of any contact with groups incorrectly described as terrorists often made potentially useful negotiations illegal. Paying lip service to democracy yet failing to support those who seek it, as the West has repeatedly been guilty of doing, has encouraged many among the disenfranchised to become cynical and desperate, and encouraged some to rally behind those who are the true terrorists. (24)

Today's bitter reality is that the region seems further than it ever was from the vision of democratic, peaceful, just, prosperous and all-inclusive societies that was the dream of the millions of Arabs and non-Arabs, Muslims and non-Muslims who took to the streets and public squares with immense hope and joy all over the region, from North Africa to the heart of the Arab lands. The bitter reality is that the Arab Spring has turned into Arab freezing winter and the ice and snow are accumulating and getting harder to de-frost as every day passes. In short, the situation is actually worse and far more disastrous now than before the self-immolation of the young Tunisian street vegetable seller Mohamed Bouazizion on the 17th December 2010, the spark that triggered these historical movements of the Arab Spring.

As Alain Gabon described the region in his powerful article Eight years on: The Arab Spring is Far from Over: Egypt, whose Tahrir Square had become the most iconic and globally mediatised emblem of the Arab Spring, its crucible, is now firmly under the yoke of an ultra-violent, fascistic and totalitarian despot far worse than his predecessor, Hosni Mubarak. Saudi Arabia, the United Arab Emirates, and Bahrain continue to be ruled by absolute or near-absolute dynastic monarchs. (25)

In the case of Saudi Arabia, the most powerful state of the region and the one with the most extensive outreach, the new one-man rule of reckless Crown Prince Mohammed bin Salman, himself an assassin and one who has committed war crimes in Yemen, constitutes a terrible regression in the nature and exercise of Saudi power, even by the democratically low Saudi Arabia standards. (26)

Yemen, whose population has for four years been decimated by an atrocious combination of foreign proxy wars, civil war, man-made famine and disease has fallen apart and collapsed, as has Syria and Libya. Some countries have fractured so profoundly that they are possibly beyond repair for the next decade or more. Iraq has not even recovered from the eight years of American occupation and the waves of violence provoked by the 2003 US invasion. It is barely coming back to life after three years of Islamic State group savagery. (27)

The Israeli-Palestinian situation has reached a terminal dead-end, essentially due to Israel's (and its allies') determination to prevent the creation of a Palestinian state, to its continued, brutal colonisation at gunpoint, to its now open Jewish absolutist supremacism, and to the Trump administration, the most unconditionally and exclusively pro-Israel of all US administrations since the creation of Israel. The Palestinian people seem fully abandoned by all, including the US, the EU and most Arab states, now that Crown Prince Mohammed bin

Salman (MBS) has aligned the Saudi kingdom with Israel. (28)

The region remains gripped by a simmering crisis that poses an even graver threat to its long-term stability: the failure of governments to fix broken systems that for decades combined oppression with state largesse to maintain stability. "Unless you come up with a new discourse politically and economically, then a new version of Isis is going to emerge," says Marwan Muasher, a former Jordanian foreign minister and vice-president of the

Carnegie Endowment for International Peace. "It [the fractures in society] is the biggest problem, and unfortunately very few leaders are paying attention to it. "If they don't, we might face another Arab Spring, this time more radical and more violent," he adds. "No one can predict when it will happen, nobody predicted when the Arab Spring happened. [But] the status quo is not sustainable." (29)

Despite the hopeless picture revealed at this moment of time in the region as a whole, I can't but emphasise some hope. The revolutions that occurred in the region and the toppling of some strong dictators have proven to so many millions around the world and around the region in particular that the seemingly unshakable and strong regimes are in reality nothing but paper that could be shredded and defeated. These repressive regimes and their cronies repress their people out fear and fragility, therefore, they have, and they know it, no legitimacy to rule. History has proven many times over that illegitimate dictators have no solid base to continue governing. I think and I want to believe that the harsh winter covering the region is going to end and the real Arab Spring, sooner or later, will come back.

The Arab Spring, with all of its failings and failures, exposed the lie that if we are to live, then we must live as slaves. It was an attempt to undermine not only the orthodoxy of dictatorship but also an international political orthodoxy where every activity must be approved by the profit logic of the "ledger."

— *Hisham Matar*

References for Plague 11: Killing the Spring

1. Khaled Fahmy, Failed Revolutionists? Qantara.de, 2018, https://en.qantara.de/content/the-arab-spring-and-the-spring-of-nations-failed-revolutionaries? nopaging=1
2. Ibid
3. Ibid
4. Ibid
5. Maria Dubovikova, Was the Arab Spring a Failure? Arab News, Jan. 2018, http://www.arabnews.com/node/1229066/columns
6. Noam Chomsky, Who Rules the World? Hamish Hamilton, UK 2016, PP. 77-78
7. Ibid
8. Michael Young, Seven Years after the Arab Spring, What has Happened to Calls for Positive Change? Dec. 2017, Carnegie, https://carnegie-mec.org/2017/12/11/seven-years-after-arab-spring-what-has-happened-to-calls-for-positive-change-pub-74983
9. Ibid
10. Nader Alsarras, Interview with Nobel Peace Prize Laureate Tawakkul Karman , 2018, Qantara.de,

https://en.qantara.de/content/interview-with-nobel-peace-prize-laureate-tawakkul-karman-we-need-to-bring-back-the-arab

11. Ibid
12. Molly Wallace, What Explains Success or Failure in the Arab Spring? Waging Nonviolence, Oct. 2018 https://wagingnonviolence.org/2018/10/what-explains-success-failure-arab-spring/
13. Ibid
14. Ibid
15. Ibid
16. Matthew Hardcastle, The Predicted Failure of the "Arab Spring", Phys.Org, Feb. 2017, https://phys.org/news/2017-02-failure-arab.html
17. Ibid
18. Ibid
19. Ibid
20. Abdeslam E. M. Maghraoui, The Failure of the Arab Spring, The Hill, 26/01/2019, https://thehill.com/opinion/international/427111-the-failure-of-the-arab-spring
21. Multiple Writers, I was Terribly Wrong-Writers Look Back at the Arab Spring Five Years on, The Guardian, Jan. 16, https://www.theguardian.com/books/2016/jan/23/arab-spring-five-years-on-writers-look-back
22. Ibid
23. Ibid
24. Ibid
25. Alain Gabon, Eight Years on, the Arab Spring is far from over, Middle East Eye, Dec. 2018, https://www.middleeasteye.net/opinion/eight-years-arab-spring-far-over

26. Ibid
27. Ibid
28. Ibid
29. Andrew England and Heba Saleh, How the Middle-East is Sowing Seeds of a Second Arab Spring, March 2018, Financial Times, https://www.ft.com/content/a6229844-1ad3-11e8-aaca-4574d7dabfb6

Chapter 12: The Way Forward

"I am the lover's gift; I am the wedding wreath;
I am the memory of a moment of happiness;
I am the last gift of the living to the dead;
I am a part of joy and a part of sorrow."

— *Gibran Kahlil Gibran*

A century has passed since the First World War, and while the rest of the world has moved on, the so-called "Middle East" still continues to have so many troubles, with a new issue arising every other day. As painful as it may be, the fact remains that the "Middle East" still has a long way to go, and the region has, so far, not risen from the ashes of the First World War.

The "Arab uprisings" that affected the region in 2011 constituted a moment of mass upheavals against authoritarian regimes and deteriorating socio-economic conditions; whereas a large segment of the protesters was composed of young women and men aspiring to democracy, freedom and the rule of law, as well as to a better and more inclusive future, recognition of their dignity and better social inclusion and economic prospects; whereas the overthrow of some regimes and, in some cases, the introduction of democratic reforms gave rise to a great hope and expectation. The majority of the population in the region is under the age of 35; whereas youth unemployment in the region is still among the highest in the world; this gives rise to social exclusion and political disenfranchisement, as well as a brain drain towards other countries; and I think, all these factors were at the root of the 2011 protests and are again generating protests in some countries; young people in vulnerable settings, without agency or prospects, can become targeted groups for radical movements.

In oil-exporting countries in particular, the global financial crisis, the decline in oil prices, demographic trends, conflict and violence have further aggravated the situation after the 2011 events; whereas the economic model typifying such countries is no longer viable, resulting in a crisis of trust that needs to be urgently addressed by the governments concerned, with a view to establishing a new social contract with their respective citizens. The increasing social impact of the decline in state subsidies, public sector jobs and public services, the spread of poverty and environmental problems, especially in remote areas and among marginalised communities, have been a source of continuing unrest and spontaneous protests in the region which are likely to continue growing in the years ahead.

Any detention that results from the exercise of the rights or freedoms guaranteed by international law, such as freedom of expression and freedom of assembly, constitutes arbitrary detention that is prohibited under international law; whereas, in significant swathes of the region, human rights defenders, journalists, lawyers, political opposition activists and religious figures at large have faced increasing systematic persecution, threats, attacks, reprisals, judicial harassment, arbitrary detention, torture and ill-treatment, and termination.

In this region, there are numerous armed conflicts and thousands of people have been murdered and disappeared and millions displaced; and ISIS/Daesh groups have committed atrocities, including brutal executions and unspeakable violence, abductions, torture and children have been recruited and used in terrorist attacks.

No conflict in the Arab-Islamic world has ever started a world conflagration of the magnitude of either WWI or WWII but the region has been at the heart of global politics and a hotbed of incessant power plays since the early years of the 20th and into the 21st century.(1)

In fact, few conflicts across the Arab-Islamic world in the past six decades have remained local, despite never escalating into a full-blown "world" conflagration. Nevertheless, they implicated internal and external actors, and had immense human and material costs, with spillover effects across the globe. The number of casualties, severity of injuries and destruction left behind by successive wars and invasions in the area are so pronounced in magnitude that they are virtually impossible to quantify. One thing is certain, and that is the fact that the Arab-Islamic world has had anything but a marginal place in international politics; the geopolitics of the Arab-Islamic world is profoundly tied to world politics and has implications far beyond the region's borders. (2)

On reflection, the 9/11 attacks at the World Trade Center marked a turning point in the region's history, as the US rallied global support for an invasion of Afghanistan and Iraq, which left aftershocks that still reverberate today.

The American invasions of Afghanistan and Arab Iraq were animated by revenge for the 9/11 attacks and rationalised by a fiction about non-existent weapons of mass destruction in Iraq and by the self-serving American chimera of "democratising" those two societies and eventually the rest of the region's Arab and Central Asian Islamic states—assumed to be candidates for integration into a Washington-dominated liberal regional system. (3)

The "New Middle East," officially proclaimed by NATO at the end of 2003, has conspicuously failed to appear, but it remains a goal of the expansionist neoconservative visionaries among the makers of American policy. In Bush's government, Secretary of State Condoleezza Rice wrote in Foreign Affairs in 2008, "Democratic state-building is now an urgent component in our national interest" reflecting a "uniquely American realism" teaching that it is America's job "to change the world," and in its own image. On the 11th September 2014 the eminent dean of the School of Advanced International Studies of the Johns Hopkins University, Vali R. Nasr, wrote in the New York Times that America "must rally the whole region to support power-sharing—and nation building. This is a tall order. But the crises facing America demand a grand strategy..." A decade of failures has passed, but the grand design has not changed. (4)

Thus the foreign policies of the United States have been stripped of a vital part of their assumed original moral content. An assimilation of modern totalitarian influences, values, and practices occurred in the United States after 2001, with state assassinations, selective drone killings, disregard of due process, torture, and permanent incarceration without trial justified by American leaders in their conduct of what has amounted to a war, not really of religions, as such, but between absolutisms, the one religious, and the other, ours, a political culture of extreme and solipsistic millenarian nationalism. (5)

One recalls the theory Samuel Huntington announced late in his career that the "next world war" would be a war of religions rather than states. The present writer dismissed this at the time as a simple projection into the future of 20th century experience and the conventional American foreign-policy thinking of the 1990s, notably that promoted by the aggressively anti-Islamic Washington neoconservatives. (6)

The war in Iraq affected the region enormously and deepened the sense of injustice, humiliation and disempowerment among Arabs. However, the dignity deficits plaguing the region were, of course, not only external. No doubt and despite the so many interferences in the region's affairs, military or otherwise, by different powers, led by the US and despite the historical injustices inflicted upon the region and its inhabitants led by the British and French at the time, have done a lot of damage to the region and its social cohesion. Yet, the damage done by the dirty hands of the ruling puppets, I believe, is far greater and deepened the region into further chaos, social and economic stagnation and suffocation. They have managed, with shrewdness, to divide the common people ever further.

And It is proven beyond doubt that authoritarian thuggery exists in the Middle East simply because foreign hegemony has established it as the way of the world. The United States and its allies have vested interests in the Middle East, and it is beneficial for them to have governments that are favourable to their cause. As such, political abuse of power is nothing new, albeit the only ones who suffer badly are the common people of the region.(7)

The thing is, the solution isn't far away when you look for it: unification is the only way forward. As long as false borders continue to exist in the region, the Middle East will not progress. The biggest thing that went wrong after World

War I was that a fake sense of nationalism came to the fore: people who were otherwise mutually related became citizens/subjects of different countries. Over the course of the century, such fake nationalist pride has only become stronger, and it is not uncommon to find the average youth of the Middle East considering themselves as Egyptians or Iraqis or Jordanians, and not as part of one coherent nation state.(8)

Back in 1957, member-states of the Arab League signed an Economic Unity Agreement (EUA) that, among other things, intended to promote "free movement of persons and capital; the free exchange of goods and products; freedom of residence, work-free use of modes of transport and civil ports and airports for all Arab citizens".(9)

That very year, six European countries decided to establish what would later be known as the Common Market. Over five decades later, the Europeans have managed to turn their Common Market into a full-fledged Union. On the other hand, the Arab states have painstakingly ensured that their divisions and differences multiply with each passing year. Sadly, the 1957 EUA has become a distant memory.(10)

This is disappointing and, more importantly, shocking. The Arab nations have a lot in common. Language, culture, religion, history — you will not have a hard time seeking unifying forces across Arab countries. In the case of Europe, though, unifying forces are nearly non-existent. Cultural, social and political differences, as well as a history of devastating wars — this is what most European states seem to have in common with each other. Yet, when it comes to integration, Europe seems to be doing better than the Arab World. (11)

And when speaking about the dignity of the common man in the region, it's another painful subject to talk or write about. They're supposedly called governments and their civil services are shocking and disgraceful. Last year (2018) I was in an Arab land to finalise some legal paperwork. What I have experienced was not a pleasant experience by any standard. People were in that government's building above each other, moving around, some with their children from one office to another, scrambling for signatures or whatever they came for. No chairs for them, no queues, nothing, and to add to the misery the building was extremely filthy. I was watching and pondering at the miserable situation and the struggle these people are facing daily with horror and disbelief. Luckily, I finished in a couple of hours, just because the people who were with me had arranged (in advance) for a Wasta to speed things up. At the same time, I felt ashamed that I had finished my paperwork with relative ease, but those people who do not have Wasta and can't afford to bribe may have to struggle for days to complete theirs, if they were lucky.

Dignity deficits, personal and collective, were the underlying cause of the revolutions. This is, of course, not dissociated from problems stemming from a lack of opportunities and employment, a sense of powerlessness and socio-economic vulnerability, but was also grounded in the humiliation and resentment felt by so many people in the region for reasons that were not economic in nature. In addition, there was also a sense that external forces were interested in manipulating the situation and redrawing regional geopolitics.(12)

Collective dignity deficits were the result of autocratic regimes, supported by foreign powers with short-term geopolitical interests. However, these regimes started to lose their grip on power when the revolts gained momentum. To the surprise of many, dictators that had comfortably ruled for decades were fiercely contested from within with fervent demands for "karama" — Arabic for dignity.(13)

There is another facet of history which is a source of frustration for many Arabs. Long before the West became a dominant force in the world, the Arab-Islamic world was a thriving centre for science, culture and civilization. This lost dimension of history only adds to the sense of disrespect that many Arabs feel from the West. While the dominant narrative about the rise of the West tells us that European civilization is founded on Greco-Latin roots, and that 'Islam in Europe' is a recent (and threatening) presence, in reality the European and Arab-Islamic worlds have been engaged in fruitful exchanges for centuries. In its golden days, the Arab-Islamic world hosted centres like Baghdad, Cairo, Cordova, Toledo, Sicily and others that attracted erudite minds from far and wide. Indeed, history shows us that no historical age or phenomena is achieved in isolation, but rather by building on the achievements and contributions of others. Just as the Arab-Islamic world built on developments of earlier empires, Europe later incorporated elements of the Arab-Islamic world. Transfers of science and technology to medieval Europe from the Arab-Islamic world paved the way for the European scientific revolution and later the Enlightenment. Great contributions were made in mathematics, astronomy, natural sciences and medicine.(14)

The "Arab world" now looks back in bewilderment, and often in disappointment.

For at least two centuries, scores of Arabs and Muslims have pondered on "where we were" builders and custodians of one the middle age's greatest civilisations, and "where we are" far from where power in the world and human achievements are. Repeatedly, that reflection gave rise to anger — at the "colonialists who plundered us", at the "local rulers who took over from them and proved corrupt", and often "at the people, the masses, who are ignorant and are condemning 'us' to our current situation". And as much as a reflection, at times, generated introspection which fuelled development (for example in the late nineteenth and early twentieth century), at other times, especially in the last half a century, reflection generated anger, which bred antagonism, aggression, and confusion.(15)

I can't stress enough that the common men of the region, irrespective of their ethnic-religious background must take their own destinies in their hands. It seems to me that the current puppets with their supporters of the West and Israel have managed successfully to create and perpetuate divisions, sectarian hatred and mistrust between historically close and co-operative communities. We must remember serious and factual facts that Arabs, non-Arabs, Muslims and non-Muslims have lived in harmony and brotherhood together for centuries. They have built great civilisations based on co-existence and above all on morality, good attitude and respect. Again, I can't stress enough that the chaos and tragedies happening today and the miseries which are unfolding daily are mainly the cause of ignorance and lack of proper knowledge which the puppets have encouraged and supported for decades for their own selfish, narrow, and greedy survival. I reject the explanation that the key to building a new stable order in today's "Middle East" is fundamentally about territory and state borders. I think we have to focus on this issue of social trust. Social trust is about communities being able to live together and share power, and that's a problem no matter where you draw the political boundary. There's no line you can draw between Shiite and

Sunni in Iraq that won't be fought over and, as the case of South Sudan shows, drawing new lines does not in itself end conflict. This suggests that the challenge is not map-making, it's politics.

It is extremely hard to swallow and painful to read and watch on live TV that we have morally and ethically deteriorated to the extent of rejoicing in the killing of our brothers and sisters. It is becoming like cannibalism or as a horror movie in slow motion. I think enough is enough. In what is happening today, there are absolutely no winners or victors, we are all losers.

Around the world, even the greatest powers have opted to be part of larger regional entities in order to manage globalisation and the competition it brings. Meanwhile, Arab countries which share a common historical, cultural and spiritual heritage and are bound by one language remain fragmented and divided and try to face individually external pressures, domestic challenges and emerging risks, in a world growing more interconnected and complex each day.

The issues confronting our people at this time are both numerous and complex, all of which have been with us for most of this century, but none of which has been resolved satisfactorily. They, therefore, remain with us and now beg to be investigated and resolved.(16)

One of these challenges lies in the ability of the various Arab countries to achieve greater integration. This objective is necessary for two main reasons:

The first is important because the absence of such arrangements as greater cooperation and coordination, and stronger and more reliable ties, could be an invitation for more divisiveness and for sharper contradictions among them. Problems such as borders and water disputes will more likely be aggravated with the lack of a reasonable regional arrangement.(17)

The second reason which makes integration even more necessary is the outcome of the old maxim which says that there is added strength in unity and togetherness. Arab integration will mean much greater power and ability to affect matters around the world than the aggregate sum of the individual Arab States.(18)

It's also highly important that we remember that when the region's elite, during the golden age of the Islamic Empire, concentrated their efforts on learning, inventions and establishing a strong scholarly culture, the whole empire was generally integrated under the banner of science and knowledge, and as a result, integrated the many ethnic groups from different backgrounds under political as well as economic unity. Nowadays, the picture is completely turned upside down. As Sayyid Jamal al-Din al-Afghani, an influential figure in contemporary pan-Islamism, said in the late nineteenth century, "It is permissible ... to ask oneself why Arab civilization, after having thrown such a live light on the world, suddenly became extinguished; why this torch has not been relit since; and why the Arab world still remains buried in profound darkness." There might be many answers to these important questions, yet I strongly believe that since the nation concerned had abandoned the seeking of knowledge, critical thinking, and innovations the demise and darkness has prevailed ever since. What we are witnessing today around the region is a total ignorance, and ignorance produces savagery and barbarism.

There are roughly 1.6 billion Muslims in the world, but only two scientists from Muslim countries have won Nobel Prizes in science (one for physics in 1979, the other for chemistry in 1999). Forty-six Muslim countries combined contribute just one per cent of the world's scientific literature; Spain and India each contribute more of the world's scientific literature than those countries taken together. In fact, although Spain is hardly an intellectual superpower, it translates more books in a single year than the entire Arab world has in the past thousand years. "Though there are talented scientists of Muslim origin working productively in the West," Nobel laureate physicist Steven Weinberg has observed, "for forty years I have not seen a single paper by a physicist or astronomer working in a Muslim country that was worth reading."[19]

For the first time since the reign of Alexander the Great, the vast region was united politically and economically. The result was, first, an Arab kingdom under the Umayyad caliphs (ruling in Damascus from 661 to 750) and then an Islamic empire under the Abbasid caliphs (ruling in Baghdad from 751 to 1258), which saw the most intellectually productive age in Arab history. The rise of the first centralised Islamic state under the Abbasids profoundly shaped life in the Islamic world, transforming it from a tribal culture with little literacy to a dynamic empire. To be sure, the vast empire was theologically and ethnically diverse; but the removal of political barriers that previously divided the region meant that scholars from different religious and ethnic backgrounds could travel and interact with each other. Linguistic barriers too, were decreasingly an issue as Arabic became the common idiom of all scholars across the vast realm. [20]

Recent unrest in the Arab world exposes the discontent among the people that has been building for decades. But is this something larger and more profound than a series of uprisings? Now that the historic seat of Arab culture and power has been upended, does this indicate a renewal or decay of the civilization as a whole? Colonel Lacey predicted the upheaval of current days and made the case for these events being the harbinger for the historical end of the Arab world. This remains a monumental claim, and Lacey recognised the incredulity with which such a claim would be met. (21)

The next question is, how could the world have missed an entire civilization collapsing before its eyes? The simple answer is that no one alive today has ever seen it happen before. Well within living memory we have seen empires collapse and nation-state failure has become a regular occurrence, but no one in the West has witnessed the collapse of a civilization since the Dark Ages. Civilizational collapses take a long time to unfold and are easy to miss in the welter of daily events.(22)

The seeds of such a collapse, if that is what we are seeing take place, might well have been sown 600 years ago, according to Lacey, with the dawning of the Renaissance throughout Western Europe. However, one can make the case that the fate of Arab civilization was set two centuries earlier, with the exile of Ibn Rushd[6] (western name of Averroes).(23) There are different reasons for Ibn Rush's prosecution, but whatever the reason might have been, the result of prosecuting knowledge is always negative.

There is often a return to superstitions in societies, the shunning of science, the supremacy of intellectual terrorism, the spread of tribal and sectarian divisions and wars, and the persecution of every free thinker to the point of exile or murder. (24)

---

[6]Ibn Rushd, often Latinized as Averroes, was a Muslim Andalusian philosopher and thinker who wrote about many subjects, including philosophy, theology, medicine, astronomy, physics, Islamic jurisprudence and law, and linguistics.

With absence of meaningful diplomatic initiatives and peaceful conflict resolution efforts to resolve the past and current problems of the region's many issues and with endurance of armed conflicts taking hold, so too the different armed groups are continuing to exploit the vacuum left by the collapse of "states", and the common man, who is the main sufferer, is left with no alternative but to face the certain fact of uncertainty and vulnerability.

What are the options left for the people in the region?

Many regimes of the region are so oppressive that people will give their lives to change them, even without guarantees that the new regime will be a lot better, as it turns out to be the case in Egypt for example. And since the "Arab Spring" started in 2010/2011, the region is going from bad to worse and in constant fighting and turmoil. People are sick and tired as well as disillusioned at the whole situation, looking at North Africa or at the heart of Arab lands the situation is miserable and in need of drastic core change. Restoring to violent means against these ruthless puppets, in my view is not an option worth exploring. The region has for long decades suffered almost non-stop from violence, killings, wars, and atrocities, and violence will defiantly breed more of the same. Therefore, enough is enough from this cycle of nonsense.

Hence, the only viable option left is a complete civil disobedience.

Civil disobedience is the active, professed refusal of a citizen to obey certain laws, demands, orders or commands of a government or occupying international power. Civil disobedience is sometimes defined as having to be non-violent to be called civil disobedience. Civil disobedience is sometimes, therefore, equated with non-violent resistance. (25)

Its earliest successful implementation was brought about during the lead up to the Glorious Revolution in Britain, when the 1689 Bill of Rights was documented, the last Catholic monarch was deposed, and male and female joint-co-monarchs were elevated. The English Midland Enlightenment had developed a manner of voicing objection to a law viewed as illegitimate and then taking the consequences of the law. This was focused on the illegitimacy of laws claimed to be "divine" in origin, including the "divine rights of Kings" and the "divine rights of man", and the legitimacy of laws acknowledged to be made by human beings.(26)

It later became an effective tool by various peoples who objected to British occupation, such as in the 1919 Revolution, however, this was never used with native laws that were more oppressive than the British occupation, leading to problems for these countries today. Zaghloul Pasha, considered the mastermind behind this massive civil disobedience, was a native middle-class, Azhar graduate, political activist, judge, parliamentarian and ex-cabinet minister whose leadership brought Christian and Muslim communities together as well as women into the massive protests. Along with his companions in Wafd Party, who started campaigning in 1914, they achieved independence for Egypt and a first constitution in 1923. (27)

For civil disobedience to have successful outcomes, the people of the region must be united in their efforts as one at all times, coordinate and communicate effectively to ensure the smooth running of the operations and to ascertain and emphasise the notion of non-violence of any shape or kind.

Regimes can be overthrown, even though dictators bring out the police and army to try to stay in power. The bad news is that the people didn't always win; when they used violence, they won only one time in four. They did, however, double their chances of success when they used a non-violent strategy. (28)

In the early 1970s, the United States got worried about Chile's democratically elected government led by left-leaning Salvador Allende. By 1973 the IA joined with the Chilean military to throw Allende out and install General Augusto Pinochet in his place. An armed struggle then developed against Pinochet's military dictatorship, but it was unable to expel him. Researchers Shandra Bernath-Plaistad and Max Rennebohm describe what worked: a non-violent people's struggle succeeded in ousting Pinochet in 1988. The movement succeeded even though Pinochet used the existence of the Chilean armed struggle as a justification to use violence against the non-violent campaign. (29)

It says a lot about people's flexibility that, even after losing lives in a violent struggle for change, they can be pragmatic and switch to something that works better. There is more and more evidence that, all other things being equal, non-violent action is more powerful than violent action. (30)

An academic study by Erica Chenoweth and Maria J Stephan — Why Civil Resistance Works: The Strategic Logic of Nonviolent Conflict — offers valuable insight. The authors use the methods of political science to test the strategic alternatives of violent and non-violent resistance across 323 cases from 1900 to 2006. They both attempt to quantify "successes" and "failures" (defined according to the stated goals of resistance movements, and discernible evidence that their actions have contributed to their achievement) and develop in-depth case studies and nuanced arguments that reflect the diversity of historical experience. This multi-method framework raises its own questions, from the inevitable difficulties faced by generalists in understanding and classifying many different examples (and some of the authors' specific judgments are certainly open to debate); but the approach seems broadly successful in neutralising any fundamental challenge to their arguments and conclusions. (31)

Chenoweth and Stephan argue that the "participation advantage" of civil resistance ensures it works better than armed resistance. The evidence, they say, shows that non-violence is capable of mobilising large sections of a population against an authoritarian regime, of undermining regime support, and even of securing significant defections from within the elite. The broader support gained by non-violent movements typically increases the cost to regimes of resisting change, and repression against non-violent movements is much more likely to backfire. But if such movements fail to achieve sufficient breadth, they may fail to achieve their goals. (32)

Non-violence is not only an effective tactic; it is a strategy and the ultimate vision. Durable ends such as peace can only come through durable means — non-violence.

Non-violent resistance and disobedience are the only way left. This may mean a boycott, a strike, tax resistance, a non-violent blockade or other forms of civil disobedience. Planning must be carefully done and discipline must be firm to avoid making the resistance vulnerable to violent provocation, in particular from the government's side. Every provocation must be answered calmly and without retaliation. The public as well as the direct action participants themselves can be moved more favourably by a well-organised, orderly expression of resistance.

A crucial part of non-violent resistance is the willingness to suffer the consequences. You are saying, in effect: "I am so determined to right this injustice that I am willing to suffer to bring about change," instead of the more common and less effective reasoning: "I am so determined to right this injustice that I'm going to make my opponent suffer for it." The willingness to accept and absorb violence and suffering can often be the cutting edge for change. When properly carried out, actions of resistance build a position of moral clarity which will strengthen your own courage and create widespread respect for your campaign. (33)

Be patient. Meaningful change cannot be accomplished overnight. Like the building of a cathedral, it requires years of work. To deepen one's analysis of injustice and oppression means to become aware of how deeply entrenched are the structures which produce them. These structures can be eliminated, but this requires a long-term commitment and strategy. Individual actions are much more effective if they are integrated in a non-violent campaign which may have to continue not only for months but for years. Along the way, there will be many experiences of failure and temptations to give up. No action should be perceived as a "do-or-die" situation for your campaign. (34)

Marx said that history sets no problems that it does not resolve. I suppose that is true in the sense that all problems of history eventually are resolved one way or another; but this is no excuse for folly nor consolation to those who suffer the consequences.

I would not even suggest that people go into the streets and demonstrate. What I am suggesting here, is that people from all spheres of work stay and remain in their homes. Not to participate in any governmental activities such as civil serving. People need to ensure that all systems of government are completely paralysed including the economic activities and the banking sector. The petroleum sector is also included in the equation. The exception to the rule is the health sector. I do not recommend or encourage health professionals and allied health professionals to participate, instead they need to ensure that life is preserved at all cost possible and they must be supported to do their jobs as much as possible. The organisers of the movement also need to ensure and send a clear message to everyone that the infrastructure, public institutions and private properties are sacred and must be protected, including all places of worship.

Final thought: let is assume, for the sake of argument, that all these ugly regimes from North Africa to the heart of Arabia which form the so-called Arab League comprising twenty-two countries, are effectively toppled. The big question arises, what then?

I will attempt to put my idea in the following steps:

1. The whole region must be, for a minimum period of two years, administered and governed by four plus twenty-two.

2. The main four representative countries to assume responsibility for governing the region are Turkey, Malaysia, Singapore, and Indonesia. One representative from each country.

3. The other twenty-two representatives are one from each country representing their lands. And those people must be chosen by their people's committees. I recommend that the representatives chosen are figures who are known to be pious, honest, knowledgeable and with integrity. So many of them can be found in forced exile or in the dark cells of the many prisons around the region.

4. After one year, a referendum should be conducted for the whole region to establish whether they want to be integrated into one political entity or not. And the twenty-six representatives must respect the outcome of the referendum

and work towards achieving a smooth running of the people's chosen outcome of the referendum.

I must remind readers that the current status quo is not a viable option. This region has been governed by the puppets for so many decades, and they've done really nothing but intensified and promoted different ills and plagues as the previous chapters described and also, they have done a great deal of damage to our cohesion and the fabric of our societies.

My final message to the people of the region is this; I have done my tiny bit by writing this book, which is a bare minimum, yet the bigger and the hardest task of all, if you agree with me, is for you to implement. That is taking the task forward by you as one, with complete unity and determination to achieve an honourable outcome for yourselves and your children.

We who engage in non-violent direct action are not the creators of tension. We merely bring to the surface the hidden tension that is already alive. We bring it out in the open where it can be seen and dealt with. Like a boil that can never be cured as long as it is covered up but must be opened with all its pus-flowing ugliness to the natural medicines of air and light, injustice must likewise be exposed, with all of the tension its exposing creates, to the light of human conscience and the air of national opinion before it can be cured.

— Martin Luther King Jr.

"I AM the free and fearless. I am secrets that never die. I am the voice of those who will not bow..."

The voice in question, raised in song amid the crowds packing Avenue Bourguiba, a promenade in Tunis, at the beginning of 2011, was that of Emel Mathlouthi.

References for Chapter 12: The Way Forward

1. Nayef Al-Rodhan, The Arab-Islamic World and Global Geopolitics: Endogenous Vs. Exogenous Factors, Open Mind,https://www.bbvaopenmind.com/en/articles/the-arab-islamic-world-and-global-geopolitics-endogenous-vs-exogenous-factors/
2. Ibid
3. William Pfaff, Why the Arab World Fights? The American Conservatives, Jan. 2015, https://www.theamericanconservative.com/articles/why-the-arab-world-fights/
4. Ibid
5. Ibid
6. Ibid
7. Sufyan bin Uzayer, The Middle-East: The Only Way is Unification, Foreign Policy In Focus, Nov. 2015, https://fpif.org/the-middle-east-the-only-way-forward-is-unification/
8. Ibid
9. Sufyan bin Uzayer, The Case of Arab Integration: Learning from Europe, Political Periscope, May 2014,

https://politicalperiscope.com/case-arab-integration-learning-eu/

10. Ibid

11. Ibid

12. Nayef Al-Rodhan, The Arab-Islamic World and Global Geopolitics: Endogenous Vs. Exogenous Factors, Open Mind,https://www.bbvaopenmind.com/en/articles/the-arab-islamic-world-and-global-geopolitics-endogenous-vs-exogenous-factors/

13. Ibid

14. Nayef Al-Rodhan, "The Islamic World and the West: Recovering Common History", YaleGlobal Online, 15 July 2014,http://yaleglobal.yale.edu/content/islamic-world-and-west-recovering-common-history

15. Tarek Osman, Arabs and Europeans-Way Forward, September 2018, https://tarekosman.com/articles/arabs-and-europeans

16. Dr. Khalid Abdulla, The Challenges Facing the Arab Nation on the Threshold of the 21st Century, http://www.alhewar.com/KhalidAbdullaChallenges.htm

17. Ibid

18. Ibid

19. Hillel Ofek, Why the Arab World Turned Away from Science, The New Atlantis, https://www.thenewatlantis.com/publications/why-the-arabic-world-turned-away-from-science

20. Ibid

21. Michael Fraley, The collapse of Arab Civilisation, American Thinker, Feb. 2011,

https://www.americanthinker.com/articles/2011/02/
the_collapse_of_arab_civilizat.html

22. Ibid
23. Ibid
24. Mohammad al-Asaad, Ibn Rushd in his darkest hour,
    The New Arab,
    https://www.alaraby.co.uk/english/artsandculture/2
    015/4/9/ibn-rushd-in-his-darkest-hour
25. Civil Disobedience, Wikipedia,
    https://en.wikipedia.org/wiki/Civil_disobedience
26. Ibid
27. Ibid
28. George Lakey, The More Violence, the Less
    Revolution, Waging Non-violence, March 2012,
    https://wagingnonviolence.org/2012/03/the-more-
    violence-the-less-revolution/
29. Ibid
30. Ibid
31. Martin Shaw, Paths to Change: Peaceful vs Violent,
    open Democracy, Feb. 2013,
    https://www.opendemocracy.net/en/paths-to-
    change-peaceful-vs-violent/
32. Ibid
33. Steps in Non-violent Campaign,
    http://www.vernalproject.org/papers/strategy/Camp
    aignSteps.pdf
34. Ibid